SIX PROUST RECONSTRUCTIONS

BY

PAMELA HANSFORD JOHNSON

LONDON
MACMILLAN & CO LTD
1958

MACMILLAN AND COMPANY LIMITED
London Bombay Calcutta Madras Melbourne

THE MACMILLAN COMPANY OF CANADA LIMITED
Toronto

ST MARTIN'S PRESS INC
New York

PRINTED IN GREAT BRITAIN

SIX PROUST RECONSTRUCTIONS

Contents

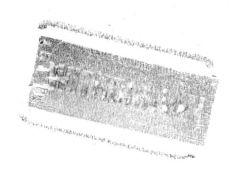

'. . . Je ne saurais trop recommander aux écrivains la vertu purgative, exorcisante, du pastiche. Quand on vient de finir un livre, non seulement on voudrait continuer à vivre avec ses personnages, avec Madame de Beauséant, avec Frédéric Moreau, mais encore notre voix intérieure qui a été disciplinée pendant toute la durée de la lecture à suivre le rythme d'un Balzac, d'un Flaubert, voudrait continuer à parler comme eux. Il faut la laisser faire un moment, laisser la pédale prolonger le son, c'est-à-dire faire un pastiche volontaire, pour pouvoir après cela, redevenir original, ne pas faire toute sa vie du pastiche involontaire. Le pastiche volontaire c'est de façon toute spontanée qu'on le fait; on pense bien que quand j'ai écrit jadis un pastiche, détestable d'ailleurs, de Flaubert, je ne m'étais pas demandé si le chant que j'entendais en moi tenait à la répétition des impar- faits ou des participes présents. Sans cela je n'aurais jamais pu le trans- crire.'

'A Propos du "Style" de Flaubert'

MARCEL PROUST

Acknowledgment

My grateful thanks are due to Messrs. Chatto & Windus, Proust's publishers in England, and to Mr. George Scott-Moncrieff, who have given me permission to use what I needed for these programmes from the text of *Remembrance of Things Past*. My work has been made easier throughout by their ready kindness and co-operation.

P. H. J.

General Introduction

WE REMEMBER the majority of great novels by the people in them. Perhaps it is not for this that we chiefly remember *À la Recherche du Temps Perdu*: if we taste the madeleine ourselves, our first involuntary memory is of an atmosphere in which girls were smiling, hawthorns and lilac were in bloom, and obsessional jealousies crumbled away the long and airless hours of the Parisian night. Yet once the memory starts to work, it is people that emerge: excavated from time past to exist in the here and now, and for as long as we ourselves shall live. In *Jean Santeuil*, Proust speaks of his characters as moving freely in time and space: it is in both elements that the greatest characters of literature move freely, or may be moved like chessmen upon the board of the reader's imagination.

When it was first suggested to me by Rayner Heppenstall that I should write an 'Imaginary Conversation' for the Third Programme of the B.B.C. and Proust came into my mind, my first thought was not simply to produce an amusing *pastiche* — though I hoped I might write something that was not dull — but to make a critical point. My intention was to show that Proust's people had been so completely regained from Time that they could continue to exist in any time; that they were so fully created as to be imaginable, in their words and their behaviour, in a good many other circumstances.

Obviously I had to demonstrate this by means of a form of *pastiche*, and in this case a somewhat peculiar form. The programme was designed for the English listener, and the English reader: it had therefore to be a *pastiche* less of Proust himself than of Scott-Moncrieff. Yet the two are so close, Proust's essence, even his speech-rhythms, are so accurately conveyed from French into English, that in my own work, as it proceeded, I found reassurance of the miracle the translator had achieved.

In the end, I wrote six programmes, not one. In *The Duchess at Sunset* and *Albertine Regained* I may appear to have made fun of a great master; I am not really apologetic about that. I regard Proust as one of the greatest of all writers; when I make fun of him, I do so where he might have made fun of himself, using much the same method as he used himself (cf. epigraph). For, as well as being one of the greatest of writers, he is in a sense the most modest. His book is not autobiographical: but in his letters to his publisher, Jacques Rivière, he equates 'Marcel' with himself by references to '*ma* grandmère', '*ma* brouille avec Gilberte'. And 'Marcel' constantly makes fun of himself, deplores himself, turns up his weaknesses like trump cards. Proust is possibly, of all great masters, the most lacking in pomposity; it is for this reason, perhaps, that he attracts so curiously personal an affection from those who know him only through his work. We cannot come so near to men who speak as gods, to Dostoievski, to Dante, to Tolstoi, even to Dickens, as we can come to men who speak as if they may be wrong, they may be mortal.

Among other things, Proust is a great comic writer, in many respects more detached than is generally realised. In others, in his approach to love and to friendship, he is far more subjective. The whole of the Marcel-Albertine story would be intolerable if it were not for the presence, beside the 'Marcel' of the story, of another shadowy Marcel, Marcel-Schlemihl, standing apart with a slightly sour, self-mocking grin upon his face. He is the 'Marcel' who has moved forward in time, who can look back, not with the detachment of the author, who is only in part the real '*moi*', but with the detachment of that second personality which maturity grafts upon us all. This Marcel-Schlemihl is noticeably a bit ashamed of himself: and when we are ashamed of our youthful selves we are forced to seek the refuge of finding ourselves funny, if we are not to find ourselves intolerable. We should be fonder of Jean-Jacques Rousseau if he had realised, when writing of his boyhood, that he was writing of a child. We are perhaps attracted to Saint Augustine because he did realise precisely that.

These six programmes are meant, then, as a work of empiric criticism, criticism through the dramatic form. In all of them there is character-criticism: and here I must say that only character drawn upon the level of psychological realism, however much it may be heightened by the writer's imagination or idiosyncrasy, can survive the chessboard treatment. We might take Dmitri Karamazov, Madame de Mortsauf, Anna Karenina, Pierre Bezhukov, La Sanseverina, Rosamond Lydgate, Mr Crawley, and put them anywhere we chose in space and time: we could not do the same with Micawber, Quilp, Mrs Gamp, Karmazinov, Mrs Proudie or Mr Slope, who are really cartoons on the level of journalism, owing their existence to the circumstances of their own time, their own world. Proust's characters continue to exist in our time, in our world. It is not true, in any deep sense, to say that we meet the characters of Dickens everywhere. When we do meet them, we are struck by their bizarreness: we feel they are unique because they do not belong to the moment in which we exist. But Bloch, Françoise, Oriane, Mme Verdurin, Norpois, Charlus — even he — are still about the world. We may meet them any day, so close are they to ourselves and to our apprehension of other beings, and when we do so we are not particularly surprised. I remember hearing, in an hotel in Brighton, the unmistakeable accents of Bloch: and turning to regard the speaker, saw Bloch sitting by the fire, dogmatically explaining to a friend that the Brontës between them wrote only one novel worth the attention of any intelligent person: and that was *The Professor*.

In these programmes I have tried to retain a certain mathematical proportion: have tried, for example, to give the subjects of 'society', 'homosexuality', the same ratios of importance as they have in the novel. Of the major-minor characters I have done scant justice to Françoise, none to the grandmother: the major characters are used in rough proportion to their significance in Proust's work.

Before passing to the six 'reconstructions', each preceded by a note of explanation, I must take the opportunity to express my special gratitude to Rayner Heppenstall, who produced the series, and to Anthony Jacobs who was 'Marcel' throughout.

The *'Petite Phrase'*, as played in the series, is from the first movement of the Sonata for Violin and Piano in D Minor by Saint-Saëns: this is the genuine *'Petite Phrase'*, identified by Proust to Reynaldo Hahn and confirmed to Jacques de Lacretelle (see *Letters of Marcel Proust*, translated and edited by Mina Curtis, Chatto & Windus, 1950, p. 297). M. Jean Laurence d'Estoux found for me Odette's song, *Pauvres Fous*, and Albertine's song, *Le Biniou*. The children of the Lycée Français recorded the nursery rhyme, *Le Furet du Bois*, heard in *Albertine Regained*. I am much indebted to Michael Head, who composed M. de Charlus's *Waltz for Eugénie*, and with sensibility and — I may add — courage, invented sections of Vinteuil's *Septuor* for the final programme *A Window at Montjouvain*.

The reader will find in Appendix A cast lists of the players in the series, in Appendix B notes of my borrowings from the Scott-Moncrieff text, in Appendix C musical themes from the programmes, and in Appendix D notes on the chronology of *A la Recherche du Temps Perdu*.

I

The Duchess at Sunset

HOWEVER many facts we may know about the England of Chaucer or Shakespeare, it is hard to imagine it with any *real ease or relaxation*. To begin with, we do not know what English speech sounded like then. We may think we do, even as we think we might now recognise the speech of Julius Caesar: but we cannot be sure. And so, as we see Hamlet and the Wife of Bath against a blur of heraldic colour rather than against a background of sharp realistic detail, we are better able to concentrate more fully upon them as individuals, related not so much to their social framework as to their immediate fellows.

As I said in the general introduction, the characters of Dickens are not transferable into the conditions of our direct experience. This is mainly because he was not presenting them on the plane of psychological realism — but there is another difficulty. It is probable that we are still too near to the eighteenth and nineteenth century in England to see its people in relief, that because we can envisage their society fairly clearly, we cannot see them except in relation to it. It happens that Proust's social background, concentrated as he was upon it, did not pin his characters by the feet so much as the social backgrounds of nineteenth-century English writers. Perhaps we know less about his society, in fact, so that it, too, becomes a blur of colour: or perhaps it is above all his particular power of creating psychological interest: but, whatever the reasons (I believe them to be complex), Albertine, Oriane, Mme Verdurin, M. de Charlus, stand out as individuals very much as

Hamlet and the Wife of Bath stand out. My idea, then, was that it would be possible to advance them several squares on the chessboard of Time, and show how they might all have behaved in 1941, in the first year of the German occupation of Paris.

This is the only one of the six programmes in which I have permitted myself wholly to equate Proust with 'Marcel'. In the book, Marcel is a Gentile: in *The Duchess at Sunset* he is half-Jewish, and this fact determines his reactions to the other characters. He is still in Paris, idle, apprehensive, wondering what to do next. It is already obvious that the magic doors are being gently but firmly closed against him: for him, the lights are going out all over Paris.

The Duchesse de Guermantes has, of course, accepted the German occupation; but with her customary caution is preserving just a degree of reserve. After all, it is conceivable that the Germans may not be the victors in the long run; there is an outside chance that they may not win the war, and she does not intend to be caught in an impossible position socially should the tide turn against them. She has a genuine affection for Marcel, but feels his presence in her house is becoming too dangerous for herself: so she sets M. de Norpois, an unequivocal supporter of Vichy, the task of persuading him to leave the country. To her the Nazis are vulgar and ridiculous, and she would like to see the back of them; but she is taking no further risks. Her nephew Saint-Loup is already in England with de Gaulle. Her old friend Swann, whom she now feels compelled, meekly and sorrowfully, to reject, is there also, broadcasting for the B.B.C. Swann's disreputable wife is in America with her daughter; the absurd Jew Bloch is there too, making a success as a playright under the *nom de guerre* of Jacques du Rozier. Oriane has a streak of real warm-heartedness and is unwilling to hurt Marcel — indeed, she restrains the Duke, who has fewer scruples. Nevertheless, she gives him delicately to understand that this is the last time her house will be open to him.

He is now in an agony of indecision. He goes to visit Mme

Verdurin. She does not share even the faint dubiety of the Duchess. Her house is full of delightful Germans who are really capable of appreciating art; nothing could be more agreeable or more stimulating. She can inspire them as she has inspired others; has she not reason to believe that she was directly responsible for the writing of *Mein Kampf*? She does not wish to hear of Bergotte's removal to a concentration camp; when forced to hear of it, she bursts out furiously that he is a traitor to France, since he wishes to see her destroyed by further war. As for Albertine — in this, as in everything else, Marcel can never discover which side she is on. There are rumours that she is in the pay of the Germans: rumours that she is working for the Resistance. Nobody will ever know.

It seemed to me that all the foregoing characters were behaving in accordance with the natures Proust gave them. My real problem was with the Baron de Charlus: and in the end I decided that he was more likely to be found on the anti-Vichy side. The son of a Bavarian duchess, allied to the Hapsburgs, he had appeared Germanophile in the first world war partly through his family loyalties and partly through sheer native counter-suggestibility.

'No doubt if he had lived in Germany the German fools defending an unjust cause with passionate folly would equally have irritated him; but living in France, the French fools, defending a just cause with passionate folly, irritated him no less.' (*T.R.*, p. 94.)

Also, he passionately despised what seemed to him the blitherings of Norpois; it struck me that he would have been as instinctively opposed to him in 1941 as in 1916: and could there be any doubt what, in 1941, Norpois' views would have been?

In the war of 1939, the Hapsburgs were finished: and in their place stood a successor for whom the Baron could have felt only contempt, a *petit bourgeois* who had never achieved a higher rank than a corporal's. Moreover, M. de Charlus, despite his maternal ancestry, was predominantly a Frenchman, the glory of France, in its reality and its myth, deeply sunken into his imagination.

With the familial allegiance removed, his racial allegiance to Germany must have become negligible.

I felt that there might be, however, other elements guiding his choice of sides. The first, and most important, was his natural bravery. He was a brave man, a man of *panache*: of all the Guermantes, he was the only one without a trace of moral cowardice. The second element may have been the decisive one: he had a fancy for a Gaullist footman.

So I decided that it was reasonable enough, and indeed honorable, to associate M. de Charlus with the Resistance movement. I simply could not see him as a hanger-on of Vichy. I could not see him, in any matter affecting France, as finally inglorious.

So I made him reveal himself to Marcel, in safety, in the open, at night, and allowed him to ask the young man what his own plans were to be. Say that he did go to England: what would he do then?

'Well, sir,' says Marcel, 'I am meaning to write a book. . . .'

By this phrase I attempted to imply the final intention of my programme. I could not hope, I had not the skill, to show Guermantes or Verdurins in their full, magical, raucous, parakeet resplendence; but I could hope to present them as the raw material, ordinary enough by ordinary sunlight, ordinary candlepower, from which Proust drew his great work.

THE DUCHESS AT SUNSET

NARRATOR: When Marcel Proust wrote *À la Recherche du Temps Perdu* he presented the study of an aristocracy in decay. He showed it, at first, overripe and golden, like a peach on a wall catching the first brilliance of the sunset. But below the Guermantes peach was the Verdurin creeper, the predatory vine of Odette and Madame Bontemps; and as the peach-tree withered the creeper overgrew it, overcame it, superseded it. By the year 1916, the conquest was complete. And the Baron de Charlus, blind, senile, riding in his carriage at the Rond Point, contemplated Time Past, and gave the roll-call of the Dead.

CHARLUS: *Hannibal de Bréauté, mort! Antoine de Mouchy, mort! Charles Swann, mort! Adalbert de Montmorency, mort! Baron de Talleyrand, mort! Sosthène de Doudeauville, mort!*

NARRATOR: *Et chaque fois, ce mot 'mort' semblait tomber sur ces défunts comme une pelletée de terre plus lourde, lancée par un fossoyeur qui tenait à les river plus profondément à la tombe.*

But to-night we shall neither grieve for nor rejoice in the fall of the Dukes and Princes of Guermantes. Since 'they stand like giants immersed in Time', and we may play with Time as we will, we shall hold them for a while at the peak of their glory: and as if we took the peach in the palm of the hand and bore it merely from one part of the garden to another, shall set them down in the year 1941, in the second year of the German occupation of France.

Madame de Guermantes is still the most fashionable hostess of the Faubourg, M. de Charlus still among the most powerful and arrogant figures of Parisian society. Madame Verdurin is yet mistress of the Little Clan, '*le petit noyau,*' whipping her lions through their paces. It is still necessary for her to soak her handkerchief in *Rhino-gomenol* before hearing the music of Vinteuil, lest her tears of appreciation induce neuralgia or bronchitis. . . . Marcel, frequenter of both salons, has not yet begun to write seriously, though he has published an article or two in the *Figaro*. It is he who will prepare us for the evening's entertainment. M. Marcel Proust!

MARCEL: It was early May, although now, after eight o'clock, it was still the light of day that, on the Place de la Concorde, was giving the Luxor Obelisk the appearance of being made of pink nougat. The moon rose in the sky like a section of orange delicately peeled, although slightly bruised. But presently she was to be fashioned of the most enduring gold.

Outside the mansion of the Duchesse de Guermantes I paused for a moment or so, wondering if it were very much too early for me to present myself. I had arrived early because I meant to stay no more than an hour before going on to visit Madame Verdurin, from whom I hoped to learn something of the mystery of Albertine.

But the windows were open wide, and as I could already hear the voice of Madame de Guermantes raised in laughter above the applauding mirth of others, I judged that she was ready to receive guests.

(The sound of a party)

DUCHESSE DE GUER: Oh no, no, Babal! I assure you, it's perfectly true. I'm sure no one can accuse me of inventing it. I haven't the imagination: I'm no Marconi, no Edison. I see, I hear, I record. I may be the Recording Angel, but I'm not the daughter of Necessity.

DUC DE GUER: Yes, Babal, I think you may accept that. Oriane never creates, she interprets.

DUCHESSE DE GUER: Besides, I had it from M. Abetz!

MME DE VILLEPARIS: What was that, Oriane? I didn't quite catch.

DUCHESSE DE GUER: Now, my dear aunt, you know I hate to repeat a joke. You make me do it on purpose, just to make a fool of me.

MME DE VILLE: You're most unfair! And I insist on hearing the joke!

DUCHESSE DE GUER: It's not even a very good one. It was simply that someone asked Herr Goering if it were true that he had a favourite Jew, and he replied, 'Why, yes, Ahasuerus! The Wandering One. I can always be sure of him moving on somewhere else.'

BRÉAUTÉ: There you are, madame!

MME DE VILLE: H'm. Not much, but it will do.

DUC DE GUER: 'Pon my word, Oriane, you mustn't tell stories like that when our young friend turns up!

BRÉAUTÉ: Which young friend is that?

DUCHESSE DE GUER: Monsieur Proust.

BRÉAUTÉ: (*Meaningfully*) Oh.

DUC DE GUER: Yes, Bréauté, you may well say 'Oh'. I often say to Oriane, ought we still to invite him here? — In these days, I mean, when you consider that perhaps his ancestry is not precisely what they call 'Aryan'. . . .

DUCHESSE DE GUER: Now, Basin, if the skies fall on me, if they take me and put me in chains, I shall continue to maintain that a man is not *wholly* responsible for his ancestors! Besides I am fond of Marcel. He is very nice. And whatever my defects, I am not altogether without loyalty —

DUC DE GUER: That's all very well, Oriane, but —

DUCHESSE DE GUER: Nor without influence — an absurd little particle, perhaps, but still . . . influence. I don't intend to let them hurt my little Marcel, while I've still got breath to put in a word in the right quarters. What says my aunt Villeparisis?

MME DE VILLE: I was very attached to his dear grandmother. I should hate to think of any harm befalling him. But why doesn't he go to England? Or to America?

DUCHESSE DE GUER: To America, like that poor Bloch! I hear his play is most successful on Broadway. But he doesn't call himself Bloch now. He calls himself — (*Overcome by laughter*) No, I can't!

DUC DE GUER: Come on, my dear; we're all waiting.

DUCHESSE DE GUER: Jacques du Rozier!

MME DE VILLE: Oh no, no! That boor!

DUC DE GUER: Now we shall have all the Cohens and Israels calling themselves Courvoisiers, or La Trémoïlles —

BRÉAUTÉ: Or Guermantes, my dear Dut-yess. Not a soul will be safe.

DUCHESSE DE GUER: Heaven forbid. But I wish him no harm. I wish harm to no human being — Oh, it's true!

DUC DE GUER: ... You may laugh, both of you, but it's true. Oriane may have a tongue like a scorpion, but at heart she's as simple and sentimental as a peasant.

BRÉAUTÉ: Good grate-ious, my dear Basin, as if any of us would ever doubt it!

MME DE VILLE: I remember M. Bloch. Once, when I was unwise enough to invite him to my 'Day', he had the impertinence to open a window without my permission. I think we taught him a lesson.

DUCHESSE DE GUER: But you're glad he's spared the fate of Bergotte?

DUC DE GUER: Of Bergotte? Nonsense. Foreign propaganda. I'll bet my boots the fellow got away.

BRÉAUTÉ: No. They took him to a camp in Germany. It seems that the gentleman had gone too far at last.

DUC DE GUER: Well, I say Master Bergotte asked for it, trying to make trouble, stirring things up again just when they were beginning to go smoothly. Besides, the camps aren't so bad as they say. It's propaganda, the lot of it.

DUCHESSE DE GUER: You may be right. All the same I do wish — for everyone's sake, I might add — that my little Marcel —

DUC DE GUER:⎫(*Mutter*) Here he is.
BRÉAUTÉ:　　⎬(*Mutter*) Talk of the devil!
FOOTMAN: (*Announcing*) M. Marcel Proust!

MARCEL: (*Narrating*) I had, in fact, delayed for some minutes my
entry into the Hotel de Guermantes, my attention having been
distracted by the spectacle of M. de Charlus, who, at the far side
of the courtyard, was engrossed in conversation with the
youngest of the Duchess's footmen. This conversation was
being conducted with an air so surreptitious, and at the same
time so solemn, that I was half-expecting it to terminate in some
kind of dramatic action, just as we half-expect that the two
figures conferring at the foot of the horrible bed, in that painting by James Pryde which is called 'The Grave', will suddenly
turn upon each other or, which would be more monstrous,
upon the spectator.

As, however, neither the footman nor M. de Charlus appeared likely to make any sudden assault upon each other or
upon my own person, I withdrew my gaze reluctantly and went
upstairs to present myself to the Duchess.

Madame de Guermantes greeted me with a comradely heartiness designed to avert my attention from the fact (which I had
not then perceived, but which became apparent in a moment or
so) that her husband was by no means happy about my presence in his house, and that I had been invited upon this occasion, not to the usual 'crush', but to a very small party of inti-
mates gathered together with all the nervous bonhomie of
Early Christians, to make a show of faith which, upon this
occasion, was to be an expression of faith in myself. Everyone
invited was 'safe', none likely to reveal the secrets of the con-
fessional.

The fact that Oriane continued to receive me was due, I have
no doubt, to a desire to prove herself gallant in the face of
danger, to give the appearance of flying, with all her loyalties

erect like an aigrette of Paradise plumes upon her rosy and marvellous brow, in the face of the Nazis; yet there was, in all this, some genuine regard for myself, something really noble and untainted by moral vanity.

M. de Bréauté, sniffing at me like a wild boar, showed an uncommon concern for my health. There was, he said, in the mountains of Northern Carolina, a wonderful new clinic for the treatment of asthma, and he insisted, there and then, upon forcing the address upon me.

Madame de Villeparisis, having asked me why I no longer came to her 'Days' and satisfied that I had no real intention of renewing the habit, told me to be sure to appear without fail on the following Friday; after which she sat down at a little table to play Patience, at which pastime she was assisted by the subtle advice, the omnipotent forefinger, of M. de Bréauté.

I informed Madame de Guermantes that the reason for my early arrival was the necessity of an early departure.

DUCHESSE DE GUER: Basin, do you hear that?

BASIN: M'm?

DUCHESSE DE GUER: I told you what would happen; he's defying the curfew and deserting us for Countess Molé! Isn't that so, M. Proust? Be a man, now. We can all endure the truth, no matter how stern it may be.

MARCEL: Well, I —

DUC DE GUER: What a woman you are, Oriane! Let the man have his secrets. Anyway, you know perfectly well why he's leaving us in the lurch. When he leaves here, he will go straight back, like a good boy, to his charming cousin of whom we've heard so much.

MARCEL: I assure you, sir, I —

DUCHESSE DE GUER: There, Basin, he assures you! I knew I was right. Ain't I right, Monsieur? La Molé has lured you to her enormous crush; and you're going to desert our humble little picnic for her saturnalia — or rather, it's something between a saturnalia and a cattleshow, full of huge, graminivorous creatures with vineleaves on their horns, all bumping and boring and mooing for their fodder. And it will be terrible fodder, you may take my word for it. Last time we were there she served a Savarin soaked in paraffin — at least I think it was paraffin; at any rate, it was some kind of volatile spirit. Basin calls her 'La Pétroleuse . . .

(The door opens)

FOOTMAN: M. le Baron de Charlus!

CHARLUS: Evening, Oriane. Evening, Basin. Evening, Bréauté.

DUC DE GUER:⎫Evening, Mémé.

BRÉAUTÉ: ⎬Good evening, Mémé.

MARCEL: ⎭Good evening, sir.

DUCHESSE DE GUER: Palamède! You're early, too! I'm so glad. If you hadn't been you'd have missed our friend here, who is in such a hurry to go to Madame Molé's that he won't even take the chair Basin's forcing into the backs of his knees.

CHARLUS: Is that true, Monsieur? Can I believe my ears? Is it possible that you have so little regard for my veto that you can sidle away into the sewers without even a clothes-peg on your nose — unless you have the article already in your pocket? — sidle away to rollick in the cesspool?

MARCEL: I give you my word, sir, I am not going to Madame Molé's this evening.

CHARLUS: You set my mind at rest. In any case, her house reeks with the Boche. There's so much heel-clicking that people take it for a typewriting-bureau.

DUC DE GUER: *(Lowering his voice)* Listen, Mémé, we're all friends here, but —

DUCHESSE DE GUER: Yes, Mémé, you really must be careful. We all know you don't mean what you say, that your heart is with us, but all the same —

DUC DE GUER: Oriane means, we are already sufficiently com-
promised. Herr Abetz said to me himself, when he found out
that Robert had joined de Gaulle in England —

MARCEL: Saint-Loup? With de Gaulle?

DUC DE GUER: Yes, the young idiot, fighting for lost causes
without a moment's concern for his family. Châtellerault's
gone, too, which is even more extraordinary, since he's the
last person one would have supposed. And with Swann over
there as well, haranguing us nightly from the B.B.C. —

DUCHESSE DE GUER: I adored poor Charles. I never dreamed he
would be so ungrateful.

MARCEL: Is Madame Swann with him?

DUCHESSE DE GUER: Why, no! She and her daughter went to
England first, but then they ran away to America. They didn't
like the air-raids. What a delicious colony there must be in New
York! The Swanns, mother and daughter, and our good
Rozier-Bloch —

DUC DE GUER: Don't chatter, Oriane! I want to talk to Mémé.
Mémé, Herr Abetz gave me the hint, when he told me about
Robert, that it would be as well for us to be discreet . . . he
didn't put it quite like that, but I understood. A nod is as good
as a wink, eh? So you must watch that tongue of yours, or piff!
We'll be in irons, the lot of us.

CHARLUS: You say we are all friends here?

DUC DE GUER: Naturally. All the same —

CHARLUS: Then in this company I am not, I take it, required to
admire the Corporal? In the last war the German soldier was
magnificent, and a German dragoon the most Phidean creature
imaginable. For the Emperor William I had the most profound
respect, which I did not, like some persons darting under the
tricolour like crabs under a rock, attempt to deny. I do not now
refuse to admit our defeat; but I am not personally attracted
towards the new master of Europe. The conquerors are de-
generating. First it was Alexander; yesterday Napoleon, today

Herr Hitler. Tomorrow, Heaven help us, it will be the sanitary orderly!

DUC DE GUER: I am only telling you that Abetz suggested we should watch our step. . . .

MARCEL: (*Narrating*) At this point Madame de Villeparisis came to join us, but for the moment said nothing, only moving her anxious eyes from Madame de Guermantes' face to my own and slowly back again, in a fixed hypnotic stare that seemed to require the Duchess to remember my presence, and consider well my potentialities as a bringer of disaster.

DUCHESSE DE GUER: . . . I don't believe it. At any rate, Basin, I don't see how we can be expected to take responsibility for our former friends. What have we to do with Swann?

DUC DE GUER: So far as Swann's concerned, his conduct towards ourselves has been beyond words. Yes, after the friendship we have shown him he ought to have remained loyal to France and to the Marshal. For you can ask Oriane — she had a real friendship for him —

DUCHESSE DE GUER: It is quite true. I have no reason to conceal the fact that I did feel a sincere affection for Charles!

DUC DE GUER: There, you see, I don't have to make her say it. And after that, he carries his ingratitude to the point of becoming a Gaullist!

MME DE VILLE: I feel that one might have expected anything from Swann since he made that low marriage. Any mésalliance is destructive. It was bad enough when the House of France married into the Medicis.

CHARLUS: But all this can't be amusing to our young friend here. Eh, Monsieur Proust? Let us hear from you how you regard the present situation.

DUCHESSE DE GUER: Yes, Marcel. After all, you must have quite an original viewpoint — I mean — well, original!

MARCEL: Well, sir, with regard to Swann —

CHARLUS: What's all this about Swann? We weren't talking about Swanns. What is your attitude to Herr Hitler and his friends, who occupy us, and occupy themselves so much with us?

MARCEL: Why, sir, I —

DUC DE GUER: Now, Mémé, leave the chap in peace! No politics here. This is Liberty Hall. That is. . . . Well, we can't perhaps expect our young friend here to see the situation in quite the same light as ourselves. And we don't want him in any doubt about your own feelings, eh?

MARCEL: After the news we have of Bergotte, Monsieur, I find my own position difficult.

DUC DE GUER: Bergotte? Bergotte? The concentration camp business? Nonsense, my boy! You've been listening to foreign broadcasts, and if you do that you may find yourself in someone's bad books. And anyway, as I was saying to Oriane, if Master Bergotte hadn't set out to be a troublemaker, all he'd get if he were in a concentration camp — which I don't admit, mind! — would be a little wholesome discipline.

BRÉAUTÉ: Which it is possible, my dear Dut'yess, that France needs as a nation.

DUC DE GUER: (*Taking up Bréauté without pause*) Precisely! Babal, you are right. If we toe the line now, we'll reap the benefit later. Mark my words, the Germans aren't bad fellows; they've points to give us all, in some respect. You can't say they haven't been correct —

DUCHESSE DE GUER: Oh, entirely! You must admit, Marcel, that their nice little frowns and charming little bows, just as if someone had put a penny in the slot —

DUC DE GUER: (*Furious*) Oriane! — The governor of Paris, for instance, isn't a bad chap. They've got to be on the harsh side now — that's the rules of war; but as they stiffen us up, so we shall civilise them, and in ten years from now France will be a world power again.

BRÉAUTÉ: Oh, in less!

CHARLUS: Stiffen us?

DUCHESSE DE GUER: How extremely odd it will seem to be Correct!

(Door opens)

FOOTMAN: Monsieur le Marquis de Norpois!

DUC DE GUER: There! That's the man to give us the facts, he'll have his finger on the pulse, all right. We'll ask him what he thinks about it. . . .

MARCEL: *(Narrating)* Feeling in no mood to hear the Ambassador's reply to the question M. de Guermantes intended to put to him, I moved away from the circle, and finding my withdrawal unremarked went to look at some new paintings by Elstir recently acquired by the Duchess. The time passed so swiftly that I was amazed, on looking at my watch, to find the hour hand pointing to ten instead of to nine-o'clock, as if the little golden needle, loosened by necromancy, had slipped from one figure to the next at the half turn of my wrist. The curfew was particularly erratic that month. There had been one notable day when it was at two o'clock in the afternoon.

I hastened downstairs to make my farewells. Madame de Guermantes, feeling that perhaps these had been accepted by her husband with rather too relieved a heartiness, urged me to return for a little while if my other appointment should not keep me too late. . . .

DUCHESSE DE GUER: . . . The others will be gone by then, and Basin and I will be alone by our own hearth. It's nicer like that, don't you think? We don't keep early hours except when we're in the country, and we shall look forward to having a really cosy chat. By the way, you haven't taken Palamède's nonsense to heart? He's as loyal to the Marshal as the rest of us, but he liked pretending he's different. I tell him, 'If you go on like this, we shall begin to believe you're a Gaullist.'

MARCEL: (*Narrating*) Assuring Madame de Guermantes that I should take nothing to heart (by which I meant that she could trust my tongue) I promised to return to her house if this were at all possible, and ran in search of a cab. I was waiting on the pavement when M. Charlus suddenly appeared at my elbow. He asked me abruptly if I were by any chance going to Madame Verdurin's, and upon hearing my reply, said he would see me there later.

CHARLUS: You will not leave before I arrive. I have something to say to you.
MARCEL: Won't you go with me now, sir?
CHARLUS: No, I shall be occupied for an hour, perhaps more. Wait for me, mind: do you hear me? . . .

MARCEL: (*Narrating*) I told him that I had heard, that I would wait; and hailing my cab directed the driver to Madame Verdurin's house on the Quai Conti.

(*Chatter and sound of a piano*)

I had hardly set foot in the hall when Monsieur Verdurin rushed upon me and drew me apart.

VERDURIN: . . . I know we can count on your discretion. You have heard about Bergotte? My wife is distracted, but as you know, she doesn't wear her heart upon her sleeve. I beg you not to mention the matter to her — the important thing is to keep her from *thinking*. Sh-h-h! She's coming now. Here's M. Proust, my dear!
MME VERDURIN: How good to see you after such a long time! I told my husband, 'It's no use asking the wretch, depend upon

it, he won't come —,' but he said to me, 'Our young friend will not desert the Faithful, especially when he learns that a certain person is to be present!'

MARCEL: Present! Is Albertine — ?

MME VERDURIN: Yes, and in good time you shall talk to her. But first you must come along and meet all my children once more. It's just like our old Wednesdays — a regular Temple of Music. Even in these grave days we keep the torch alight. . . .

(Door opens: music and chatter)

MARCEL: (*Narrating*) Madame Verdurin opened the double doors of the salon with an air of desperate gallantry, readmitted me to the little clan. They were all there, the Cottards, Brichot, Saniette; Ski was seated at the piano, and leaning over his shoulder, like the marmoreal fold of fabric sculpted upon a funeral urn, was Albertine, who, perhaps to avoid acknowledging my entrance, was watching the keys with the rapt attention of a great cat contemplating a dust-bath of sparrows. I would have gone straight to her side, but Madame Verdurin detained me.

MME VERDURIN: Have you seen Charlus? Is he coming tonight?

MARCEL: He told me he might be a little late.

MME VERDURIN: When did you see him? He didn't come with you?

MARCEL: We met at Madame de Guermantes'.

MME VERDURIN: Is that where you've been, with all those bores? I admit, I should find it quite intolerable. If there's one thing I cannot endure, it's being bored —

(Ringing little bell to command attention)

Ski! That will do for now. I can't hear a word M. Proust's saying. . . .

(Music stops)

MME VERDURIN: So the Guermantes still ask you to their circuses, do they?

COTTARD: What's that about circuses?

MME VERDURIN: Why, Professor Cottard, I was merely raising my eyebrows at the idea of M. Proust wasting his intellect upon the lions and tigers of the Faubourg.

COTTARD: I'll bet my boots he goes for the *panis* rather than the *circences*, eh, Monsieur? I expect that keeps its standard. Here, however, we have food for the mind, and no rationing, either!

MME VERDURIN: You're sure Charlus is coming, M. Proust?

MARCEL: Quite sure, Madame.

MME VERDURIN: I thought he wouldn't stay away. I told him that unless he honoured us with a visit I might find no opportunity for giving him news of our friend, Morel. After all, people can't expect me to run after them! If they want something, they can always apply to me. They know where I live. It's no secret.

MARCEL: What news is that?

MME VERDURIN: Of Morel's whereabouts. I heard yesterday, through Captain von Sternberg. . . . You don't know the Captain, he's a recent addition to our little group. People say to me, 'But the Germans, they are still our enemies,' . . . to which I reply, 'There are no enemies in the world of the Mind!' Von Sternberg is a brilliant poet and a charming man. He's writing a little cycle of songs for Ski to set to music. He's coming tonight and you shall meet him if you . . . or if you would rather not, it would be easy to arrange that you didn't. It's up to you. . . . What's that, Monsieur Saniette? Speak up, we can't hear a word you're saying. Have you got something in your mouth?

SANIETTE: I was only asking M. Proust if he'd heard the news about Bergotte.

MME VERDURIN: Don't mention that name here! . . . I will not think about Bergotte. I refuse to torment myself!

VERDURIN: (*In an undertone*) There, you fool, don't you know better than to distress her? Now she'll cry for a week, and drive us all to distraction.

SANIETTE: I only thought, if there was anything we could do, if any of us had any influence. . . .

MME VERDURIN: Influence? Let me tell you this, M. Saniette! My heart bleeds for Bergotte. I mourn him as an artist. I mourn him as a disciple. But whatever you may think of me, I cannot play the hypocrite. As a man, I consider him a traitor! Yes, a traitor! France was defeated in battle by an enemy not lost to generosity. Under the Marshal she has a hope of retrieving her glory. But Bergotte will not let her be! He wants her torn in pieces by civil war, her cities laid in ruins. . . . Yes, he would sacrifice her art, *he*, an artist, would sacrifice her art —

VERDURIN: Sidonie, Sidonie, calm yourself. You know how you'll suffer for this.

COTTARD: Take care, Madame! With your high blood pressure you can't afford to indulge the emotions.

VERDURIN: And it was you, Saniette, who began it all! Watch out, or you'll find yourself in disgrace.

SANIETTE: I beg your pardon. I only meant to express —

COTTARD: Anyone would have thought you meant 'to despatch'. You'll despatch our hostess if you upset her like that again. Eh, M. Brichot? What do you think?

BRICHOT: Of Maître Bergotte? I am of the opinion of our hostess that the gentleman, like his predecessor, M. de Voltaire, was not sufficiently content to cultivate his own garden but encroached too far upon the tender green plants of his neighbour. Whether it be Frederick the Great or Herr Reichkanzler Hitler, the boundary line is better observed.

COTTARD: Léontine! Don't stand about like that! Either take a hand in the conversation or stay outside. Since the topic's been introduced, you'd better have your say with the rest. What do you think?

MME COTTARD: I really don't know, my dear. Like Madame Verdurin I feel sorry. . . .

MME VERDURIN: Well, well, let's not pull long faces as if somebody were dead! Our good Bergotte will probably appear on the foreign wireless programmes before long, anyway, and we shall have wasted our tears in vain. (*Rings her bell*) Ski! I command you to play for us.

PIANIST: What shall I play?

MME VERDURIN: Anything, anything!

(The pianist drifts into music)

No, no, no! Not the Vinteuil! (*Piano stops*) You know the effect it has on me, even now. Struggle as I may, I cannot stop weeping, and if I weep too copiously —

COTTARD: Struggle as you may? *Sein Kampf!*

MME VERDURIN: That reminds me! (*Tinkles her bell*) My children — all of you — gather round. Your Mistress has something to tell you. You won't believe it, but it is true. Do you know that, but for me, Herr Hitler would never have written *Mein Kampf*?

Yes, yes, you may exclaim, but it is simple fact! As long ago as 1922, when I was in Munich, I went to a gathering of Bohemians, intellectuals, revolutionaries — all sorts of queer people. There I was introduced to a shabby young man with the most magnetic blue eyes and a harsh, disturbing voice, who began to address me as if I were a meeting — a mass meeting, as if I were a hundred thousand people! I can't *tell* you how fascinating it was. When he had finished I said to him, 'My dear young man, you have the gift of words — you have verve, inspiration — have you ever thought of writing a book?'

MARCEL: (*Narrating*) The attention of the little clan was so gripped by this recital that I was able at last to slip away and go in search of Albertine, who was standing apart at a window, her grave and luminous gaze fastened upon the starless sky as upon some face the meaning of which she had understood and forgotten, and now understood once more.

ALBERTINE: Marcel! I hoped you would be here tonight, but I was afraid you would not.

MARCEL: My little Albertine.... (*Quickly*) But if you had really hoped to see me you'd have written to me, called on me, before this.

ALBERTINE: I don't know what you will think of me. I hardly like to explain.

MARCEL: There is nothing to explain. You wanted first to be sure what the Verdurins would do, whether they would receive me.

ALBERTINE: Oh, no! Now you are going to be cruel, and torture me with your horrible suspicions. As if I don't know you!

MARCEL: Let us go out into the garden. I must talk to you privately....

(*Sounds of the party retreat*)

ALBERTINE: My dear boy, I'm sure I can't guess what you have to say to me. As for me not writing or calling, I might blame you for the same thing. After the Germans came, you never sent me a word or sign. I though you might have gone to England.

MARCEL: I should have gone, but for you. Don't think I'm referring to our love — that is over. We both agreed that our lives should sever, that if we saw each other again it should be as friends, as dear friends, but as nothing more. Anything else would have been inexpressibly painful.

ALBERTINE: Then I don't know what you *are* talking about! Oh, it's the same old story, you question me and hint at me till I don't know whether I'm on my head or my heels!

MARCEL: Have you met Captain von Sternberg?

ALBERTINE: Von who? Oh, if it's some German or other.... Mother Verdurin has the house full of them.

c

MARCEL: He writes poetry.

ALBERTINE: And sings it, too, that's the worst of it. He has a voice like a corncrake.

MARCEL: But, Albertine, my darling — or rather, my dear friend, for I mustn't call you any more by our old names — if you can't remember the Captain, how are you able to remember the quality of his voice?

ALBERTINE: I didn't say I didn't remember him. I simply didn't remember him by name.

MARCEL: The Verdurins have accepted the situation? '*Travaille, famille, patrie?*'

ALBERTINE: No doubt about that.

MARCEL: And you?

ALBERTINE: I don't bother my head about politics. I've better things to do.

MARCEL: You heard about Bergotte?

ALBERTINE: Yes.

MARCEL: Well?

ALBERTINE: I will confess to you, since we are alone, with only the trees to hear us, that it has made me terribly unhappy. I can't get it out of my mind.

MARCEL: Yet you are content to come to this house?

ALBERTINE: For all you know, your little Albertine may have her reasons. I know you think she's stupid, rattlepated, but one day she may surprise you!

MARCEL: How? In what way? Are you working against *them*?

ALBERTINE: I don't know what you mean.

MARCEL: Or for them? If you held my life in your hands, what would you do with it?

ALBERTINE: I'm sure that if I were ever in such a position I should cherish your dear life as if it were my own. What a Marcel! What a Marcel! Do you think me quite without gratitude? If ever I become clever I shall owe it entirely to you: and if ever I become good-hearted and generous, as you are, it will be

through your example. (*Pause*) But I am not working for anybody. I haven't the least idea what you mean.

MME VERDURIN: (*Calling*) Albertine! Where is my little piece
of Perfection?

ALBERTINE: (*Whispering*) They tell me it's the name she used to
give Madame Swann. Now, it seems, it's descended upon me.

MME VERDURIN: Albertine!

ALBERTINE: (*Calling back*) Yes, Madame?

MME VERDURIN: Ah, there you are, deserting us all, letting M.
Proust rob us of your company! Captain von Sternberg is here,
and wishes to see you. He says you are to go with him to a
ball.

ALBERTINE: Tell him I won't be a moment.

MME VERDURIN: He's waiting, my dear!

MARCEL: So this is the Captain whose name you don't remember!

ALBERTINE: (*Calling*) I'm coming, Madame. (*To Marcel*) Yes, I
admit it, I told you a lie, but only because I was afraid you
might think badly of me, that you might not understand. You
don't know how terrifying you can be with those great eyes of
yours, blazing away like lamps! Yes, I do know the Captain,
but I don't like him. I let him take me out for what I can learn
from him. . . . Anyway, why shouldn't I have a bit of fun?
One's only young once, and I'm sure I don't see why I should
immure myself like a nun because of some stupid war which is
no concern of mine!

MARCEL: (*Pause*) My poor little Albertine. . . . Do you realise . . . ?

ALBERTINE: What?

MARCEL: That now I shall never know, in any conceivable context,
which side you are on?

MME VERDURIN: (*Calling*) Miss Perfection! Come here at once.
We're waiting for you. . . .

MARCEL: (*Narrating*) Albertine gave a nervous, impatient toss
of her head, tapped her foot once or twice to the ground and

then darted away from me towards the house. I followed her in, and would have pursued her to the drawing-room had I not caught a glimpse, through the door, which was slightly ajar, of M. Verdurin's study, of the Mistress and Monsieur de Charlus.

CHARLUS: (*Fading in*) I should, of course, have been delighted to visit you for the sake of your company alone, Madame, and for the excellent company you keep. They are all there, are they not? All your performers . . . but I understood that you had news for me.

MME VERDURIN: Why, yes, to be sure: but it will keep until later. There are some new additions to the little clan whom I want you to meet — Captain von Sternberg, for example, is a charming young man who should be much to your taste, a true artist, if only he is able to accept the guidance I can give him.

CHARLUS: I am not charmed, Madame, by these dandies who appear to spend their lives between the barber and the breeches-maker.

MME VERDURIN: You don't want an introduction to the Captain, then?

CHARLUS: Perhaps you are afflicted by intermittent deafness. I stated that I was not charmed by him, and you may therefore take it that I am in no great hurry to make his acquaintance. (*Violently*) Your news, Madame! Where is Morel?

MME VERDURIN: He is serving his country as an artist should.

CHARLUS: How?

MME VERDURIN: With modesty, with generosity, in a realisation that true art knows no frontiers. Herr Goebbels has personally invited him to perform for the troops of the Reich in Germany. He has already played for the Fuehrer himself.

CHARLUS: For the Fuehrer himself!

MME VERDURIN: I thought I should astonish you. I believe Morel played his own arrangement of the *Liebestod* from *Tristan*, the Vinteuil Sonata, and a fantasia upon the Waltz Song from *The Merry Widow*. . . . Monsieur le Baron, you are not looking well. Surely, being of our mind, you can only rejoice with us —

CHARLUS: Madame, I am perfectly well. I was simply taken aback for a moment by the beauty of the prospect. *The Merry Widow*. . . . Can one get in touch with him? Do you think your absurd Captain with the moustaches is a person who might be entrusted with a message?

MME VERDURIN: You shall ask him yourself. But wait. . . . I thought you would not welcome the introduction?

CHARLUS: I shall tolerate it, if it is in a good cause, as politicians abroad are said to tolerate, or even to encourage, at election time, the embrace of malodorous and unenfranchised babes in arms.

MME VERDURIN: So far as influence in the right quarters goes, I think you will not find the Captain unenfranchised. . . . So will you accept my offices?

CHARLUS: I will accept them, Madame, on condition that you make the introduction correctly. Though I realise you are not in society, I must remind you that *I* must not be introduced to him but *he* to *me*, who am Duc de Brabant, Demoiseau de Montargis, Prince d'Oleron, de Carency, de Viareggio et des Dunes. . . .

MARCEL: (*Narrating*) By the time I made my way back to the drawing-room Albertine had disappeared; Madame Verdurin informed me that she had returned home in order to change into her gown for the ball. I talked for a little while with Brichot and the Cottards and then took my leave, only to find once more that M. de Charlus was close upon my heels. I told him I had been invited to look in upon Madame de Guermantes upon my way home, but that I was doubtful whether the invitation had been sincerely meant.

The Baron, however, insisted somewhat irritably that I

should do as I had been commanded, and adding that he himself would be returning there for a purpose of his own, suggested that we should share a cab. He had a *laisser-passer* that was in good order. Recalling his remarks to the effect that he had something to say to me, I waited for him to begin; but he remained silent during the drive, his lips violently twisted as if in irony or displeasure. Upon re-entering the Hôtel de Guermantes, M. de Charlus told me to go upstairs by myself, and not to mention to the Duchess that he had accompanied me.

CHARLUS: I shall see her later, perhaps. There is a matter of business to which I must attend.

MARCEL: (*Narrating*) I found Madame de Guermantes, as she had promised, at her own hearth, for the night was cold for May and a small fire had been lighted. She and the Duke, however, were not alone; a guest who had arrived after myself had not yet taken his departure. M. de Norpois rose as I entered, held out his hand, bowed his tall figure and fixed his blue and glacial eyes, now delicately threaded with blood as a map with rivers, upon my face. His bow was both cordial and abrupt, a recognition of old friendship coupled with intimation of the hope that I might not, at this stage of European history, be tempted to overstep its bounds. Having greeted me, he at once resumed his conversation with the Duchess and her husband. . . .

NORPOIS: As I was saying, Madame, the hour has come for France to make up her mind whether she desires or does not desire to realise her national aspirations. If she waits much longer she will risk being too late. The unity of our country is essential, and I believe that this — provided it is possible to check the few agitators and mischief-makers — may well be achieved.

DUCHESSE DE GUER: And yet I am sad for France.

DUC DE GUER: That's true; strictly between ourselves, mind, Oriane has doubts that are still unresolved.

DUCHESSE DE GUER: You think, Monsieur l'Ambassadeur, that the enemy will be sufficiently generous to permit us to arise from our knees?

NORPOIS: As I said to Monsieur Abetz yesterday: 'Sir, your master has it in his power to be the Caesar of Britain or the Cromwell of Ireland. Which will be his choice?'

DUC DE GUER: And his reply?

NORPOIS: He simply bowed his head. But I knew that I had moved him. I sensed his good-will. Nevertheless I think we must not try it too far. Monsieur!

DUCHESSE DE GUER: Monsieur Proust, the Ambassador is speaking to you.

MARCEL: I beg your pardon.

NORPOI: What are your plans, Monsieur?

MARCEL: I — I have no plans at the moment.

NORPOIS: A word to the wise. There is the case of the son of one of my friends which, *mutatis mutandis,* is very much like yours. He, too, has chosen to 'stick to his post', as the saying goes, and without caring what people might say, he has settled down to 'brave the storm'.

I happen to know, the powers that be — no names, no pack-drill — would be prepared to put no obstacles in the way of his departure, might, in fact, be prepared to facilitate it. A friend of mine in the American Embassy assures me that his country is always prepared to give asylum to young men like him and yourself, and if you wished me to put in a word for you I should be pleased, for the sake of your excellent father, to do what I could.

MARCEL: But Monsieur, I —

NORPOIS: Oh, you must not take this as a positive *ukase* on my part! But I think our friends here would agree with me.

DUC DE GUER: Of course.

DUCHESSE DE GUER: I confess I should feel happier, Marcel — you don't mind me calling you by your first name? We're such old friends now — I confess I should feel happier if I thought you were in a country where your talents could flourish more healthily! You'll be cross with me, Basin, I know, but I do feel that the present fashion in 'Kultur' may stunt our friend's intellectual growth. Besides —

DUC DE GUER: Besides what? Damn it, Oriane, no spies here! You can speak plainly to the man. He's like me — he appreciates bluntness. Don't you, Monsieur — eh?

DUCHESSE DE GUER: Oh, Basin, why will you *insist* on plain speaking? — It's always the people who shout for it the loudest that detest it the most. Anyway, there's nothing to be plain about. Is there?

DUC DE GUER: No need to hedge, Oriane. You know why we wanted Monsieur Proust to come back here, meet us alone in the bosom of the family, as it were. We hear things. We're not in with the 'nobs', of course, but a few little tips do come our way. Frankly, Monsieur, we think you should pack your bag. In your own best interests.

NORPOIS: If I may intervene in a friendly spirit, my young sir, and without beating about the bush, you are blessed in your friends. They are loyal. They are true. And they will, if you insist, continue to receive you —

DUCHESSE DE GUER: We're honoured to receive him — ain't we, Basin?

NORPOIS: — but! — this is the point. It is conceivable that you may unwittingly cause them some embarrassment. I repeat my offer to mention your name to the American Ambassador.

MARCEL: If you consider, Monsieur, that I am likely to go the way of Bergotte —

NORPOIS: Ah, Bergotte! I have heard the rumours, but doubt their veracity. For the man's own sake, I hope he is in safety; but I could not consider him a loss to literature. He cannot place to his credit — does not carry in his baggage, if I may use the term — a single novel that is at all lofty in its conception.

You disagree? Well, well, we must not quarrel with the pioneering enthusiasms of youth. I don't know if you are following the fashions of literature in England. There are a number of young men grouped around various periodicals of whom the adventurous young speak well, for instance. . . .

MARCEL: (*Narrating*) Realising that I had received my dismissal, that the doors of the Hôtel de Guermantes were about to be closed upon my contagious person perhaps for ever, I took my leave of the Duke and Duchess, bowed low to M. de Norpois, and accepted from all three pressing invitations as meaningless as the lover's insistence that, after death, his beloved shall join him in Elysium. Sad at heart I went slowly down the great staircase and into the courtyard where, owing to my own preoccupation, I nearly collided with M. de Charlus and the Duchess's footman, who were continuing the conversation they had begun earlier in the evening. I was just in time to catch a few words. . . .

CHARLUS: You're sure you can get it to England? You will not forget what I told you? Your memory is sound?

FOOTMAN: I've got it safe in my head, M. le Baron.

CHARLUS: And mind you watch your step! Not a breath to the others! They're not with us, remember that.

FOOTMAN: You can trust me, M. le Baron.

CHARLUS: You're a good fellow. By the way, what's happened to that brother of yours, the one with the charming little nose, who lived at Illiers?

FOOTMAN: He got over to join de Gaulle, M. le Baron.

CHARLUS: Good lad. Get along with you now, and — (*Bellowing*) Monsieur!

MARCEL: (*Narrating*) He pursued me across the cobbles and caught my arm in a cruel grip.

CHARLUS: Eavesdropping, were you? Can't I hold a private conversation without a dozen little gentlemen creeping about me with their ears cocked?

MARCEL: I beg your pardon. I didn't see you until I was almost upon you.

CHARLUS: You will walk with me for a little. It is safer to talk in the street, where one can put a wall of space between oneself and the enemy. . . .

MARCEL: (*Narrating*) We walked slowly by the river, upon which the moon was now casting her first indecisive and watery rays. M. de Charlus had transferred his grip from my arm to my shoulder, his manner that of a friendly policeman who conducts to jail a criminal with whom he feels great sympathy, but whose escape he has no intention of permitting, less he lose his promotion.

CHARLUS: (*Fading in*) Since you have heard so much, you may as well hear more. Your racial peculiarity, I fancy, ensures my safety: should you feel inclined to tattle to the Gestapo in the hope of buying favours for yourself, it will be your word against mine. And mine will be believed. My Germanophile sympathies are well known — and the better believed because I am open in the expression of my distaste for the Nazis. The officer-class trusts me; I have a respect for the Prussian and he, for his part, is prepared to take the place of the Glorious Archangel Michael as my protecting angel.

MARCEL: But, sir, why should you run such risks? What has made you change your mind?

CHARLUS: Like the rest of them, you cannot bring yourself to believe my simplest statements. Frederick the Great I can accept; I could accept the Emperor William and the Emperor Franz Josef (who, by the way, always addressed me as Monsignor); but I do not care to see France in the grip of the sanitary orderly — or the corporal, if you will. It's a single step.

MARCEL: But Morel —

CHARLUS: I shall be obliged if you will not take that name upon
your lips. It has become so much bile upon my own. I had to
give Madame Verdurin the impression that I meant to write to
him; but the only words I could write would shrivel his eyes
in his head. *Morel!*

MARCEL: I'm sorry. (*Pause*) Surely Madame de Guermantes is in
some sympathy with us?

CHARLUS: Have you no brains at all? Have they been addled by
fright, or by adoration of your charming cousin (who, I believe,
is in the pay of the Gestapo, but my information may not be
exact)? Madame de Guermantes is always loyal to the winner.
She will be loyal to this one, so long as he remains; and then as
loyal as a leech to the next. There is no difference between her
drawing-room and Madame Verdurin's — save that Oriane does
not yet invite the Obersturmbannfuehrer to her 'days'. Oriane
takes the long view, and doesn't propose to compromise her
future more than is strictly necessary — which, perhaps,
sets her a step above Madame Verdurin and the woman who
attends the toilet in the Champs Élysées. Their 'salons' are
open to all the rag-tag and bob-tail, to tail-coats and jack-boots
alike.

MARCEL: Tonight, I received my dismissal from the Hôtel de
Guermantes.

CHARLUS: Exactly. And Madame Verdurin will kick you out of
doors tomorrow.

Where will you go? To England? If that's your fancy, I can
send you an introduction to a cousin of the young person with
whom I was conversing just now — the cousin is a friend of
mine, a delightful fellow with a breadth of judgment uncommon in his class. He's with de Gaulle now, and when I've done
my work here, I may join him. Now then: let us be businesslike.
If you go to England, what will you do there? What will be
your plans?

MARCEL: Well, Monsieur, I have been meaning to write a book. . . .

(*A silence*)

NARRATOR: The moon rising to her full illumines them as they lean for a moment upon the parapet of the Seine; the small young man, slender, his great black eyes mournful with time past and time to come; the tall, bulky man, purse-mouthed, the light just striping the silver pigeons' wings of his hair. . . .

CHARLUS: A book? About what? A romance? A history? I hope you'll give us something better than that pretentious little volume of yours with all those scribbles by Madeleine Lemaire. . . .

MARCEL: It will be a book about Time. . . .

NARRATOR: *Si du moins il m'était laissé assez de temps pour accomplir mon oeuvre, je ne manquerais pas de la marquer au sceau de ce Temps dont l'idée s'imposait à moi avec tant de force aujourd'hui, et j'y décrirais les hommes, cela dût-il les faire ressembler à des etres monstrueux, comme occupant dans le Temps une place autrement considérable que celle si restreinte qui leur est réservée dans l'espace, une place, au contraire, prolongée sans mesure, puisqu'ils touchent simultanément, comme des géants, plongés dans les années, à des époques vécues par eux, si distantes — entre lesquelles tant de jours sont venus se placer — dans le Temps.*

They stand like giants, immersed in Time.

II

Madame de Charlus

NOTE

I SEE no hope of solving completely the chronological problem of *À la Recherche du Temps Perdu*. (See notes, Appendix D.) Even if we allow for the expansion and revision of his original draft, made between 1907–1912, Proust was peculiarly careless. His world, the world of his book, was suspended in the hanging gardens of his mind: he timed it as he pleased.

To make a start at all, I think we must assume that 'Marcel' was born in the same year as Proust, that is, in 1871. I shall not go further into the matter here, but for the purpose of *Madame de Charlus* I assumed that the Duc de Guermantes was born in 1837, the Baron de Charlus in 1840 and Oriane, then Mlle de Guermantes, in 1848. (This would make their respective ages, at the time of the final party given by the Princess de Guermantes in *Time Regained*, 83, 80 and 72.)

There is only a single reference to the marriage of M. de Charlus: it occurs in *The Guermantes Way*, II, 272–73.

' "Yet, Oriane, if you take the case of your brother-in-law Palamède you were speaking about just now; no mistress in the world could ever dream of being mourned as that poor Madame de Charlus has been." "Ah!" replied the Duchess, "Your Highness must permit me not to be altogether of her opinion. People don't all like to be mourned in the same way, each of us has his preferences." "Still, he did make a regular cult of her after her death. It is true that people sometimes do for the dead what they would not have done for the living." "For one thing," retorted

Mme de Guermantes in a dreamy tone which belied her teasing
purpose, "we go to their funerals, which we never do for the
living!" M. de Guermantes gave a sly glance at M. de Bréauté as
though to provoke him into laughter at the Duchess's wit. "At
the same time I frankly admit," went on Mme de Guermantes,
"that the manner in which I should like to be mourned by a man
I loved would not be that adopted by my brother-in-law." The
Duke's face darkened. He did not like to hear his wife utter rash
judgments, especially about M. de Charlus. "You are very particular. His grief set an example to everyone," he reproved her
stiffly. But the Duchess had in dealing with her husband that sort
of boldness which animal tamers show, or people who live with a
madman and are not afraid of making him angry. "Oh, very well,
just as you like—he does set an example, I never said he didn't, he
goes every day to the cemetery to tell her how many people he
has had to luncheon, he misses her enormously, but — as he'd
mourn for a cousin, a grandmother, a sister. It is not the grief of a
husband. It is true that they were a pair of saints, which makes it
all rather exceptional." '

We know only two others things about Mme de Charlus, that
she was a Bourbon princess, and that she brought her husband
the estates of Brézé. (Mlle de Brézé, incidentally, was the niece
of Cardinal Richelieu and the wife of the Duc d'Enghien, later
the Prince de Condé. The Duchesse de Guermantes was a 'great-
grand-daughter of Mlle de Montpensier'. I suspect that Proust
had sometimes played with the idea of working out a precise
genealogical structure for the Guermantes, but never had the time
to put it into practice.)

We know of Charlus that he mourned her, but rather as a
brother for a sister than as a husband for a wife. We know
that, despite his violence, his scatological sadism, he could be
generous and kind. It seemed difficult to believe that he would
have distressed his wife by an open display of his predilec-
tions: constructing the story of his marriage with Gide's

story in mind, I was careful to leave 'Eugénie' innocent of her betrayal.

My second experiment was in the choice of setting.

Edmée de la Rochefoucauld, in *Le Disque Vert* (1953) speaks of Proust's horror of his own time: and indeed, he concerns himself hardly at all with the history of his own day except where he cannot possibly ignore it (the first world war) or where, as with the Dreyfus affair, he can use a national upheaval for an artistic purpose. It seems to me that the great artist rarely writes of the world which lies immediately about him, since he cannot get it into perspective. The novelist is not the journalist — the event on Monday, the report on Tuesday: he needs time in which to think. The dogma that precise contemporaneity is desirable, is a contemporary invention of the unthinking. George Eliot set her novels thirty–forty years back from her own time: so did Dickens (*Pickwick, Little Dorrit, David Copperfield*), so did Balzac and Stendhal. The only great novelist who was actively engaged in portraying his contemporary scene was Dostoievski: yet although *The Possessed* is immediately contemporary, his finest novel, *The Brothers Karamazov*, is set back twenty years.

In this programme, however, I wished to see whether I could show M. de Charlus against a background of historical events, so I chose the Siege of Paris and the Commune. The result of taking Marcel's eye off Charlus in this way is, I am aware, often un-Proustian: but I daresay Charlus himself was frequently un-Proustian when unobserved by Proust: as I have said before, 'my' characters are only intended to represent the raw material of the artist. In any case I was deliberately attempting to do something un-Proustian (that is, to show his people caught up by the drama of history) without losing the Proustian spirit of the programme as a whole.

One of my difficulties was to find an idiom for the 'old woman' who tells Charlus of the death of the valet, Pinaud. Proust had a poor ear for working-class speech, as can be observed in the scene in Jupien's brothel (*Time Regained*, 139–142, *Le Temps Retrouvé*, xiv, 141–144): all I could do was to borrow his own doubtful idiom, varying it as much as I could with an eye to greater plausibility, while not altogether destroying the sound of Proust's voice.

I had to remember that Charlus himself was young — no more than twenty-nine years old — and to reduce the full flow of mature Charlusian imagery accordingly. I had also to remember not to destroy the listener's sympathy with him — at least, not until the end, when, though truly mourning Eugénie, he cannot resist pretending that he has just composed, for a footman, the little waltz he had once dedicated to his wife. I hoped even so that, appalling as this action might seem, he would not forfeit sympathy altogether. For Charlus's desires were compulsive and he could not struggle against them. He was no stronger than Gide: but I think he was kinder.

Towards the conclusion of this programme, M. de Charlus happens to mention to Swann that he knows a nice little woman who would adore to meet him. She is, of course, Odette de Crecy: a fact which leads directly to the third 'reconstruction' in my series, *Swann in Love*.

MADAME DE CHARLUS

MARCEL: For a long time I used to go to bed early. Blowing out my candle, I allowed the unpublished diary of the Goncourts, that Gilberte had lent me earlier that evening, to slip from my fingers, and almost at once fatigue closed my eyes; yet, to my surprise I did not instantly fall asleep. I believed that my wakefulness was caused by the little Athene owl who, in her tree at Tansonville, kept making her meaningless and plaintive exhortation of the night; but even as I told myself that this was so, I felt my left hand reaching out to the book I had abandoned and my right fumbling along the rim of the bedside table for matches with which to rekindle my watchlight. For a moment the print danced with the candle-flame, black on the white page, as black and as white as the evening habit of M. de Charlus, whose name was set down before me, and as I drew the candle nearer to my eyes, a particle of crimson wax, fallen from its lip, set in his buttonhole the rosette of the Legion of Honour. As I began to read, the sounds of the Present, the voice of the bird in her mysterious turret of leaves, the fingering of the breeze through the hedge of pink hawthorns that gave out their pungent sweetness into the night like the breath of a girl opening her lips to declare her love, were overpowered by that voice from the past, the voice of the elder Goncourt who had known Verdurin, the critic of the *Revue*, and the young Charles Swann, then only twenty-two years old, and the young Baron de Charlus: had known them before my birth in a world as foreign to me as the world of Thaïs or Augustine, since, of those yesterdays in which we had no part, one is as far from us as another. The date was April 7th 1868. . . .

D

GONCOURT: ... April 7th, 1868. Dined ... with the Princess and
Sainte-Beuve, the Princess vivacious in a gown of china-crêpe,
the delicious colour of limetrees in the early sunlight of spring,
amethysts about her Renaissance brow and on her full and
creamy bosom. A woman, when she is a masterpiece, is indeed
the first of all works of art. Windows open to the evening, the
violet light thin above the trees and the air smelling of violets,
which, *ma foi,* had no existence but in the colour of the night
and the jewels of the Princess! She spoke to us of *Manette
Salomon,* which she had been reading for the second time,
praising the world of artists which, she said, we had created as
if we were gods with the power to create men. This pleased us
deeply, but during the exchange Sainte-Beuve remained mute,
gazing down at the plate before him, a delicate circlet of rose and
gold with iridescence of goldfish, the rim encrusted with rosy
vines, veined as it might be by the silverpoint of Leonardo. We
felt the hostility of the Sorbonne even in the silence of our
friend, and were glad when the Princess, by speaking of the
recent marriage of the Baron de Charlus to Mlle de Montagnac,
changed the subject. The Princess merry at the expense of the
Marquise de Villeparisis, that soi-disant Bohemian who, though
despising rank and nobility and counting nought of worth but
talent, intelligence, virtue, had yet contrived to marry her
nephew Palamède to the estates of Brézé. . . .

PRINCESSE MATHILDE: (*Fading in*) Estates of Brézé, which are
almost a royal domain, you know. But that's not all. Have you
heard that she's betrothed her niece —

GONCOURT: Mademoiselle de Guermantes?

PR. MATHILDE: As you say, Mademoiselle de Guermantes —
Oriane — to her other nephew, the Prince des Laumes?

GONCOURT: Upon my word! That's news to me.

PR. MATHILDE: Who is quite the wealthiest, noblest, and most
eligible bachelor of the Faubourg!

SAINTE-BEUVE: Now let me see ... Mademoiselle de Montagnac.

Surely she must be of the collateral branch of the family of Jean de Montagnac?

GONCOURT: Jean de Montagnac. Oh, wait a minute, wasn't he the priest —

SAINTE-BEUVE: Precisely. Who commissioned from Enguerrand Charonton, in the fifteenth century, that great Coronation of the Virgin at Villeneuve-les-Avignon.

PR. MATHILDE: Quite so. And you, Goncourt, if I know anything about you, will count it her greatest claim to distinction. Mind you, she's also a Bourbon — not that it matters to me! I only love and understand and *sense* what is modern — but there it is: she is.

SAINTE-BEUVE: I fancy myself that Brézé will prove to be the greatest distinction of all in the eyes of the Marquise de Villeparisis.

GONCOURT: But surely the Marquise herself married for love?

PR. MATHILDE: Eventually. It was most creditable. But first of all she became Duchesse d'Havré — thereby embracing the world; so when her second chance came she was in a financial position to embrace Paradise.

GONCOURT: Princess, Princess, you are very wicked!

SAINTE-BEUVE: I hear that Mademoiselle de Montagnac is two years older than the Baron. He's twenty-eight, isn't he? How is it that she's appeared so little in society?

PR. MATHILDE: Delicate health, or so I'm told. And such shyness! It's almost morbid. She was so shy that at one time she even thought of becoming a *religieuse*.

GONCOURT: What a wife for the wild young gentleman who could take his pick of any woman in Paris!

PR. MATHILDE: Who *has* taken his pick, I dare say, and tired of peonies may now be content to pin in his buttonhole the simple marguerite. . . .

MARCEL: Laying the book aside before reading on, but not permitting my eyes to close since it was now my intention to read until morning, I tried to visualise Madame de Villeparisis in the autumn hour before the beauty of her face and of her limbs had withered, to leave her looking, as I had known her, like an old apple woman nodding over her wares, as wrinkled and rosy as they: to behold Mlle de Guermantes as a girl, her cheeks fresh with youth but still of that peculiar pink which sometimes merges almost into violet, her finespun hair, like some marvellous golden lichen, or masterpiece of spun sugar, arranged flat on her brow, in the fashion that shocked and puzzled the Courvoisiers.

(Oriane's high and rippling laugh)

MME DE VILLE: What's the matter, Oriane?

ORIANE: Oh, my dear aunt, you were looking so solemn, almost like Father!

MME DE VILLE: Well, I don't like to see you smoking cigarettes like a cocotte in a railway carriage! If only the Duchesse d'Angoulême could see you!

ORIANE: Oh, oh, if only! Or the poor little Courvoisiers! I shock them so terribly, simply by being intelligent. You can't imagine how they dread intelligence! To them it's a sort of burglar's jemmy by which people they don't know from Adam force the doors of the most reputable drawing-rooms. When they knew I had allowed my face to be drawn by Gavarni, who made me look exactly like an odalisque, I must say . . . they nearly died!

MME DE VILLE: They probably will die when they hear you are to marry Basin. I know they were hoping you'd marry an artist, or a free-thinker, or some sort of scalliwag, and so pass into the category of detrimentals.

ORIANE: They never can see that nothing matters but cleverness and niceness. And Basin agrees with me.

MME DE VILLE: I fear Gilbert doesn't, though. He really will be an absurd brother-in-law for you to have; always prating about rank. When he heard that you'd allowed young Swann to take

you to dine in a public restaurant with M. Viollet-le-Duc and
that flashy fellow Gautier, he said to me, 'I wish Oriane would
bear in mind that she is, after all, the great-grand-daughter of
Mlle de Montpensier!'

ORIANE: But who could have been more Bohemian — up to a
point — than La Grande Mademoiselle? I can hardly see Marie-
Gilbert manning a cannon — even supposing Gilbert would
let her! When does Charlus return, by the way?

MME DE VILLE: At the end of the month. It will be too hot in
Algeria after April, and indeed, I think it was rather selfish of
him to take Eugénie, when she's so delicate and feels the heat so
much.

ORIANE: I hope he's faithful to her. He's such a terror, poor
Mémé! He can hardly look at a woman without wanting to
swallow her up.

MME DE VILLE: (*With constraint*) He has that reputation, I am afraid.

ORIANE: And Eugénie is one of those large, stately, meek creatures just like beautiful cows who simply ask to be swallowed.
(*Pause*) Basin will not be faithful to me.

MME DE VILLE: My *dear* child! (*Pause*) Well, if by chance he is
not — and I am sure my nephew will know his duty — he will
at least care for the conduct of your home. He thinks you very
beautiful. And he is proud of your wit. After all, the wit of the
Guermantes. . . .

ORIANE: Ah! But there's no such thing! It's just an absurd reputation like the Biscuits of Rheims or the Porkpies of Tours.
(*Pause*) And if there were such a thing, does any Guermantes
possess it but myself?

MME DE VILLE: Oriane! You really must be less mischievous
when you have a drawing-room of your own!

ORIANE: But my drawing-room is going to be quite delightful!
I shall invite only people who please me, and when *I* entertain
the Princess Mathilde I shall not surround her with all those
boring Bonapartists, as the Courvoisiers do. Do you know

what Viollet-le-Duc said to me? He said, 'For a really agreeable evening, the mistress of the house must have a lover and the lover must not be there.' If needs be, I shall dismiss Basin and pack him off to the Jockey.

MME DE VILLE: I think, my dear, you will not find Basin so adaptable a husband as you anticipate. There is a lion-like quality about my favourite nephew.

ORIANE: There is a lion-taming quality about me.

FOOTMAN: Madame la Princesse de Guermantes-Bavière!

PR. DE GUER: My dear Aunt Madeleine! Oriane!

ORIANE: How splendid you look, Marie-Gilbert! I like the raven plumes — most successful! One wouldn't dream of saying 'Nevermore'.

MME DE VILLE: You look very flushed. Have you been hurrying?

PR. DE GUER: I've only just learned — in fact, I overheard my footman talking — and I came straight to see you — about something that happened just before Palamède's marriage. Did you know that he was forced to *pay* to have it hushed up and that — ?

ORIANE: Marie, you must try to begin at the beginning. We are all agog.

PR. DE GUER: But didn't you know? It seems that one of those horrible creatures of the night — one can't call them *men* — made a suggestion to him in the Bois, and Palamède turned round and beat him almost to death! He's got to pay compensation and have him cared for in hospital!

MME DE VILLE: Where did your footman hear all this?

PR. DE GUER: From Mr Haydon's valet. Mr Haydon was with Palamède when it happened. Isn't it dreadful? And he does so detest that sort of thing. Fancy the creature having to be paid to keep quiet! It's repulsive.

ORIANE: Well, I suppose Mémé had to keep it from Eugénie somehow. She'd have been so shocked, poor dear. She has no idea what the world is like.

PR. DE GUER: I really think you should have *less* idea, Oriane. Oh, Aunt Madeleine, how superb Palamède must have looked, turning on that monster! So tall and handsome, with his eyes flashing —

ORIANE: I hope the monster was not very ugly and small. It would make the whole thing seem unfair.

PR. DE GUER: Oh, nonsense! You'd make fun of anything.

(*Eagerly*) Have you any news from Mémé, Aunt Madeleine?

MME DE VILLE: Well, don't y'know, I had a letter this very morning. It's very hot in Biskra, and Eugénie rests most of the day. Palamède says the Arab children are charming. They play on little flutes. . . .

(An Arab tune, played on a flute)

CHARLUS: My dear, you look tired. I've let you walk too far.

EUGÉNIE: It's only that the sun is so hot, Palamède. I feel as if someone were holding a burning-glass to my face.

CHARLUS: There's some shade under the wall here.

EUGÉNIE: Such pale shade! I never saw shade as pale as that.

CHARLUS: Sit down on the bench.

EUGÉNIE: Here? I could go a little further, I think. Do let us walk a little further!

CHARLUS: Don't you like it here?

EUGÉNIE: There's such a smell from the goats. And that boy makes my head ache.

CHARLUS: The little musician? (*Calling out*) You, there! Hold your noise!

(Flute playing stops)

Come here! Will you come here, sir, when I call you?

LASSIF: (*A charming intonation*) Ill? The poor lady is ill? I could fetch her some milk. . . .

EUGÉNIE: Oh, no, child, though you're very kind. What is your name?

LASSIF: My name is Lassif. I am twelve years old.

EUGÉNIE: Who is that little girl over there?

LASSIF: She is not little. She is Rhadra, my big sister.

EUGÉNIE: (*Very faintly*) How . . . pretty . . . she is. . . .

CHARLUS: Eugénie! There — put your head down — right down . . . so. That's right. Don't be afraid, I have my arms around you.

LASSIF: It is as I said. She is ill.

CHARLUS: (*Roaring*) Go away, you little rascal! And don't stand there hovering about! (*Change of tone: to his wife*) I was a selfish dog to bring you here. There! Do you feel better?

EUGÉNIE: Yes . . . I'm all right now. I'll just sit here quietly for a moment. . . . The wood-pigeons, they never stop their cooing, do they? It is such a little noise, but it goes through my head.

CHARLUS: I said, I am a selfish dog. I should never have brought you to this place.

EUGÉNIE: But M. Haydon said you would like it so much, that the people were so charming! And indeed they are, and I should like it too, if I didn't get so tired.

CHARLUS: (*Angrily*) I should not have allowed Willy to persuade me. I should have had more sense, and so should he.

EUGÉNIE: Please don't be angry with him. You and he are such good friends. It is pleasant to see you together, so like brothers. If he were here you could both go for long walks and you would enjoy it so much more.

CHARLUS: (*Half-laughing*) I'd be a curious fellow if I brought him on a honeymoon!

(*Flute begins again, farther off*)

Curse that boy! I'll go and teach him —

EUGÉNIE: No, stay here with me. He is such a pretty little boy. He means no harm. His sister is beautiful too, but he has the better eyes.

CHARLUS: His sister is an Ouled-Naïl.

EUGÉNIE: Why, do you know them?

CHARLUS: I know of them. The porter at the hotel pointed her out to me. Boy! You — Lassif! Stop that damnable wailing and come here!

(Flute stops)

EUGÉNIE: You mustn't be cross with him. He is very little for his age, and so very thin!

LASSIF: Monsieur wants something?

CHARLUS: What would a certain little rascal say if Monsieur were to put him over his knee and beat him till he howled for mercy? Eh? What would he say?

LASSIF: He would not like that at all, Monsieur.

CHARLUS: Then to avoid such a contingency, the little rascal will run as fast as those matchstick legs can carry him back to Monsieur's hotel and tell the porter to send a carriage at once for Monsieur.

LASSIF: A carriage? To this place?

CHARLUS: Of course to this place, idiot! And the little rascal may ride on the box, if he pleases. Be off with you!

LASSIF: I shall obey Monsieur.

CHARLUS: (*To Eugénie*) There, my dear, no more exertion for you to-day. You shall lie in your room and I will sit beside you. Or, if you prefer to sleep, I might walk a little myself.

EUGÉNIE: I am a great drag upon you already, Palamède.

CHARLUS: No. You are my wife.

EUGÉNIE: It seems strange that I should be . . . and that you should love me. As perhaps you do. . . .

CHARLUS: (*After a pause*) I have never loved any other woman. Isn't that enough? (*Pause*) Is it not enough?

EUGÉNIE: I have always been doubtful of people. I never thought I was handsome. And I was never very much in the world.

CHARLUS: (*Teasing*) You were Rapunzel in her tower at Brézé, waiting for a lover to admire her hair.

EUGÉNIE: My hair is getting thin, I think. I don't know why. It's since we came here. I shall be better when we are back in Paris. . . .

MARCEL: It was forty years after this that Morel showed me a letter, glazed and brittle with age, which he had purloined from the bureau of his patron, a letter written by M. Charlus himself to the dearest friend of his youth, the Englishman, Willy Haydon, and returned to him by Willy's executors in a sealed box containing the whole of the correspondence between them. It began: 'Eugénie asks me if I love her, and I can only reply that I have never loved another woman. This seemed to me sufficient. . . .'

CHARLUS: . . . 'Eugénie asks me if I love her, and I can only reply that I have never loved another woman. This seemed to me sufficient to ensure our happiness, but she needs something more of me and I cannot give it. As she lies exhausted on the day-bed, with the shadow of the palm-leaves lying as sharp as razors across the blind, for here you cannot shut the world away and Africa frets at you even in the grains of sand that stick between your toes, I kiss her beautiful eyelids and am torn with such a strange pity that the tears run from beneath my own. She speaks of you with such tenderness. If ever we have a son, she says, she would like him to resemble you; but I think we shall have no son. How she loves me! She gives me all the nobility, the gentleness, the exquisite goodness and humility of herself; she holds nothing from me. But my peace of mind, alas, is not in her gift. You ask me if I am happy, and I tell you no. Without you, I could not be. Yet there is a voluptuous harshness in this place which fascinates me and makes me unwilling, even for her sake, to depart, though I fear I may kill her if I have not the strength to rouse myself from this hashish dream of heat and eternal summer.

'To-day, when she was faint on one of our walks, we were succoured by a charming little scoundrel, twelve years old, his flesh tender as spring chicken through the rents in his burnous, a little flute player who was all concern for us but who nevertheless picked my pocket before he bade us farewell. . . . I shall seek him out and chastise him, for if it is the will of the Lord that he shall be a Good Samaritan, it must also be His will that I, His earthly vessel, should drive the devil out of him. . . .'

MARCEL: . . . 'for if it is the will of the Lord that he shall be a Good Samaritan, it must also be His will that I, His earthly vessel, should drive the devil out of him. . . .' In May Monsieur and Madame de Charlus left Biskra, and after a tour of Sicily and the Italian lakes returned to Paris, where, before many months had passed, the young couple had established a devoted ménage. Eugénie's health had apparently improved, and when she walked in the Bois on Sundays between her husband and the handsome, high-shouldered young Englishman who, with his slanting blue eyes and charming medical stoop, as if he desired to catch not only the murmur of one's lips but of one's heart, was like a brother to them both, she was admired for the delicate crescents of colour that had appeared upon the waxen fruit of her cheeks. Oriane, who was now the Princesse des Laumes and whose drawing-room was already the smartest and most talked-of in Paris, since she thought nothing of inviting to her 'days' both the Princesse Mathilde and Monsieur Fromentin, was loud in praise of her new sister-in-law, being perfectly genuine in this inasmuch as she was charmed by Eugénie's air of race and of rustic simplicity and saw in her not the faintest shadow of a rival.

(Distant motif on flute)

In the spring of the following year, M. de Charlus left his wife, who would not for a second time risk the heat, and returned for a few weeks to the scene of their honeymoon where, every day, he wrote to her the tender and poetic letters so characteristic of the gentler borders of his spirit, assuring her that though he had Willy to keep him company, yet he could not help but see her gracious shadow on every path they had trodden together, as if she were for ever slipping just ahead of him, round the bend of a wall crumbling in the merciless sun, or through the sparse shadow of a trinity of palm-trees enamelled in jade and encrusted with peridot and gold.

(Flute motif dies away)

When he came back to Paris it was as a husband refreshed, a lover with springing heels and tossing crest, and Eugénie, at her Wednesdays, often had the pleasure of displaying, in loving, almost girlish pride, some token of the thought for her to which he delighted to devote his unique artistic taste and sensibility.

(Sound of voices, chatter, laughter: the laugh of Oriane)

ORIANE: My beloved Eugénie, it's delicious and it's absurd! To think of Mémé, who looks like Rupert of the Rhine and Genghis Khan rolled into one, painting a fan for you! Oh look, Aunt Madeleine, do look! One would really think it was done by a woman!

MME DE VILLE: Really, one never comes to the end of Palamède's surprises. What's this, the terrace at Guermantes with a border of white peacocks? And the motto — I must put on my spectacles. It's so fine I can't read it.

EUGÉNIE: *Post Nubila, Phoebus:* 'after the clouds, the clear sun'. He painted it for me to celebrate his homecoming.

ORIANE: There's simply nothing he can't do! Paint like Watteau, write verse as well as Gautier, compose little tunes as charming as Chopin's! Marie-Aynard, he must compose a lullaby for you when the time is ripe.

MME DE MARS: It would be so nice of Mémé, so *very* kind! I should be honoured. . . . But, Oriane, not at the top of your voice!

ORIANE: Nonsense! The first of my Guermantes kinsfolk to propose an heir! Marie-Gilbert has no luck, Eugénie has no luck as yet, I have no luck — though of course, it's early days, as they say —

EUGÉNIE: Oh, please! People will hear you.

ORIANE: But Marie-Aynard is to give us a Marquis or Marquise de Saint-Loup! Which is it to be? What shall you call him or her?

MME DE MARS: Aynard says that if it is a boy, it shall be Robert. If a girl, another Oriane.

ORIANE: (*Singing*)   'Gloire à Robert,
                    Marquis de Saint-Loup,
                    Gloire au bébé. . . .'

EUGÉNIE:
               } Sh-h-h-!
MME DE VILLE:

ORIANE: Anyway, I can't finish it on the spur of the moment. We must wait for Palamède. Isn't he coming, Eugénie?

EUGÉNIE: Oh, yes, but he went out with M. Haydon, so he may be late.

FOOTMAN: (*Announcing*) M. le Prince des Laumes!

ORIANE: Well, Basin! Have you come to take me home?

BASIN: Get your duds on, my dear, I've got the carriage waiting. Eugénie, my dear girl! Where's my little brother? Don't tell me I've missed him!

EUGÉNIE: I'm sure he won't be long now, if you can wait just a little while.

ORIANE: Yes, do stay just for ten minutes, Basin.

BASIN: My dear, if we're late again at Mme du Bellay's we shall both catch it, I tell you!

ORIANE: The only thing we are likely to catch at Mme du Bellay's is pneumonia. She has all her windows and doors wide open, as if she were always expecting to call for help.

BASIN: Oh, come now, she's not a bad old girl, and after all, she's a Mortemart.

ORIANE: And *was* she angry in England when the ambassador sent Princesse Murat into dinner before her! — though of course, as it happens, he was perfectly right, because over there precedence is given to the closest connection of a *reigning* monarch. Not that I really know anything about that sort of thing; Mémé's the authority.

FOOTMAN: Monsieur Haydon!

EUGÉNIE: Willy! I thought you were never coming. Is Palamède with you?

HAYDON: He's on his way, Madame, hotfoot, I do assure you.

EUGÉNIE: Oriane, Marie-Aynard, may I present to you Mr Willy Haydon, our dearest friend? He and Basin have already met. Willy, let me present you to my sisters-in-law, the Princesse des Laumes, the Comtesse de Marsantes.

HAYDON: Enchanted, Princess: Madame de Marsantes, your servant.

EUGÉNIE: Aunt Villeparisis — where is she?

ORIANE: Gone to talk to some aged Royalty in the corner — I didn't catch her name — she's showing her your fan. Well, Mister Haydon, your blue eyes are the talk of Paris, d'ye know that?

HAYDON: Oh, Lord, Madame, I can't think why that should be. There are only two of them.

ORIANE: Any protégé of Mémé's is instantly credited with being a crowned head incognito, or at the very least a criminal of international repute. I suppose you are not Monsieur Vautrin?

BASIN: Oriane! What sort of a joke is that?

ORIANE: A little bird tells me that Mémé is now spending all his time at the Cour d'Assise, studying life in the raw. You know — the murder in the rue Monthabor! He was seen yesterday at the trial. Monsieur de Goncourt saw him there, and told my dear Charles Swann.

HAYDON: Yes, that's so. Firon will be convicted and sentenced this afternoon. I couldn't drag Palamède away; he was rooted, simply rooted to the spot.

EUGÉNIE: I think it's horrible. I don't know what fascination he finds in these dreadful things.

FOOTMAN: The Baron de Charlus!

(*A chorus of greeting*)

EUGÉNIE:⎫ Oh, my dear, I thought you were never coming!
BASIN: ⎬ Here's my young brother, consort of murderers!
ORIANE: ⎭ The Baron Vidocq!

CHARLUS: Good-evening to you all! Eugénie, my dear, you must forgive me; I meant to be with you an hour sooner. How are you feeling? Has the headache gone?

EUGÉNIE: Thank you, dear, yes. It's quite gone away.

CHARLUS: Well, Basin, I hardly seem to set eyes on you these days — what, you're not in instant flight?

BASIN: Time flies, my dear fellow, and so must I. But first, how's my little brother? Our poor Mamma used to tell me I must always keep an eye on you, but it's hard to do it when you're always on the wing.

HAYDON: I say, Palamède, did they sentence Firon? Do tell us all about it!

CHARLUS: My boy, what a scene! You know how dark it grew this afternoon? — And I tell you, that courtroom, with only the narrow rays of the lamps on the judge's table to pierce the gloom, was like one of those adorable nightmares we loathe and don't want to relinquish. When the President pronounced sentence, Firon's mistress screamed and fainted. He'd listened to his fate quietly enough, but all at once he bounded up like a tiger on to the bench behind him, and with a gesture of violence and desperation — magnificent! — sent a last kiss in her direction. It was horrible — superb — capital, I assure you!

EUGÉNIE: Palamède, don't. You make me shudder.

CHARLUS: And Firon himself — a wild boar of a fellow! Hideous but fascinating. I had a strange feeling that if I could have spoken with him we should have understood each other.

ORIANE: The blood-spiller and the blood-curdler. I don't doubt it. What do you make of such a husband, Eugénie?

EUGÉNIE: He is always saying such things.

ORIANE: And then running home from his blood-bath to paint the most delicious fans for you!

CHARLUS: Well, Willy, you took to your heels and deserted me. What was the meaning of that?

HAYDON: I thought Madame de Charlus would be anxious about you, so I appointed myself an advance courier.

EUGÉNIE: Mr Haydon is so kind, Oriane. He is a great comfort to me.

CHARLUS: As he should be, my dear. The whole world would conspire to be a comfort to you, if it knew how good you were.

ORIANE: There's the right sort of husband to have! Basin never says such beautiful things to me. Well, we must make our round of farewells. . . .

(Noise of party dies away. Pause)

CHARLUS: . . . Surely the most successful of your Wednesdays, Eugénie? Has it tired you too much? You stand up far too much of the time, you know. You should adopt the old court custom of my Aunt Villeparisis and sit behind the Patience table. Shall you go and lie down?

EUGÉNIE: No, I don't think so. I thought we might dine quietly by ourselves and perhaps have a little music? You play so beautifully.

CHARLUS: Not to-night, it's impossible. I promised to dine with Willy at Voisin's. Afterwards, we may see Swann. But you shall have some music all for yourself soon — that is a promise.

EUGÉNIE: All for myself?

CHARLUS: Only for you. I am writing a little piece, to be dedicated to my wife.

EUGÉNIE: Palamède. . . .

CHARLUS: My love?

EUGÉNIE: I shall like that. But I wish . . . that you weren't so far away.

CHARLUS: Far away? I told you, I shall only be at Voisin's. That's only around the corner, as they say!

EUGÉNIE: I didn't mean in space. I think I meant . . . in spirit.

CHARLUS: (*Gently*) Is my spirit not near to you?

EUGÉNIE: I wish I didn't *doubt* so much. . . . But I expect I'm being very silly. Mémé — must you go out?

CHARLUS: No help for it. Willy has some problems to settle before he goes back to England to play the young squire, and after all his kindness to us — how can I not be kind to him?

EUGÉNIE: No, no, you're perfectly right. I was being selfish, as wives are. But if they were not selfish they would not be loving, I think . . . so perhaps selfishness isn't altogether a fault?

CHARLUS: You could never be at fault. You are my gentle saint. . . .

(*Footsteps along a street*)

CHARLUS: 'Pon my word, Swann, she's a pretty little woman! And not at all a common girl — she must come of decent parents. I could see Willy's eye brighten as he looked at her. Are you going to her later?

SWANN: On the stroke of midnight. My little Delphine adores romantic hours! She'll never let me escort her home after we have dined in case people should think she wasn't respectable. She is rather Botticelli, don't you think? Though oddly enough it's not a type I at all admire. She had an eye for you too, I fancied — I can't have that. We know your reputation.

CHARLUS: You misjudge me. I've quite done with all that sort of thing. Even if I still wanted to run around with women, I couldn't do it; Eugénie might hear of it and it would kill her.

E

No, my boy, I've grown respectable. Here's a cab coming; shall we take it?

SWANN: I'd rather walk. The air's delicious with all these lilacs about — how fine it is this year! And I swear I smell syringa. There must be a bush in one of these gardens.

CHARLUS: The tragedy of spring: the bush of flowers whose existence we cannot swear to.

SWANN: You're out of spirits to-night, Mémé.

CHARLUS: A little. How ever many friends we have, it is hard to spare a single one.

SWANN: When does Willy go?

CHARLUS: Next month.

SWANN: You and Eugénie will miss him.

CHARLUS: He is leaving me a bequest — his valet, a gigantic fellow with the absurd name of Horace Pinaud. My fatal kindness of heart! I would as soon have a buffalo in the house; he will certainly trample all my shirts and rip up my trouser-seams with a great blast from his nostrils. But Willy doesn't want to leave him destitute. . . . (*Pause: footsteps continue*) Oh, well, I shall contrive to endure him. By the by, did you see the attacks upon Flaubert in the *Gaulois* and *Constitution*? They called him a scoundrel and a moron.

SWANN: Oriane says they don't understand him. She said the other night, 'Flaubert, that arch enemy of the bourgeois is bourgeois through and through —' (*Clock begins to strike midnight*) Gad! How the time's flown! I must take a cab after all. Hey! Cabby! Cabby!

(*Clop-clop of hooves approaching*)

Can I drop you anywhere, Mémé?

CHARLUS: No thank you, my dear chap. I shall continue to enjoy the lilacs and the putative syringa.

(*Cab stops*)

SWANN: Twenty-five, rue des Cygnes, and look sharp about it!

CABBY: Right, sir.

(Cab moves off. Last stroke of midnight)

MARCEL: When Willy Haydon returned to England, the grief of
M. de Charlus was such that for two months he retired completely from society, keeping only the company of his wife,
who, though comforted to have him so closely at her side,
sensed his misery without knowing the cause: and in the selflessness of her nature prayed each night, with hands folded
over her patient and beautiful eyes, that some joy might come
to assuage it, even if this joy were to take him once more from
herself and leave her desolate. For she was one of those creatures, rarest of all upon this earth, rare as the aurochs or the
white rhinoceros, who are genuinely able to love another
better than themselves, who would rejoice, even while weeping,
to see the beloved in the arms of another woman, if that woman
were able to reinvigorate him with happiness. After a while,
however, she was pleased to discover that he derived some
curious easement from the absurdities of Pinaud, who had been
Willy's valet, and who, in his incongruity, appeared to afford
M. Charlus some palliation of his melancholy. . . .

CHARLUS: . . . What are you muttering about under your breath,
you Gascon from the Batignolles? Can't you so much as press
my trousers without growling over them like a tiger over a
lump of bleeding flesh that brings the juices to his muzzle and
boils his slaver up?

PINAUD: Monsieur le Baron wouldn't like it if I didn't keep my
thoughts to myself. Thought is free.

CHARLUS: A free-thinker, eh? You'd like to see the last king
strangled with the guts of the last priest?

PINAUD: *(Mumbling)* There's them that says we was created equal
and not to press each others' pants.

(Charlus gives a shout of laughter)

(*Louder*) Yes, Monsieur, and when Badinguet falls over on his napper, which he will do — Monsieur gave me to understand what I said was privileged —

CHARLUS: Badinguet? If you mean his Majesty the Emperor, then kindly say what you mean.

PINAUD: It's what we call him. . . . *When* he falls over on his napper there won't be no more pants-pressing. Every man will press his own.

CHARLUS: It is possible that you may be right: but until that fortunate or unfortunate time, according to one's point of view, you will keep your place and try to impress me with the skill that seems to have impressed Mr Haydon. (*Suddenly*) Eh? Eh? What do you say, young ruffian? When the next liquidation comes to pass — yes, I know that's the revolting phrase you use, — you'll string me up to the nearest lamp-post, eh?

PINAUD: (*A change of tone*) Monsieur le Baron should not let me presume. M. Haydon, like most young Englishmen, was a bit too free and easy. He gave me a lot of rope, as he called it.

CHARLUS: Because you're a handsome scoundrel, eh? Well, that won't weigh with me.

PINAUD: I beg Monsieur to pardon my freedom. (*With conceit*) My looks are my mother's fault. I shall try to please him.

CHARLUS: Till the next liquidation? Till the night of the lampposts? Come here. Come here, when I tell you!

PINAUD: Monsieur! My ear!

CHARLUS: So you'd fancy yourself as a delicious executioner, eh? Isn't that so?

PINAUD: My ear! You're hurting me, Monsieur!

CHARLUS: (*Violently*) Be off with you, and don't let me see your idiotic face till to-morrow. Go and tumble the bitches of Belleville — I wager that's your game? Eh? Isn't that what you do on your day off?

PINAUD: If Monsieur pleases. But I can take the women or leave them. Like my master that used to be, Monsieur.

CHARLUS: (*After a pause*) It is only for his sake that I keep you. Remember that.

PINAUD: He was a fine young gentleman, Monsieur, a regular sport. He and I used to have many a joke together. . . .

(*Pause*)

EUGÉNIE: . . . The autumn in Paris is so sad. I've been lying here all day watching the rain dripping over the little statue in the garden — poor little god, so full of tears!

CHARLUS: The doctor says that when you feel stronger you should go to Guermantes or Brézé. How would you like that?

EUGÉNIE: No, not now. I'm peaceful where I am. And you are with me.

CHARLUS: You look so tired.

EUGÉNIE: It has been a long day, so many hours without you. Mémé. . . .

CHARLUS: My dear? What is on your mind?

EUGÉNIE: You won't be angry with me? (*Pause*) Sometimes I am jealous.

CHARLUS: (*Rather sharply*) Of whom?

EUGÉNIE: Of the people on whom you lavish so much care and kindness — oh, how abominable I am being! — and of the people who admire you.

CHARLUS: Tell me.

EUGÉNIE: Even Willy Haydon, who was so good to us — how horrible it was of me to grudge the time you spent with him! But I couldn't help it. And even now — I am sure you will laugh at me — you seem to spend so many hours training poor Pinaud to his work —

CHARLUS: I can't put up with him for ever, my dear, and if he has no training he will be forced back to which ever sad gutter Willy took him from. And yet, he can brush a silk hat with any valet at Versailles!

EUGÉNIE: Sometimes when women look at you, I am jealous. So many love you! I know it.

CHARLUS: My dear good girl!

EUGÉNIE: And sometimes your eyes seem to rest upon other women with a passion that is not in them for me. People are spiteful, too. They hint things to me. . . .

CHARLUS: What things? (*Loudly*) I must demand to know!

EUGÉNIE: No, you mustn't be angry. . . . They hint that you have many mistresses.

(*Pause*)

CHARLUS: (*Slowly*) I swear to you, by the Holy Michael and his angels, that I have none.

EUGÉNIE: My dear . . . it is hard for me to say such things, because I wasn't brought up to be free of speech, like Oriane . . . but you are so virile, so strong! It must be hard for you . . . to have a shadow wife.

CHARLUS: (*Moved*) You say that to me? My dear shadow! I want nothing better.

EUGÉNIE: (*Sighing*) Be patient with me. And thank you.

CHARLUS: To prove it, I have brought you a gift; the little piece I said I should compose only for you.

EUGÉNIE: Palamède! How lovely! And how kind!

CHARLUS: Now what is there to cry about? I shall play it to you. Lie there quietly, just as you are, with the lamplight in your lap.

(*He plays to her a little waltz: it is in the style of the period, wistful and romantic, but it has a touch of originality. When it is halfway through, Marcel begins to speak*)

MARCEL: It was true that in his own fashion M. de Charlus cared deeply for his wife, his tenderness strengthened by the anguish that grew about his heart like a slender but tenacious bindweed, as her health once more began to wane. Yet he could not match her selflessness, nor spare her that inevitable cruelty which a

man wreaks upon a loving wife through the mere fact of pre-
ferring some other person to herself, even if that preference is
unexpressed by so much as a single word or even a single
wandering glance, and when, in the summer of the following
year, the Emperor declared war upon Prussia, M. de Charlus
astounded the Guermantes by refusing to take his wife from
Paris, insisting, despite her doctor's reassurance, that she was in
too sickly a condition to make even the short journey to the
neighbourhood of Combray.

The truth was that Horace Pinaud, after some violent
quarrel about a satin waistcoat he had failed to send to be
cleaned, had quit the service of the Baron and had flung off in
martial fury to join the National Guard of the XIIIth District:
whereupon the Baron, trembling in delightful terror at the
thought of this young warrior bred upon the precepts of
Messelier and Babeuf, could not now endure the thought of
leaving the capital while there was still a chance of meeting his
ex-protégé out of barracks.

BASIN: (*Fading in*) Really, Mémé, I can't see what there is to keep
you here! I can understand that Eugénie might be lonely at
Brézé, but if she went to Guermantes she'd have Marie-Aynard
and the baby to keep her company. We shall win the war all
right in six weeks, but on the other hand, there's no need to run
unnecessary risks.

CHARLUS: My good Basin, I have every faith in our Chassepôts
and our Mitrailleuse, and I don't expect to see M. de Bismarck
storming into Paris at breakfast time to-morrow. Eugénie is
perfectly comfortable here, and as for these donkeys of doc-
tors, who would let her traipse all over the countryside on
foot —

ORIANE:— but Palamède —

CHARLUS: — I prefer my own judgment. M. Palikao is confident,
they tell me, and so am I.

ORIANE: Really, Mémé, if you weren't so high and mighty, I should tell you you were a donkey yourself!

BASIN: Oriane! Now seriously, I'm very fond of my brother and I hardly think one should speak to him as if —

ORIANE: Don't glare at me, Basin! I shall not be intimidated. Nobody is asking Eugénie to trudge the roads on foot, with her household goods in a wicker basket. Mémé is obscuring the issue.

CHARLUS: My charming cousin, whom I respect and admire above all women, excluding — perhaps pardonably, as a husband should — my own wife, there is no need for Eugénie to travel at all. A whiff of grapeshot, as it were, and this curious adventure of Isidore, or Badinguet — as the plebs choose to call the Emperor — will be over. I have not the least doubt of it. . . .

MARCEL: And indeed, M. de Charlus, while privately considering his country ridiculous to indulge in a military adventure at a time of growing civil discontent — since he no more believed the Mitrailleuse would distract the attention of the discontented than he would believe a display of fireworks likely to distract the attention of a lean cat with a pigeon in view — had no doubt that France would be victorious, pointing out tirelessly in the drawing-rooms of the Faubourg the superiority of the Chassepôt rifle, with a range of 1,200 metres, to the German Needle gun, with a range of 600: figures he had received from the lips of Pinaud and which seemed to him, such was their source, as liquid and marvellous as the pearls of La Fontaine falling from the lips of Berma. When, in August, rumour from the Bourse announced the defeat of the King of Prussia and the capture of 25,000 prisoners, only the Princesse des Laumes, who was much influenced by her occasional daring appearances at the dinner-table of M. de Goncourt, forbore to cheer; and when that unbreathing twilight which precedes defeat made

still and silent the streets of Paris, turning to stone even the
very leaves upon the trees, was the sole Guermantes able to
draw consolation from the mere fact of having been right.

When M. Palikao, the Minister of War, confirmed the defeat
of MacMahon and on the following day announced the defeat
and capture of the Emperor at Sedan, it was Oriane who called
upon M. de Charlus at an unexpected hour, to make assault
upon his obstinacy, to beard, as she put it, the mule in his den.

*(Charlus' waltz for Eugénie, played rather hesitantly
by Eugénie upon the piano)*

EUGÉNIE: *(Through the music)* Oh, Palamède, how badly I play!
I was so poorly taught at the convent. Poor Sister Pélagie
could never play anything with more than four sharps herself,
— she used to turn any piece with five into two flats. *(Makes a
mistake)* Oh, dear! *(She pauses)*

CHARLUS: C natural, not C sharp. C natural. *(Eugénie begins
again)* There, you are doing quite nicely! You are improving
very much.

(Door opens)

SERVANT: Madame la Princesse des Laumes!

(Eugénie stops playing)

CHARLUS: Oriane? At this hour? It's twenty-past eleven. What
the devil. . . .

ORIANE: My dearest Eugénie! My dear Mémé! No, don't look at
me as if I were the ghost of Banquo! I know it's late, but they
told me downstairs that you hadn't gone to bed.

CHARLUS: It would be a pleasure to see you, my dear, whatever
the hour.

EUGÉNIE: Come and sit by me, Oriane. How delightful you look,
even in these sad days! I think it was so brave of you to come
through the streets. Paris is so sinister at night. They tell me

they are turning the Tuileries gardens into a great stables in case . . . in case we should be besieged.

ORIANE: (*Briskly*) Which we shall be, there's no doubt of it. Mémé, do you propose to stay here?

CHARLUS: I am not, my dear cousin, in a state of animal panic.

ORIANE: So I see. Eugénie, my love, how are you keeping?

EUGÉNIE: Oh, I think — much as usual. I have to rest a great deal.

ORIANE: Mémé: Basin and I shall go, naturally, to Les Laumes: Marie-Aynard has been there for the past week. Guermantes is already overrun. We shall have the jackboots plunging all over our gardens and sleeping in our beds. I want you both to come with us.

CHARLUS: We shall do nothing of the kind. (*Grandly*) I do not desert the capital of my country when she is threatened.

ORIANE: Bravo! That is the sort of speech I adore people to make on balconies. But we are not on a balcony now.

CHARLUS: (*Infuriated*) By God, Oriane, do you take me for one of your miserable played-out little Royalties or cowed Grand Dukes, that you dare to speak to me like that? I can hardly order my cousin out of my wife's house, but —

EUGÉNIE: Oriane, oh, please! He is so terrible when he is angry — oh, please —

CHARLUS: (*Sobering*) My own Eugénie, I am not angry with you. (*To Oriane, harshly*) But as for you, coming here in the middle of the night to subject me to that insulting and trivial badinage which passes for wit —

ORIANE: There, there, Mémé! I am sorry. I humbly apologise. Look! I am sweeping you such a curtsey as no woman ever made to any man except, perhaps, *Le Roi Soleil*. (*Meekly*) It is a beautiful curtsey, Palamède, but a little too deep for comfort. I do hope you will be generous and raise me up. For otherwise I shall have to spend all night upon your floor, and the servants will look so strange when they come and find me there in the morning. I expect they will sweep me out with the ashes.

CHARLUS: (*Laughing despite himself*) Get up, Oriane, and don't be an idiot. There! I give you permission to rise. Now then, sit down and tell me what all this is about.

ORIANE: Ouch! It is dreadful, you know; I am sure I have a touch of rheumatism in my knees, which makes me dread to think of what I shall be like at thirty. (*Pause*) Mémé, if you won't leave Paris, I beg you to let me take Eugénie with me to Les Laumes.

EUGÉNIE: Oh, no! I don't want to leave Palamède. My place is at his side. I must stand by him!

ORIANE: My dear, I don't want to sound cruel: but 'stand' is just what you cannot do. You're not strong enough. You need rest and quiet. To lie at someone's side in a time of danger, or even to *sit* there, isn't enough.

EUGÉNIE: But I am feeling far stronger! I can't bear to be sent away!

ORIANE: (*After a pause*) Palamède: aren't I right? (*Pause*) If *you* have ties in Paris, you must stay. But it isn't fair to Eugénie to keep her there.

CHARLUS: (*After another pause*) Yes, you are right.

EUGÉNIE: Oh, no, please! I am sure it is not God's will —

CHARLUS: She is right, Eugénie. You will go to Les Laumes with Oriane, and I shall join you as soon as I can. Since Marie-Aynard is there, you will be able to play with her little boy; you will like that.

(*Eugénie is sobbing*)

As Oriane says, I myself have ties here. . . .

MARCEL: Eugénie had not been a week at Les Laumes before the Prussian encirclement was completed, and Paris was cut off from the world outside save for the meagre flutterings of news borne by the fantasy of balloon or of carrier pigeon, which seemed like messengers in some sinister fairy-tale. In the Bois de Bologne, the oxen, pigs and sheep that had been driven to pasture cropped the grass to a grey and sullen stubble, the colour of thunder or of the sound of the cannon that rolled by day and by night through the fretful waking, the tumultuous slumber, of the new Republic. M. de Charlus, seeking comfort from his young warrior behind the barracks square, pleading with his eyes for the assurance that Pinaud and his gallant comrades would at length break out and drive the Prussians from the gates, had his optimism rudely dashed.

PINAUD: (*Calling sharply*) Who's that? Who's that, slinking around behind me, eh? Come out, where I can see your face! (*Change of tone*) Well, well, well, if it isn't the Baron! I hope he's in the pink, because he'll need all his strength pretty soon, he can bet his life.

(*Faint booming of cannon now and then, through this scene and the following scene between Charlus and Swann*)

CHARLUS: Moderate your tone, my good man. It is an honour I do you, seeking you out simply for your well-being. I feel responsible for you, Pinaud. If any harm came to you, I should not like to think it was through any lack of brotherly care on my part.

PINAUD: All right, all right, but look here, let's get out from under this lamp! I don't want every Tom, Dick or Harry goggling at me. Well, do they give you horsemeat yet at the places you go to eat? They say it'll be dog and cat next — brrr! And rat omelette, always providing there's an egg left.

CHARLUS: Pinaud, my good lad. . . . I must say they've made a fine-looking soldier out of you! Yes, indeed. . . . Tell me, Pinaud, we shall have them in the end? We shall force them back?

PINAUD: Force 'em back? You watch this lot: you watch those old boys, Rochefort, Gambetta and that crowd, old Arago, who must be a hundred and ninety — they'll make peace quick enough. And then —

CHARLUS: (*Stiffening again into his old arrogance*) You are becoming something of an oracle. I fancy your voice of doom booming in the caves of Delphi, indistinguishable from the thunder of the immortal surf. And then — well, what then?

PINAUD: (*With grinning ferocity*) Then the people will take over. And the pants-pressers will show the gents who've got the pants a thing or two. (*Feigning bonhomie*) But don't you go worrying or losing sleep. If I can help the Baron when the time comes I won't say I shan't do it. If the Baron is as nice as he's always been to me....

SWANN: ... An extraordinary Christmas, Mémé; I never expected to see anything like it. To dine at Voisin's and be served with the elephant from the Zoo! — which I must say was not too disagreeable, though I hardly think my poor little Delphine could have stomached it. To-day I was able to take her a wing of chicken from the last of poor Goncourt's fowls, and she thanked me for it far more prettily than she did for the Fabergé snuffbox I was weak enough to give her a year ago. Poor child, her hunger is making her look even more Botticelli than before. Have you news of Eugénie?

CHARLUS: None. But I thank God, Swann, that she is spared this. We are living in a cage of wild beasts, waiting for the invasion of beasts that may possibly not be so wild as ourselves. One can only hope so.

SWANN: Flaubert told me that near Mantes, a peasant had strangled a Prussian and torn him to pieces with his teeth.

CHARLUS: If it were only from hunger, one might excuse him. However, *we* are still dining.

SWANN: The people have the cats and dogs. The elephant, so far as I can see, is reserved for Voisin's. It would have seemed a curious social distinction not so long ago. I say, my dear fellow, you look far from well!

CHARLUS: There is nothing wrong with me but worry. How

bitter it is to-night! The trees are fossilised with frost. I hope Eugénie is keeping warm.

SWANN: They will look after her. I am sure they will. They are all so fond of her.

CHARLUS: A shell fell in the garden of our house this morning, a spent one, but it knocked the nose off the little god Eugénie liked so much. How horrible the sky is, lit by those eternal fires, and yet how magnificent! I could fancy that I am Dante and that you are Virgil, leading me by the nose through the circles of my own atrociously vindictive Hell. . . .

(Sound of cannon dies away)

(Eugénie's waltz, played rather stumblingly)

ORIANE: *(Softly)* Eugénie? *(Playing stops)*

EUGÉNIE: Oriane? I was almost half-asleep at the piano. Isn't that queer?

ORIANE: I want to talk to you. Why *did* you insist on going to early Mass to-day? You're not strong enough.

EUGÉNIE: I pray for Palamède.

ORIANE: God would listen to *you* at some more reasonable hour.

EUGÉNIE: It's so terrible, month after month, without news!

(She begins to cry)

ORIANE: You will have news soon, my dear. That's why I've come to tell you; but you must prepare yourself, because the news that ought to bring him back to you is tragic news for France.

EUGÉNIE: Oh, what is it? What is it?

ORIANE: *(Bitterly)* We have capitulated. When the Assembly meets again they will be like the Burghers of Calais with ropes about their necks.

(Pause)

EUGÉNIE: *(Whispering)* I know I am very wicked, but I can only be glad that the siege is over and Palamède will come back. God will be angry with me.

ORIANE: It strikes me that the good God is going to be angry with far too many people to spare any of his wrath for you. We should all be far happier, Eugénie, if we resisted religious vanity. Now lie down for a while and try not to excite yourself.

EUGÉNIE: (*Crying out*) How do we know he is even alive?

ORIANE: Somehow, I cannot imagine Mémé being otherwise. . . .

MARCEL: But though M. de Charlus, at the earliest opportunity, sent messages of love and reassurance to his wife, he did not join her at Les Laumes. He informed her, in a style as sturdy and as massive as Cicero's, a style at variance with the simple domestic phrases which characterised the main body of his letter, that he felt it his duty to stand at the heart of his country at her time of sorrow and humiliation, even until the conquerors, if such should be their will, had stabled their horses in the cathedral of Notre Dame.

It was not that he did not desire to see Eugénie, nor that his sensitive imagination was unmoved by visions of her loneliness; but alas, we may love those, and suffer on account of those, who bore us horribly, as Madame de Charlus had from the first days of their marriage bored her husband. It is an error to suppose that affection is inevitably killed by tedium; sheer tedium may be an element of our bondage, and there are many men who experience the deepest feelings of tenderness while attempting to stifle, in the presence of their unsuspecting wives, the most body-racking of yawns.

The truth was that the Baron, not altogether hypocritical when he claimed a feeling of responsibility for the future career of Horace Pinaud, was too worried concerning his protégé to stray far from his vicinity, for Pinaud was constantly uttering his gasconades against the 'swells' who had betrayed the working-men of France to the King of Prussia, predicting an early reckoning, and hinting that rebellion was rife even in his own battalion of the National Guard. Now M. de Charlus, while not believing a word of all this and having complete confidence in the authority of M. Thiers, was yet fearful that this young Desmoulins might, by boastful rashness, get himself into trouble with his superior officers; and so it was not until the National Guard of the XIIIth District had in fact revolted, and the Commune had been proclaimed, that he fled, with tears in his eyes, to take refuge at Versailles.

BASIN: (*Fading in*) Mémé! My dear little brother! 'Pon my word, I thought I'd seen a ghost. I tell you, we were giving you up for lost. When I came here to offer my services to M. Thiers, I made sure of finding you. Have you been in Paris all through the fighting, among that pack of wolves? By God, there's a reckoning ahead, I can tell you that! We shall hang them in their own dirty red flags. But my good chap, what's your news? Eugénie's pining for you, poor girl, and she's not getting any better. What times we live in, eh? What a world! But never mind, the piping times of peace will soon be with us again, after there's been a bit of salutary blood-letting. . . .

MARCEL: M. de Charlus did not enter Paris with the advance guard of the victorious Versaillais, but stole back there one night early in June and made his way through the broken streets, in which the pall of gunpowder lingered still and the reek of burned-out fires hung on the air with the bitterness of faded chrysanthemums, towards a lodging-house near the Porte Saint-Denis, which he had visited on previous occasions.

(*Repeated knocking at a door*)

OLD WOMAN: (*She is both surly and afraid*) Who's there?
CHARLUS: A friend.
OLD WOMAN: Whose friend? What do you want?

CHARLUS: News of a — an acquaintance of mine.

OLD WOMAN: Oh, you do? Wait till I bring my candle. I like to see who my friends are. . . . (*Gasps*) Oh! I've seen your face before, lurking around here.

CHARLUS: A young acquaintance of mine, in fact, a former employee, had his lodgings in this place.

OLD WOMAN: No one but me lives here now, so you can stir your stumps and be off with you.

CHARLUS: A young man. Horace Pinaud.

(*A clatter*)

OLD WOMAN: *Merde!* You be off, why don't you? You've made me drop my candlestick.

(*She fumbles with matches*)

CHARLUS: Where is he?

OLD WOMAN: Only the good God knows, and He won't tell you.

CHARLUS: Don't light the candle again — I said, let it be! Damn you, you hag, where is Pinaud?

OLD WOMAN: I know by your voice, you're a gentleman. You ask the other fine gentlemen what happened to him — the murderers!

CHARLUS: (*Softly*) If you don't tell me what you know I will wring that old neck of yours and stamp you into the gutter. *Where is Pinaud?*

OLD WOMAN: They shot him up against the cemetery wall, him and a hundred others, the butchers! I saw them march him up there with a batch of 'em, and the ladies from Versailles was watching, such ladies they were, they spat in our chaps' faces and dug at them with their pretty sunshades like they was beasts. I cried out to him, 'Horace!' hoping he'd hear me, because wild he may have been and rough, but never a penny of rent did he owe, he had a good heart, he treated me as if I'd been his own grannie; but he couldn't hear me what with the

F

jeering and the screeching, and he never saw me . . . and now
he's dead, take that to your cheek, and get out of here, clear out,
clear out, (*Rising to a shriek, then fading*) clear out! . . .

(*Pause*)

CHARLUS: Willy lost, Pinaud dead, Eugénie. . . .

ORIANE: (*Fading in*) '. . . may be dying; she is very sick, and the
doctor says she must have a nurse day and night. When you
receive this letter, Palamède, come at once. I have run out of
excuses, which she is always demanding, for your continued
absence and I assure you that my imagination is beginning to
fail me. . . .'

MARCEL: One summer evening, when the lilac in the garden of
the château of the Prince des Laumes was solid as a wall of
violet pumice-stone against a sky opaque with its continance of
rain, when the sound of the little fountains trickling from terrace to terrace was the only sound in the hushed and halted
world, M. de Charlus, at a signal from the nurse, stepped into
his wife's room and seating himself at the bedside, began gently
to stroke her hand. She awoke quite easily and calmly, turned
upon him the brown river-light of her marvellous eyes, now
alas, so sunken that they seemed to rest upon the bones of her
cheeks, and spoke to him with a smile.

EUGÉNIE: Palamède? . . . How nice . . . my dear. Now I shall be
happy.

CHARLUS: Forgive me.

EUGÉNIE: If I have anything to forgive . . . I can't possibly
remember what it was. How handsome you look! Does Oriane
know you are here? She has been very kind to me.

CHARLUS: Eugénie, I should have come before. I should have
come when the siege was raised. But a friend — a very dear
friend of mine — was ill; and he died.

EUGÉNIE: My poor Palamède.

CHARLUS: But I should have come. He was killed in the fighting, when the Commune was defeated. He was so young; it was like the sun going out. But I should have come to you.

EUGÉNIE: You were always so loyal to your friends.

CHARLUS: You should curse me.

EUGÉNIE: How could I, when I love you? And we musn't talk about sad things, because you are here, and I feel so happy, and I am sure I am going to get well! Mémé!

CHARLUS: My dear?

EUGÉNIE: It was so quiet a little while ago, and now, listen, all the birds are singing! I expect it's because there is going to be a storm. I used to love storms when I was a child at Brézé, they didn't frighten me at all. — What are you doing?

CHARLUS: Laying my head between your hands.

EUGÉNIE: You're still sad! I can't understand why you should be. I am so happy I could dance, if only I were stronger. Perhaps I shall be strong, soon. . . .

MARCEL: It seemed at first as if the return of M. de Charlus had wrought a miracle, for Eugénie's health seemed to improve from that moment, and she herself to burst into new and delicate flower, a flower touched, perhaps, by wintry sunshine, but light enough to move as the breeze of pleasure blew upon it. This was, nevertheless, a false flowering, destroyed by the winter of the material earth, for with the first frost she took to her bed again, excusing herself by saying that she could not get warm *at her back* in such big rooms, even by the most splendid of fires, and that she felt better and far stronger with pillows at her shoulders and the eiderdown up to her chin. M. de Charlus left her scarcely for a moment during these last months of her life, contriving for her such an ingenuity of little pleasures that she declared herself, at the end of each, day to be exhausted not by sickness but by delight: framing for her with his own hands in ivory and gold a copy of that great *Coronation of the Virgin* donated by her ancestor to the Church, pressing into a garland behind a sheet of glass the autumn leaves and berries she so greatly loved, composing a sonnet especially for her birthday, and playing for her, as often as she desired to hear it, the little piece he had dedicated to his beloved Eugénie.

She died quite peacefully, between a smile and a yawn, one evening towards the end of January, and M. de Charlus, as he folded her hands, which had now the colour and dryness of ancient linen, gave thanks to God for the happiness of her end: for it had not been an hour ago since she had stirred herself from a lax and comfortable silence to draw him down to her, and to speak in his ear, like a schoolgirl confiding some small, important secret to a trusted teacher, or perhaps to a friend a little older than she, in the bare, religious quiet of a convent dormitory. . . .

EUGÉNIE: (*Whispering*) Palamède ... listen ... there is something I must say to you. . . . I have to say it now, because tomorrow I might so easily forget. . . .

CHARLUS: (*Brokenly*) Yes, my love?

EUGÉNIE: I know now that I did you a great wrong.

CHARLUS: And how was that?

EUGÉNIE: I told you . . . that I was doubtful. I was always doubtful, as a girl. I was wrong to doubt you when you said . . . that you loved me. I know now ... I am convinced . . . that you have loved me as much as I love you. . . .

(*A silence*)

MARCEL: The sorrow of M. de Charlus, so profound that it seemed to cast upon him a minatory blackness which was like the hood of a Franciscan friar, weighed almost as heavily upon his cousin, the Princesse des Laumes, who, though she had thought her sister-in-law silly, gullible and rather too pious for good taste, had yet loved her more sincerely than she would have loved a woman closer to her own nature. During the first six months of mourning she went seldom into Society, and it was only with difficulty that Swann, by promising to introduce to her M. Victor Hugo, prevailed upon her to dine with him once more at the house of M. de Goncourt.

ORIANE: . . . You, M. Hugo, who know so much about grief, who have taught us that God will not hang the fruit of sorrow on a bough too weak to bear it, will understand the sadness of my poor cousin, a widower so young, with his heart in the grave at a time when it should be springing with youth and with the seasons!

SWANN: I have never known our princess so sad, and I have so little comfort for her!

ORIANE: My dear M. Swann is a comfort simply because he walks and breathes.

HUGO: 'If we must suffer, let us suffer nobly.' They were my words. They must still be the only consolation. For in doing anything nobly we become proud; and pride is among the most restorative of the emotions. M. de Goncourt, you looked at me strangely; I hope I did not seem to speak in cynicism. Nothing was further from my thought.

GONCOURT: I was simply thinking that I should like to be courageous enough to ask you to speak to the Princess as you did to me, after my dear brother left me. You made me feel that he still lived, that he still hung upon my words, as I used to hang upon his.

HUGO: (*Strongly*) I am an old man. For myself I believe in the presence of the dead. I call them the Invisible Ones. . . .

(*A silence*)

MARCEL: We may mourn with all our hearts, yet be betrayed by forces beyond our control, may apprehend, even across the staling and sickly lilies heaped upon the bier, some *ignis fatuus* which calls us to premature and shameful joy; even as M. de Charlus, darkly rigid as a forest pine in the chapel at Guermantes, the traces of tears congealing in their salty florets upon cheeks still puffed with grief, could not detach his interest from a charming little acolyte, a fiery-haired Gabriel with a censer, whose duty it was to assist the committal of the mortal remains of Eugénie, Baronne de Charlus, to their eternal resting place among the bones of her kinsmen. In a sense he was not to be blamed, for when we speak of the 'love' of such a man for his wife, we are using the word 'love' in the context of our own nature rather than of his. The nature of the love between the man and woman who have first come together as strangers must contain, whether in great degree or small, an element of sensual desire, and unless we ourselves share the taint of M. de Charlus, it is an hypocrisy for us to speak of 'love' as existing in any such relationship where desire is not, nor has ever been. The tenderness he felt for Eugénie, which, for many years, was to bring the tears to his eyes whenever he spoke of her, was infinitely more like the love of a brother for a sister, a son for a mother, than of a husband for his wife; but in this case was imbued with a quality of darkness, of guilt, of hyperaesthesia, by the unspoken belief of the world that it must be founded upon the joy of the flesh.

(For a few seconds, the sound of a flute)

After the funeral was over, M. de Charlus travelled for many months abroad, and it was not until the late summer that he resumed his position in the social life of the Faubourg St. Germain.

(Noise of a party: chink of cups and plates: the laughter of Oriane)

CHARLUS: *(Fading in)* I see my Aunt de Villeparisis has had her chairs re-covered in the most enchanting tapestry; to sit on one would be like lowering one's backside into a bed of strawberries, an experience surely more voluptuous in the breach than in the observance.

MME DE VILLE: They're fine, ain't they? I was determined upon Beauvais, and I hunted Paris for the stuff. Palamède, will you take a dish of tea?

CHARLUS: No, thank you. I must be off again soon.

ORIANE: To tame the lions of the Faubourg, I expect. People have been getting quite out of hand since you went away, accepting the most extraordinary invitations and turning up in houses expressly under your interdict.

CHARLUS: Really, Oriane, I can never understand this nostalgia for the gutter that seems to afflict so many of our acquaintances. I could understand the mania for visiting the Iénas or the Israels if it were sheer kindness of heart that prompted it, such as one may feel for some orphan child or some elderly cousin a little soft in the head, but as people are not particularly kind even when they find themselves in these drawing-rooms, the charitable explanation falls to the ground.

ORIANE: He's back in his old form, ain't he, Basin? I swear it's a joy to listen to him!

BASIN: Yes, but I say, we can't stand listening even to my young brother if we're going to get to Madame Leroi's 'on the dot', as they say. Do make your farewells, Oriane! You know it will take you a couple of hours to change your dress. . . .

(*His voice dies away*)

SWANN: Mémé! It's capital to set eyes on you again! By the by, I want a word with you. Let's step over into that corner where we can be screened by the immense posterior of Madame d'Hunolstein. . . .

(*His voice fades: chatter rises*)

CHARLUS: (*Voice sharpening again*) . . . A most delightful little woman, Swann, a Madame de Crécy, whom I met a week or so ago, I am most anxious to introduce her to you. She would be so delighted to meet a man of your culture, for she is very humble and anxious to learn. . . .

MME DE VILLE: My dear nephew, you and M. Swann must really stop hiding yourselves in corners! We simply can't spare you, after all this long time!

CHARLUS: It seems strange to see so many unfamiliar faces.

MME DE VILLE: Unfamiliar? But Mémé, there isn't a soul here whom you don't know!

CHARLUS: I mean, all these new servants: for instance, there was a charming little maid scurrying by the lodge as I came through the courtyard, and I see you have a new footman, a big, blond, squareheaded fellow like a German, who took my stick from me. . . .

MME DE VILLE: Oh, that would be Pépin; his father used to be my coachman. (*Hurriedly*) I really do not think you would care for him at all —

CHARLUS: (*Overriding her*) I have been thinking, my dear aunt, that my own chairs would look delightful in that Beauvais tapestry. I suppose you haven't a scrap of it left that I could use for matching? If you could find one, perhaps you would send Pépin over with it to-morrow. . . .

(*Chatter dies: a pause*)

MARCEL: And so, for M. de Charlus, life began to assume once more its normal aspect, to open its Book of Hours and permit him to step back, as it were, into the painted pages, to follow the winding paths through the pastel seasons, past so many rivers dotted with little skiffs, past so many meadows where charming haymakers combed the golden grass, past so many shepherd boys lovely as lines of Theocritus as they herded

sheep as round and as white as guelder roses, until he came to
the castle of the Court of Love

*(Eugénie's waltz. M. de Charlus playing it, and speaking
as he plays)*

CHARLUS: ... You have enough intelligence, I suppose, not to
imagine that it is from want of society, from any fear of solitude
and boredom, that I have recourse to you. It is merely that it
amuses me to attempt to put a little cultivation into a mind
bare as the Russian steppe, to sow in virgin soil, perhaps, a seed
of appreciation of the finer things of life. For why should a
footman not be changed into a man of culture by the revelation
of art, as Zenelophon the beggar-maid was changed into a
queen by the revelation of the condescension of her King,
Cophetua? Don't pick your nose, Pépin, it is a disagreeable
habit, and shows a great want of respect for myself, especially
at the moment when I am playing for you a little piece composed
for you alone — for it pleases me, upon occasion, to make a
truly preposterous gift to one unworthy — a piece to which I
have devoted the flower of my talents and that I have dedicated
to Ignace Pépin, footman, protégé, by the grace of God, of
Monsieur le Baron de Charlus, Duc de Brabant, Damoiseau de
Montargis, Prince d'Oléron, de Carency, de Viareggio and des
Dunes. . . .

(The waltz comes to an end)

III

Swann in Love

NOTE

THE aim of this programme was twofold — the evocation of an atmosphere, and the bringing of Swann into the full light, without the shadow of Marcel falling always across him. *Swann's Way* (II) contains more consecutive dialogue than the other books (the great party scenes in *The Guermantes Way*, *The Cities of the Plain* and *The Captive* consist mainly not of conversation but of monologue and commentary) and for this reason I used more of the Scott-Moncrieff text than I used in the other programmes. Also, I used far less invention of incident, simply dramatising incidents upon which Proust merely touched, and in 'Annette' making a character out of what is only a hint. (*Swann's Way*, I, p. 300.) My only real innovation was the presentation of Odette in relation to Charlus.

All the same, the programme presented considerable difficulties. Proust, writing to Jacques Rivière, describes himself as anti-romantic: yet the essence of *Swann*, despite its ultimate harshness and disappointment, is romance itself. It is romance *en grande tenue*, flowered and scented and jewelled: it achieves a sort of superlative iron-hard prettiness, never cloying, always remote. Between the reader and this romance is a plate-glass window, as alluring and as forbidding as the aquarium-window of the restaurant to which the poor set their faces, while Marcel dined in the light and warmth within.

What I attempted was to do away with that window, without destroying the magic of the remoteness itself; and as I could not do it by imitating Proust, I had to be content with selection and re-arrangement of what he had already written, and by an extension of his own commentary.

Where I did feel that the 'reconstruction' had achieved something of my intention, was in its emphasis of the ordinariness of Odette. She was entrancing, but she was ordinary; she had no mind, no insight, no generous impulse. 'Life had given her good parts, but she could not play them.' (*Time Regained*, p. 400.) The same could be said of Captain Dreyfus: and of all characters about whom the drama of life crystallised, asking from them nothing but that they should stand still, that they should *be*.

SWANN IN LOVE

MUSIC: (*Violin and piano: the 'Petite Phrase'*)

MARCEL: Swann was dead: the charming figure who had thrown
his courteous and enchanted shadow so momentously across
the scenes of my childhood and my growing-up: Swann, whose
widow had married a man he despised, and who was to continue
the tally of her lovers into old age: whose beloved daughter,
between whose hands he had placed, like a jeweller's box of
gilt and satin, the trust of preserving his memory, was in
deliberate process of obliterating, from the set-scene of the
new world she was building for herself, not only his image but
his very name.

Young Swann, the easy, unassuming friend of dukes and
princes, the unassuming connoisseur of art, always the moderate
man, hating exaggeration in any shape: young Swann with the
arched nose and green eyes under a high forehead fringed with
fair, almost red hair dressed in the Bressant style, had vanished
first beneath the travesty of sickness and age, and at last beneath the grosser disguise of death.

His friends, too, were growing old. But the Baron de Charlus,
once Grand Master of the Faubourg, terrible in pride, could no
longer maintain so carefully his own disguise, and, stripped of
his long-guarded secrecies, was naked and defenceless, like a
nymph before stag-hounds, to the whispered mockeries which
would soon be as bold and open as the voices in the drawing-
room of Madame Verdurin — as still, at that time, she was.

It was at a music party at her house that I heard the Baron
speak of Swann once more. He and I and Professor Brichot had
been chatting idly together, waiting for the return of our
hostess. . . .

CHARLUS: I am not interested in history. This life is sufficient for me, it is quite interesting enough, as poor Swann used to say.

BRICHOT: What, Baron, did you know Swann? I wasn't aware of that. (*Diffidently*) Er . . . tell me . . . was he that way inclined?

CHARLUS: (*After a pause; with lofty scorn*) What a mind the man has! So you suppose I only know men like that, do you?

BRICHOT: (*Heartily*) In any case, Swann was never what you'd call a beauty, eh?

CHARLUS: (*Rounding on him*) Hold your tongue, Brichot — ! You don't know what you're talking about. In those days he had a complexion like a peach and, (*Tenderly, finding a fresh note for each syllable*) he was always quite charming. The women were madly in love with him.

BRICHOT: Did you ever know his wife?

CHARLUS: Know his wife? Why, of course I did! — It was through me they met.

MARCEL: May I ask you, Baron, how did that come about? I've so often wondered —

CHARLUS: But there was no need to wonder, my dear young friend! You could always have asked me. I have always been accessible to the young, anyone will tell you that. Oh, it was ages ago — the dark ages — in fact, the 'Seventies — when she was playing 'Miss Sacripant' at one of the 'Little Theatres'. Some fellows from the club took me 'behind the scenes', as they say, to make her acquaintance, and then nothing would do for them but that we should each of us take a woman home with him.

BRICHOT: Ha! That's a good one. That's very good indeed.

CHARLUS: Oh, I assure you, Professor, all I wanted was to go to sleep; but malicious people would have it that I went to bed with Odette. Of course, she took advantage of the slanders to come and pester me, and I thought I might get rid of her by introducing her to Swann. I invited him to join us in my box at the theatre. I'd whetted his appetite, I assure you — I'd told

him I wanted him to meet a lady whose favours, if not absolutely impossible to obtain, were at least exceedingly hard . . .
and though he wasn't much taken with her at first. . . .

(*Acoustics of the theatre: coughing, fluttering of programmes*)

CLEANTE: *Que voulez-vous dire, et qu'entendez-vous avec cette
faculté de vos amies?*

TOINETTE: *Quel est donc votre dessein?*

BERALDE: *De nous divertir un peu ce soir. Les comédiens ont fait
un petit intermède de réception d'un médicin, avec des danses et
de la musique; je veux que nous en prenions ensemble le diver-
tissement, et que mon frère y fasse le premier personnage.*

ANGELIQUE: *Mais, mon oncle, il me semble que vous vous jouez un
peu beaucoup de mon père.*

BERALDE: *Mais, ma nièce, ce n'est pas tant le jouer, que s'accom-
moder à ses fantaisies. . . .*

ODETTE: You know, Baron, I'm beginning to find *Le Malade*
rather a bore. Not that a silly little thing like me has any right
to have opinions about the great classics, isn't that so?

CHARLUS: Patience, my dear. It's nearly over. And I have a friend
I want you to meet. . . .

(*Acoustics of the theatre*)

BERALDE: . . . *Toute ceci n'est qu'entre nous. Nous y pouvons aussi
prendre chacun un personnage, et nous donner ainsi la comédie les
uns aux autres. Le carnaval autorise cela. Allons vite préparer
toutes choses.*

CLEANTE: *Y consentez-vous?*

ANGELIQUE: *Oui, puisque mon oncle nous conduit.*

(*Applause. Music of the ballet beginning. A knock on the
door of the box*)

SWANN: May I come in?

(*Door opens*)

CHARLUS: My dear Charles, how late you are! Odette, allow me to present M. Charles Swann, one of my oldest friends. Charles, may I present Madame de Crécy, who is bored to distraction with *La Malade* and dying for some conversation?

ODETTE: Oh, M. Swann, you mustn't listen to him! How presumptuous it must seem to you that someone like me should criticise a great writer!

SWANN: Why, to be bored is never a crime so long as the boredom's real! It is only boredom assumed that gives offence.

ODETTE: I'm afraid that's far too clever for me. Is M. Swann very *very* clever, Baron?

CHARLUS: You shall discover that for yourself, Odette. Well, how shall we pass the rest of the evening? Shall we take supper at Wéber's?

ODETTE: Now what I should love, would be to sit here just for a little while, just the three of us, and talk quietly! I'm sure they'd never turn you out, not an important man like you, they'd never dare, would they? (*Fading out*) I'm perfectly certain they'd never have the nerve. . . .

MARCEL: M. de Charlus told me, that evening so many years later, that he and Swann and Odette had sat in the box till the last light was extinguished in the theatre, and had then walked for a while in the streets full of the smell of that spring rain, which seems to bear with it lilac from far-off country gardens, like an aviator who flies with a cargo of flowers; and at last they had left Odette at her little house in the Rue Lapérouse, and strolled on together towards the Champs Elysées.

CHARLUS: She's a ravishing creature, my dear Charles, I do assure you. What do you think of her yourself? How does she strike you?

SWANN: (*Thoughtfully*) She's beautiful in her way. But her profile's too sharp for my taste, her skin's too delicate, her cheekbones are too prominent. Her whole face is too *tight*. You expect the skull to break through the skin.

CHARLUS: Her eyes are fine, don't you think so?

SWANN: Too large, too heavy. And she looks so mournful! I admire softer women . . . rosy women. Healthy ones. Madame de Crécy has such a bad-tempered air. Who is Crécy, if I may enquire, Mémé?

(Fade)

MARCEL: For the first time I learned from M. Charlus who Odette's first husband had been; and that, moreover, he was an old acquaintance of my own. On my visits by the little train from Balbec to Madame Verdurin's country house, La Raspelière, I had not infrequently broken my journey at Grattevast for the purpose of greeting an old and impoverished nobleman by the name and style of Pierre de Verjus, Comte de Crécy; and had also, on several occasions, entertained him to dinner at Balbec.

CHARLUS: And you never connected him with Odette?

MARCEL: Why, no, sir; I thought she'd simply adopted the style 'de Crécy'—

CHARLUS: You mean, in the same way that a little chorus girl born Marie Lenoir will take the stage name of Mélusine Lafayette, or Mélisande La Vallière. Precisely. But Odette's name, oddly enough, was not the trade name of a cocotte. She had every right to it. Her husband's title was one of the highest — though she succeeded in draining him of his last farthing, of course. Why, for years Swann used to make the poor devil a small allowance — it ceased when Swann died, of course, so I imagine Crécy was more than commonly grateful for the dinners you 'stood' him, as the saying goes.

MARCEL: Did Swann never know, sir, that you had enjoyed his wife's favours?

CHARLUS: What an idea! Why, my dear fellow, he was as jealous

G

as a tiger; he'd have killed me on the spot, if you'd suggested a thing like that.

MARCEL: Was he always jealous of Odette?

CHARLUS: Not at the last; and not at the first. Indeed, I didn't think he would take any serious interest in her; she was not his kind at all, not at all his sort, to be sure. And in the beginning, it was she who made all the running. . . .

(The scratching of a pen, the rustle of paper)

ODETTE: *(Reading)* 'Dear M. Swann. . . . Since our meeting at the theatre I have been wondering timidly whether I might ask a favour of you. M. de Charlus has told me that you are a great connoisseur of art — of which I know so little but would love to know so much! I am only an ignorant woman with a taste for beautiful things, but the moment I saw you I had a wild fancy to become, if I might say it, your pupil. May I be permitted to call upon you? I am sure I should know you better when once I had seen you in your home. . . .'

SWANN: *(Reading her letter)* '. . . So comfortable with your tea and books — am I right? I am being bold, I know, but from all that people tell me of your wonderful collection. . . .' *(Ruefully, half-annoyed)* The devil take it, Mémé! — Look at this! — What shall I do?

CHARLUS: Does a man who has loved as many women as you need advice?

SWANN: I'm sure she's an idiot. Still, I suppose I can hardly say no. . . .

(Fade. The chinking of tea-cups)

ODETTE: How nice it is here! I think you must be the most fortunate man in the world. How I envy you, with all these wonderful books and pictures, and your beautiful china, and your brilliant, smart friends. . . . You can't know what it means to be lonely.

SWANN: (*After a slight pause*) Try one of these little cakes with the pink frosting. I sent Rémi to Bourbonneux to buy them specially for you.

ODETTE: Oh no, no more! I've been as greedy as a child, I know I have. And now I must go, out into the hard world, warming myself with the memory of all this comfort and beauty in the firelight. . . . I believe even your fire burns more prettily than other people's!

SWANN: (*Without undue pressure*) If you're certain you have to go. . . .

ODETTE: Listen, I couldn't interrupt your work for a moment longer! It's been enough for me just to find my way into your house even for a little while. If you knew how I'd dreamed about seeing you in your natural 'habitat'— isn't that the phrase? (*Voice fading as he shows her out*) Have I been just a little clever for once? . . . Oh, yes, my muff, thank you. . . . If I have, it's all through your influence. . . .

(A pause)

SWANN: (*Emphatically*) Mémé! No doubt about it. She's an idiot.

CHARLUS: You won't, of course, receive her again.

SWANN: (*After slight hesitation*) She's not precisely unamusing. She means to visit me to-morrow afternoon. How on earth can I stop her, without hurting her feelings? She looks at me with that imploring gaze, under the velvet pansies on her bonnet, with those black strings tied under her chin, and I feel a brute to put her off. . . .

(Fade. Odette fading in)

ODETTE: Charlus! Does he like me? Did he say anything about me? Am I a success?

CHARLUS: I hope so, my dear. Indeed I do.

ODETTE: Ah! That means you want to get rid of me. How cruel you men are!

CHARLUS: Not at all. I have a prodigious concern for your future, and you should have the sense to realise it. I want to see you settled in life.

ODETTE: He's such a very smart man! I think he's quite charming. You've no idea how hard it is to find a man who's clever *and* a gentleman. Does he admire me?

CHARLUS: What a question! Could anyone fail to?

ODETTE: You could. And you did. How uncomplimentary of you!

CHARLUS: On the contrary, I admire you supremely. And so will Swann. He is enraptured, by the way, by your bonnet with the velvet pansies. I should continue to wear it, if I were you, when pleading your cause. . . .

(Odette fading in)

ODETTE: But won't you — I know I oughtn't to ask — come just once and take tea with me?

SWANN: I should be delighted, if only —

ODETTE: If only you hadn't to work on that important essay of yours! I wish you'd tell me more about it. I'll be a good pupil in time, if you'll only bother just a little with me. — Do come to tea!

SWANN: But, you see, if I don't finish my first draft this week —

ODETTE: Now you're going to laugh at me . . . but this painter who keeps you from seeing me —

SWANN: Vermeer.

ODETTE: Yes, that's it — I'm afraid I'd never heard of him till now. Is he alive still? Can I see any of his things in Paris? Then I'd know what goes on behind that great brow of yours that works so hard. Wouldn't it be a dream if one day I could help you in your work! — Please spare just one 'Five o'clock' for me!

SWANN: My dear, I assure you it's impossible —

ODETTE: Oh, why do you keep me at such a distance? Do tell me. I'll listen patiently. I'll be as quiet as a mouse.

SWANN: (*Gravely*) Well, you see ... I have a terrible fear of forming new friendships. It seems curious to you, I know, but it has grown into a positive dread of becoming involved in some hopeless passion. And that I couldn't bear. I know you will understand.

ODETTE: You're afraid of falling in love? How funny that is, when I'd give my soul to find just a little love somewhere!

SWANN: (*Touched*) Ah, things surely can't be so bad as that!

ODETTE: I know! Some woman must have made you suffer. And so you think the rest are all like her. Charles. ...

SWANN: My dear!

ODETTE: I've never used your Christian name before. It slipped out. I'll be more careful next time, I promise.

SWANN: I liked it on your lips.

ODETTE: She can't have understood you, that woman! You're so, so different from ordinary men! That's what I liked about you when I first saw you, that you weren't like everybody else. Please come to tea with me!

SWANN: (*Hedging*) Oh, but it wouldn't be right for me to take up your time.

ODETTE: But I never have anything to do! I'm always free, and I'll always be free when you want me. At whatever hour of the day or night it may suit you to see me, just send for me. Will you do that?

SWANN: It would be a presumption on my part —

ODETTE: Listen — Do you know what I'd simply love above all things? I'd love to introduce you to Madame Verdurin — I go to her every evening. Do you know her? She has a wonderful salon, a regular Temple of the Arts! I know a clever man like you couldn't help being quite fascinated. Doctor Cottard goes there — Madame Verdurin says he's a better diagnostician than Potain, even! And there's a pianist who leaves Planté and Rubinstein sitting, and there's an artist whom we call Monsieur Biche who paints wonderfully — Oh, I'd love it! Only fancy if I found you there one night, and thought it was perhaps a little for my sake you had gone! ...

MARCEL: Perhaps at that time, recalling this conversation, thinking of her when he was alone, Swann did no more than call her image into being among the countless others of his romantic dreams; yet imperceptibly that image was to spread and bloom like a lamp turned slowly upwards, so that its radiance first shadowed and finally obliterated all others, drawing the whole concentration of his desire upon its secret and mysterious flame. Even now, he could not resist the granting of the small pleasure she required of him; and so he allowed her, one night, to take him with her to the Verdurins'.

(Sound of voices chattering; Madame Verdurin's cutting through)

MME VERDURIN: Well, my children, to-night we are to see the famous Swann!

COTTARD: Swann? Swann? Who on earth is Swann?

MME VERDURIN: Dr Cottard, I'm afraid you don't always listen when we talk to you. Swann? Why, Odette's friend, of course.

COTTARD: Ah! Good. Good. That's all right, then, but who is he? What does he do? Eh, Verdurin?

VERDURIN: According to Odette, he's extremely 'smart', as they say: and you know how my wife feels about *that* sort of thing.

MME VERDURIN: People in society are such bores. Bores! There's nothing worse than a bore. But Odette's such a little piece of perfection, I don't believe she would saddle us with people who can't fit in with our ways. Eh, Madame Cottard?

MME COTTARD: Oh, no, indeed. I'm sure she wouldn't! Odette is so kind, so thoughtful for other people!

MME VERDURIN: What do you say, Monsieur Biche?

ELSTIR (Biche): Why, I'd trust her good sense any day! When are they coming? Are they in love? If they are I must make another sketch of her; he'd like that. I hope they're in love. Nothing amuses me more than matchmaking.

MME VERDURIN: Indeed, I hope they're not! I don't want Odette snatched away from our little clan. You, there! What are you doing? Don't you sing for your supper any more? Let's have some music from you.

(*Piano music sounding through general chatter; transcription of the Liebestod, from Tristan*)

MARCEL: Swann was enchanted by the unfamiliarity, the novelty, of the company in which he found himself that evening. Because delight and the desire for delight was in him, he found everything and everyone delightful, and was in a passion to give pleasure in return for the pleasure he was himself receiving. He asked eagerly to be introduced to everyone, including an old friend of the Verdurins', a palaeographer by the name of Saniette, whose shyness and simplicity had made him a favourite butt for the discourtesy of his hosts.

(*Music and chatter*)

SWANN: It is a great pleasure to me to meet M. Saniette, with whose work I am of course acquainted.

SANIETTE: The honour is mine, I do assure you. My work is nothing at all, nobody cares for it, but it is an amusement for me, that is to say, not an amusement precisely, but an interest.

(*Music breaks off. Chatter and laughter*)

MME VERDURIN: (*Shouting peevishly*) What are all those good people laughing at over there? There's no sign of brooding melancholy down in your corner. You don't suppose I find it very amusing to be stuck up here all by myself on the stool of repentance?

VERDURIN: Now, Sidonie, no one has forgotten you. — M. Swann, do you mind if I light my pipe?

SWANN: (*Murmuring*) No, no, of course not.

VERDURIN: No ceremony here, you know; we're all pals. Ski, you sit down at the piano and let's hear from you again. I'm sure M. Swann has never heard the sonata we've just discovered —

MME VERDURIN: (*Screaming*) No, no, no, not my sonata! I don't want to be made to cry till I get a cold in the head and neuralgia all down my face like last time!

(*Laughter*)

ODETTE: (*Murmuring over laughter*) Madame Verdurin's so amusing! This happens whenever he sits down to play, and she does it better and better every time!

COTTARD: Now, Madame, I assure you you won't be ill this time, and if you are — then we shall cure you!

MME VERDURIN: Oh, Dr Cottard, will you really?

MME COTTARD: I'm sure my husband won't let you suffer, Madame Verdurin, he wouldn't dream of it!

MME VERDURIN: Well, if he swears to keep his word, I shall give in.

(*Applause*)

Odette, come and sit near me, on the little sofa.

ODETTE: I have my own little corner, haven't I?

MME VERDURIN: And I fancy you can make room for M. Swann there, can't you? M. Swann, you don't look comfortable. Come and sit by Odette. . . . Odette, you can easily move up a little — That's right!

(*Silence. The Vinteuil Sonata begins*)

MARCEL: The year before, at an evening party, Swann had heard a piece of music played on the piano and violin; and his imagination had been caught by some phrase or harmony — he hardly knew which — that had opened and expanded his soul; just as the fragrance of certain roses, wafted upon the moist

air of evening, has the power of dilating our nostrils. Sitting by
Odette on the little sofa, he heard the phrase again, the secret,
airy and fragrant phrase he had loved. . . .

(*The 'Little Phrase'*)

And now at last he could enter into possession of it, could ask
the name of the music, he could take it home, study it, and
acquire its secret. . . .

(*The music ends rather quietly: clapping: the chatter soars
up again*)

MME VERDURIN: (*Screeching*) Isn't it charming, M. Swann?
Doesn't my little wretch play it superbly? Somebody run and
fetch him some orangeade, he's earned it!

SWANN: (*Under the chatter: to Odette*) Did you hear that little
phrase? I've fallen in love with it.

ODETTE: I'm not sure. Which was the one you meant?

(*Swann hums a bar or two*)

Oh, yes, yes! There, now you've sung it to me I shall get it on
the brain! I shan't have a moment's sleep for hearing it in my
head all night.

SWANN: It was with you I recognised it. I am glad it was with you.

MME VERDURIN: (*Calling out*) It looks to me as though someone
was saying nice things to you, Odette!

ODETTE: (*Simply*) Yes, very nice.

SWANN: (*Whispering*) You are charming.

ODETTE: I like you to say so. Perhaps you don't think I'm quite
so silly, any more.

(*She hums the 'Little Phrase'*)

SWANN: It was with you I recognised it. I am glad it was with
you. . . .

MARCEL: Madame Verdurin had feared, out of her jealousy, that the attachment of Swann and Odette would draw both of them away from her circle; but this did not happen. To her surprise and gratification, Swann never failed them, and as he never spoke of his distinguished friends, her terror of his 'smartness' was for the time allayed. Meanwhile, he was happy. Odette was a delight to him, but still a delight within his control. As he infinitely preferred to her style of beauty that of a little working girl, as fresh and plump as a rose, with whom he was simultaneously in love, he liked to spend the first part of the evening with her, knowing he was sure to see Odette later on. This little girl used to wait, not far from his door, at a street corner. . . .

(Sound of carriage wheels: clipclop of horses' hooves)

SWANN: Rémi! Stop.

(Carriage draws up. Door opens)

Annette!

ANNETTE: Oh, Monsieur! I thought you'd never come!

SWANN: Jump in, there's a good girl. Quickly.

(He shuts the door)

Are you cold? Why, you're trembling all over! Let me warm you up.

(A gasp and a giggle)

Rémi! Off you go.

(The carriage moves on)

There! Aren't you warmer now! Let me rub your hands. Why, what have you done to yourself?

ANNETTE: It's only a little scratch. My thimble slipped.

SWANN: *(Kissing her finger)* I'll make it well again. Isn't that better?

ANNETTE: Much better! Oh, it's been such a long, weary day!

I've been thinking and thinking about you. I suppose you didn't think of me.

SWANN: Of course I did.

ANNETTE: And even now, you're going to leave me alone again almost at once. I do wish I could stay with you.

SWANN: Even a few minutes together is better than nothing. Isn't it, Annette? Don't you think so? (*Pause*) How charming! You've done your hair a new way. Do you remember the princess who spun gold out of flax? I believe you've spun flax out of gold. How clever of you! You were always so clever with your fingers. And you smell like a meadow full of bean-blossom. . . . Yes, you do . . . you do. . . .

ANNETTE: Oh, please, please. . . .

SWANN: Hold me in your arms. How strong you are! . . . In a minute we must part.

ANNETTE: I don't want us to part. Shall I see you to-morrow?

SWANN: Perhaps. I can't be quite sure. There may be something. . . .

ANNETTE: I'll wait on the same corner and hope for you. I shan't move a step till you come. No, I shan't!

SWANN: But I don't want my meadow catching cold and all the bean-flowers dying. . . .

(*The carriage slows up*)

Heigh-ho! Here we are. The time's been much too short. Rémi, take Mademoiselle home and return for me at midnight. *Au revoir*, Annette.

ANNETTE: To-morrow! Promise you'll come to-morrow!

SWANN: I'll send you a little note. I promise. Good-night, my dear.

(*Swann crosses the pavement. He rings a bell. A door opens*)

VERDURIN: Ah, Swann! Good evening. I am my own manservant to-night, as you see.

(*Door closes*)

SWANN: Forgive me — I'm afraid I'm a little late.

VERDURIN: Well then, come along, come along! My wife wouldn't hear of the music starting till you arrived. . . . Sidonie! Here's M. Swann!

MME VERDURIN: I'm furious with you, sending me such wonderful roses this morning! Because now, of course, I musn't be furious with you for being so late!

SWANN: Forgive me, Madame. An unexpected caller —

MME VERDURIN: No explanations now, if you please. You go to your own place, next to Odette, and you shall justify yourself later.

(The chatter at the Verdurins' rises)

SWANN: (*Whispering*) You are beautiful to-night, Odette.

ODETTE: I was so sure you weren't coming! It's been such a long day, and I've been thinking and thinking about you.

SWANN: How delicious! You've done your hair a new way. . . .

MARCEL: Night after night Swann would take her home in his carriage and leave her at the gate of the tiny garden. Sometimes she would pluck a flower and thrust it into his hand, and he would hold it pressed to his lips during the drive home. He would escort her to her gate, but no further. Twice only had he gone inside to take part in the ceremony — of such importance in her life — of 'afternoon tea'.

In her little lobby, the walls covered with a gilded garden trellis against which bloomed a screen of great chrysanthemums, she would come to receive him, in her tea-gown of pink silk that left her neck and arms bare.

ODETTE: Now come and make yourself thoroughly comfortable! You shall see, I shall make everything nice for you. Lift up your head — there — you shall have a cushion behind it. . . . Now isn't that better! And another for your feet. . . . Lift them, silly! I want to plump it up. Isn't this cosy, Charles? Do you like my beautiful orchids?

SWANN: The cattleyas are fascinating. They look as though they're made out of scraps of silk and satin.

ODETTE: Yes, don't they? How clever you are, finding the right words for everything! I never knew such a man. *I* always say they've been made out of the lining of my opera-cloak. Yes, do prowl round and look at things. . . . I want you to see all my silly little bits and pieces. Do you like my silver dromedary? Isn't he a handsome creature? And my toad — it's jade, you know. I adore my toad, (*To the ornament*) . . . don't I adore you, my love? Don't I give you a kiss sometimes on your great, big, ugly head? . . . (*She kisses it*) There! Like that! (*Pause*) Oh, Charles, you don't know how delightful it is to have you here!

(*Rattling of tea-cups*)

Lemon or cream?

SWANN: Cream, if you please.

ODETTE: A cloud! There, is that right?

SWANN: (*A pause for sipping*) Most excellent!

ODETTE: You see, I know just how you like it!

MARCEL: And Swann, going home, sitting bolt upright in his brougham, unable to repress the happiness with which the afternoon's adventure had filled him, kept repeating to himself:

SWANN: What fun it would be to have a little woman like that in the place where one could always be certain of finding, what one never can be certain of finding, a really good cup of tea!

MARCEL: Meanwhile, Odette was writing him a note.

ODETTE: (*To rustle of paper, scratch of pen*) 'You had scarcely been gone a moment when I found your cigarette-case, lying on the cushions where your feet had rested; so I am sending it back to you with this letter. But why, why did you not forget your heart also? I should never have let you have that back.'

(The 'Little Phrase', haltingly, with one finger on piano)

CHARLUS: Well, and what do you think of her now? She's got a way with her, eh? Don't you agree?

SWANN: Why yes . . . she's quite charming . . . in her fashion, of course.

CHARLUS: One would say, unique. And she has a mind. She's not a great intellectual, not a blue-stocking, of course, she'll never keep a School of Wit, but —

SWANN: I admit, she's not altogether a fool. But I wish I could fathom her tastes. Why, for heaven's sake, does she admire *Serge Panine?* She has an absurd little piece she plays on the piano, quite delightfully, with a wrong note here and there. It's called *Pauvres Fous*, by Taglia . . . Tagliafico, I think it is. You've no idea how touching she looks, like Saint Cecilia. . . .

(Piano: Odette stumbling daintily through Pauvres Fous)

MARCEL: More important, perhaps, was a second visit Swann paid her a little later, when he found her none too well, weary, and rather sullen. He had taken her an engraving he had promised her, and as she leaned over it, gazing with bended head out of her great weighted eyes, he was struck by her resemblance to Zipporah, Jethro's daughter, in Botticelli's Sistine frescos. At once her beauty was enhanced, made more precious in his sight, and he began to reproach himself with his failure to appreciate her true worth. Also, for the first time, he had sensed in her not, perhaps, as yet, an indifference, but the possibility, however slender it seemed, that she could become indifferent to himself.

ODETTE: Oh, yes, it's all very clever, I suppose. I like the girl's hand — that's what you'd call well-drawn, isn't it? But I can't say it excites me.

SWANN: You look a little sad to-day. Come, what can I do to amuse you?

ODETTE: I don't know. What is there to amuse one? Life's such a bore sometimes.

SWANN: Would it bore you to play for me?

ODETTE: Not if you want me to very much. What shall I play?

SWANN: Our own little phrase?

ODETTE: Oh, *that*. . . . No, I'm too tired. I've got a headache. Some other time. . . .

MARCEL: One evening, when he had taken Annette, his 'other little girl', all the way to the Bois, he was so late in reaching the Verdurins' that Odette, supposing he did not intend to come, had already left. Seeing the room bare of her, Swann's heart was wrung with sudden anguish.

MME VERDURIN: You're not going already, are you, M. Swann? Why, you've only just arrived.

SWANN: Forgive me. I — I only looked in for a moment. . . . If you'll excuse me. . . . Perhaps to-morrow? Good-night.

(*Good-nights are said all round. A door closes. Pause*)

VERDURIN: Sidonie! Did you notice the face he pulled when he saw she wasn't here?

COTTARD: Whose face? Who pulled what face?

MME VERDURIN: D'you mean to say you didn't meet him on the doorstep, Cottard? — The loveliest of Swanns?

COTTARD: Why, has M. Swann been here?

MME VERDURIN: Just for a moment. Oh, we had a glimpse of a Swann tremendously agitated! In a state of nerves. You see, Odette has left.

COTTARD: (*Awed*) Do you suppose she's 'gone the whole hog' with him? 'Burned her boats'?

MME VERDURIN: No, no, no! There's absolutely nothing in it. If there had been she'd have told me. She tells me everything. It's only a Platonic affection, she says — she swears she wouldn't permit anything else. (*Pause*) And yet, mind you, he's exactly the sort of man she wants.

VERDURIN: I beg to differ. I am only half satisfied with the gentleman. I feel he poses.

MME VERDURIN: (*Furious*) Poses? Poses? Why should anyone want to 'pose' in *my* house? I tell you, if I thought our Swann had any ideas of *that* sort in his head. . . .

(*Fade*)

(*Steps in hall*)

FOOTMAN: Monsieur! Monsieur Swann!

SWANN: Eh! Who's that? Is that you, Albert?

FOOTMAN: Madame de Crécy left a message for you, sir. She said I was to tell you that she would most likely stop to drink a cup of chocolate at Prévost's on her way home. That would be about an hour ago, sir, because I remember hearing the clock strike while we were talking. . . .

(*Door opens*)

SWANN: Thank you, thank you. . . .

(*Door closes. Street noises. Swann's steps. Hooves idly stamping. Carriage door opens*)

Rémi! Drive to Prévost's as quickly as you can. . . .

(*Carriage door closes. Rémi calls up his horses. Wheels, clip-clop of horses*)

SWANN: Rémi! Can't you go any faster. . . . Damnation, do

people think they own the streets? . . . Oh, God, oh God, why are we crawling like this?

(*The 'Little Phrase' begins. Stops as carriage slows and stops*)
    (*Door slams. Street noises. Swann's feet across pavement. Café door opens — noise of laughter, voices, chink of cups and glasses*)

(*To himself*) Odette . . . Odette . . . Odette. . . .

MARCEL: Odette was not at Prévost's.

    (*Noises of a café; tinkle of glasses, chatter*)

SWANN: You! Waiter! Has Madame de Crécy been here to-night? You must know her — Madame de Crécy. . . .
WAITER: Would that be the dark lady, sir, in black and white, with the orchids —
SWANN: Yes, yes. Where is she?
WAITER: Oh, she went out again, sir. It must have been an hour or more — perhaps not an hour.

MARCEL: He sought for her, his dreams of terror painting her face upon a thousand faces, and seeing always the dissolution of the mask and the smile of a stranger. In desperation, he called for the coachman's aid. . . .

    (*Sounds of the street*)

SWANN: Rémi! I must find Madame de Crécy! You go that way — try all the cafés, don't miss one, mind — I'll go the other way. Then meet me on this corner — you can wait here till I come.

    (*The 'Little Phrase'*)

MARCEL: The little phrase, rising from the darkness and heat of his mind, tormented him, overwhelming all other sounds of the

H

night, as if the whole world had fallen silent to be punished utterly by the rapacious music. As he walked — half walked, half ran — along the streets, he was pursued by the voices of lovers undesired.

PROSTITUTE ONE: (*In a thin, faint voice*) All alone, dearie? I'm lonely, too. . . .

SWANN: Not you, not you. . . . Odette. . . . Odette. . . .

(*The music rises*)

PROSTITUTE TWO: (*Soft, cajoling voice*) Is the gentleman looking for somebody? For somebody to love. . . .

SWANN: No, no, no! Odette. . . . Odette. . . .

MARCEL: And then, as if by a miracle, the thousand faces that were hers and not hers blended into the face that was hers alone; and he saw her hurrying to meet him, black and white, the orchids trembling at her breast, her hands outstretched.

ODETTE: (*Sharply*) Charles!

(*Music ceases*)

SWANN: Ah!

ODETTE: Oh, I'm so glad we've found each other! I went into Prévost's, but there wasn't room, so I thought I'd go to supper at the Maison Dorée —

SWANN: But I looked there! Why didn't I see you? I can't understand it. Where are you going now?

ODETTE: Home, of course! I'm looking for my carriage. . . . Oh, here it is!

SWANN: I shall come with you. Rémi! Follow on behind, will you?

(*Opening of carriage door: rustle of silk. The door closes. Odette's coachman calls to the horses. Carriage moves off*)

ODETTE: You know, it gave me a terrible start, coming on you like that! I was so cross about missing you, and of course, I didn't know where you'd go when you found I wasn't —

(*A heavy jarring. Odette shrieks. Coachman: 'Whoa, there!'*)

SWANN: It's all right, my dear, it's all right, I assure you it's all right —

ODETTE: What happened? Oh, what happened? I thought we were going to turn right over!

SWANN: The horses shied. . . . It's all right now.

(*The carriage goes on*)

Don't be frightened. Let me put my arm round you, just to steady you . . . so. . . . Now, whatever you do, don't say a word — just make a sign, 'Yes' or 'No', or you'll be out of breath again. You won't mind if I put the cattleyas straight on your bodice? I'm afraid of them dropping out — I only want to pin them a little more securely.

ODETTE: (*A smile in her voice*) No, not at all. I don't mind in the least.

SWANN: No, no, no, no! What did I tell you? You mustn't speak, or you'll be out of breath again. Really and truly now, you don't mind me doing this? Look, there's a little pollen spilled over your dress — may I brush it off with my hand? Seriously, I'm not annoying you, am I? May I sniff your flowers to see whether they've really lost their scent? I don't believe I ever smelled any cattleyas before. . . . May I? Tell the truth, now?

ODETTE: (*In a whisper*) Stupid, stupid. . . .

SWANN: How long your lashes are. May I touch your lashes?

ODETTE: Charles. . . .

SWANN: I'm not annoying you — you promise me? . . . Your lashes and your great eyes. . . . My dear!

ODETTE: Charles . . . Charles. . . .

(*For a moment or so, only the sound of the horses' hooves*)

It's time to say good-night. We're almost home. . . .

(The carriage stops)

SWANN: I may come with you, may I not? Don't make me leave you! Tell me I may come in, tell me.

(The 'Little Phrase', slowly and simply. Piano only)

MARCEL: Yet he was so shy in approaching her that, after this evening which had begun by his arranging her cattleyas and had ended in her complete surrender, whether from fear of chilling her or because, perhaps, he lacked the audacity to formulate a more urgent requirement than this, he resorted to the same pretext on the following days.

SWANN: Oh, how unfortunate! The cattleyas don't need tucking in this evening. But this one isn't quite straight, I think. . . . If you will permit me. . . . If you're sure I'm not annoying you. . . .

MARCEL: And now, every evening when he had taken her home, he must follow her into the house; and often she would come out again in her dressing-gown, and would kiss him before the very eyes of his coachman, saying:

ODETTE: What on earth does it matter what people see? Why should we care? The whole world may look if it likes. . . .

MARCEL: From this time onwards, the image of Odette obsessed the whole of his imagination. No other woman had for him now the slightest meaning; it was as though she alone gave him vision, and that any face but hers had come to seem to him like a page on which the words written long ago are now smudged and meaningless, and even so, perhaps, were in a language unknown.

(Sound of sobbing)

SWANN: Ah don't, Annette, my little dear! I can't give you the things you ought to have. I'm not the slightest use to you. You must find a nice boy, a good boy, and marry him, and be happy in a little house as pretty as you are. . . .

ANNETTE: I don't want anyone else. I don't, I don't!

SWANN: Listen, I shall give you a little present and you must take it from me without being proud, or you'll make me very unhappy. You have been perfectly delightful and I shall never forget you, as long as I live. . . .

(*Music: Odette stumbling through Pauvres Fous*)

My darling Odette, tell me why you love that piece so much? I want to know exactly what goes on in that little head of yours. I want to follow your thoughts, as if I were exploring some strange countryside with a map and compass.

ODETTE: I don't know why I love it. I just do. I've put it in my Will that they're to play it at my funeral.

SWANN: I forbid you to talk of your funeral!

ODETTE: Forbid! That's a big word . . . but I can't refuse you anything, can I?

SWANN: Then you shall play our own '*Little Phrase*' for me.

(*Odette stops Pauvres Fous and blunders through the 'Little Phrase'. Then she stops, and giggles*)

ODETTE: But how can you expect me to play when you keep on holding me? I can't do everything at once. Make up your mind what you want: am I to play the phrase, or do you want to play with me? (*She bursts out laughing*)

SWANN: You shan't laugh. I forbid you.

ODETTE: Oh, I can't help it, I can't!

SWANN: You shan't laugh. . . . (*He kisses her. A long pause*)

ODETTE: (*Meekly*) Whatever you say, I must do. Isn't that it?

SWANN: My darling, my love. . . .

MARCEL: This was the Swann I never knew, the Swann recreated for me by the countless memories of men and women who spoke of him and of the greatest love affair of his life. M. de Charlus told me that at this time Swann knew nothing of Odette's past, never, even in the back of his mind, seemed to wonder what her life might have been. He had once heard someone refer to her as a *cocotte*, a 'kept woman'; yet at the recollection of her honesty, her simplicity, her embarrassment at being caught out by Madame Verdurin in a small white lie, the idea seemed to him preposterous. He delighted in her simply as she appeared in his eyes; and if he realised that it would be absurd for him any longer to try and cultivate her mind, or her tastes in literature and art, was able to find a rare and inexhaustible pleasure in her very triviality.

ODETTE: Your Vermeer, did he make a lot of money?

SWANN: No one knows.

ODETTE: But it would be interesting to know, wouldn't it?

SWANN: To look at the paintings is enough. One doesn't need any more.

ODETTE: Oh, I can't make you out! You never seem to care for the really interesting things. In my opinion. . . .

RÉMI: (*Coughing*) May I speak to Monsieur a moment?

SWANN: Of course, Rémi.

RÉMI: If it wouldn't incommode Monsieur, I should be glad if he would let me take my half-day to-day. My sister at Puteaux is ill.

SWANN: What's wrong? Nothing serious, I hope?

RÉMI: No, no, only her old trouble, but Monsieur knows how she does fret herself.

SWANN: Very well, then. Get along with you.

(*Pause*)

ODETTE: Oh, Charles, I can't think why you fuss so over your servants! Grab, grab, grab, that's all they care about. You'll never get a ha'porth of thanks.

SWANN: Don't be angry. I'm going to take you driving this afternoon, and then I shall see the springtime and you all at the same moment and not know which is which, and everyone will envy me.

ODETTE: (*Sharply*) You don't go talking about me to people, do you?

SWANN: Why do you always make me promise not to mention your name? And why don't you want to go into society?

ODETTE: Well. . . . You see, long ago I had a quarrel with a certain girl, and she revenged herself by saying nasty things about me.

SWANN: Oh, come, darling, people don't all know your friend!

ODETTE: But can't you see, a word of scandal spreads like a spot of oil; people are so horrid! Anyway, I go where I want to go. People in so-called 'society' never seem to me to know the really smart places.

SWANN: (*Puzzled*) But tell me, my love, what do you mean by that?

ODETTE: Why, just fancy, at your age, having to be told what the smart places are in Paris! Well, there are the balls, for instance —

SWANN: What balls?

ODETTE: Why, silly, the balls people give in Paris — the smart ones, I mean. Herbinger's, for example — oh, *you* know, that great swagger, fair-haired boy in one of the jobbers' offices. . . . Charles! Oh, what *have* you got there? Oh!

SWANN: Do you like it?

ODETTE: Oh, I never saw you with a single eyeglass before! I really think it's tremendously smart! How nice you look with it! Every inch a gentleman. All you want now is a title. Here, come and give me a kiss. . . .

MARCEL: Meanwhile, because for him their salon had become an essential symbol of the love of Odette and himself, holding for ever, as it were, within the curtained brightness, the precise moment when he had looked at her in the first wonderment of recognition, Swann's delight in the society of the Verdurins and his reverence for their wit, their taste, their brilliance, continued to increase. In the whole of their circle there was not a single one of the 'Faithful' who loved them, or believed he loved them, more than Swann. And yet, when M. Verdurin said that he was not satisfied with Swann, he had not only expressed his own sentiments, but had unwittingly discovered his wife's.

MME VERDURIN: Swann's nose will be out of joint to-night, I fear!

COTTARD: Out of joint? What joint? A leg of mutton?

MME VERDURIN: Don't play the fool, Cottard! I'm telling you that Swann is going to take a back seat for once. Odette is bringing us a new acquisition to our little circle — none other than the *Comte* (*with emphasis*) de Forcheville!

SANIETTE: Oh yes, that's my brother-in-law.

VERDURIN: What? Is this some ridiculous joke?

MME VERDURIN: *Your* brother-in-law, Saniette?

SANIETTE: Why, yes, yes, certainly; *certainly*. My wife's brother, or rather, to be more precise —

COTTARD: But isn't he enormously the swell?

SANIETTE: I don't know. He may be. I never saw much of him.

FOOTMAN: M. Charles Swann!

SWANN: Good evening, Madame Verdurin. Monsieur. Dr Cottard. How are you, M. Saniette? Quite well, I hope?

SANIETTE: Oh yes, thank you, surely, surely. We were just saying —

MME VERDURIN: We were saying, we are to have a new acquisition to our little Clan.

SWANN: (*Distrait*) Splendid, splendid. I hope I'm not too early. Madame de Crécy hasn't arrived. . . ?

MME COTTARD: How are you, M. Swann? I was just saying to my husband —

SWANN: Oh, Mme Cottard! How do you do?

MME COTTARD: I was just saying to my husband, I do *hope* we shall see M. Swann to-night because —

FOOTMAN: M. le Professeur Brichot!

MME VERDURIN: Ah, Professor! How delightful to receive you at my house, for the very first time! My dear, you know our great scholar —

VERDURIN: I am charmed. Most delighted.

MME VERDURIN: Professor Brichot, may I present to you Dr Cottard. . . . M. Charles Swann. . . .

BRICHOT: Delighted, delighted —

SWANN: (*Whispering*) Is this the Mistress' new aquisition, Cottard?

COTTARD: (*Whispering*) Oh, no, no. Of course, Brichot's a great *savant*, as they say. But this new fellow's a '*de*'—

SWANN: I beg your pardon?

COTTARD: A *de* — D — E. . . .

FOOTMAN: Madame de Crécy, M. le Comte de Forcheville.

MME VERDURIN: Odette, how perfect you look! And is this your guest? (*A chorus of greeting*) M. de Forcheville, I can't say how honoured we are. . . . Any friend Odette brings to our little circle. . . .

FOOTMAN: (*Above the noise*) Madame, dinner is served.

MME VERDURIN: M. Swann, you will take in Madame Cottard. . . . Odette, M. de Forcheville will give you his arm. . . .

(*The chink of china; chatter of voices*)

SWANN: (*Under cover of talk*) Odette, I thought you were never coming! How on earth did you come to meet Forcheville? You never told me you wouldn't be alone. . . .

ODETTE: Be quiet! People are staring at us. You know I hate to be conspicuous.

FORCHEVILLE: (*A high-pitched, affected voice*) I say, Doctor, quite original, Madame Verdurin's white dress, eh? *Toute blanche*, eh?

COTTARD: Who's M. de Forcheville talking about? Blanche? Blanche of Castille? Ha-ha! Ha-ha!

MME COTTARD: What was the joke, dear? I didn't quite catch.

FORCHEVILLE: Blanche de Castille? Very good, very good!

MME VERDURIN: What are you to say to a scientist like that, eh? Is that the way you go on in your hospital, Dr Cottard?

BRICHOT: (*A loud boring, pedantic voice*) I think I heard the Doctor speak of that wicked old humbug, Blanche of Castille, if I may so express myself. . . .

MME VERDURIN: Professor, professor!

BRICHOT: Goodness gracious, Madame, I would not dream of shocking the reverent-minded, if there are any such, around this table, but with reference to that particular lady . . . I recognise, moreover, that our ineffable and Athenian — oh, how infinitely Athenian — Republic, is capable of honouring, in the person of that obscurantist, old she-Capet, the first of our Chiefs of Police. Yes, indeed, my dear host, yes, indeed! The Chronicle of Saint Denis, and the authenticity of its information is beyond question, leaves us no room for doubt on that particular point. I have given my attention to it, you may be sure, and the inference is exact. Who runs may read, and all the rest of it. . . .

FORCHEVILLE: Who is that gentleman, Madame? I didn't catch his name. He seems to speak with authority.

MME VERDURIN: What? Do you mean to say you don't know the famous Brichot, celebrated all over Europe?

FORCHEVILLE: Oh, that's *Brichot*, is it? It's always interesting to meet well-known people at dinner. No dull evenings in this house, I'm sure.

BRICHOT: . . . No one could be more fitly chosen as Patron by a secularising proletariat than that mother of a saint, who let

him see some pretty fishy saints besides, as Suger says, and
other great Saint Bernards of that sort; for with her it was a
case of taking just what you pleased. . . .

FORCHEVILLE: Ah, very good! By Jove, that's good! Food for
thought, eh?

MME VERDURIN: (*Sharply*) M. Swann, you don't look very lively
to-night. Don't you feel well?

BRICHOT: . . . Indeed, if we regard the lady attentively, with our
eyes and ears open, as it were, we shall see how apt for her
would have been the old tag, *Aut inveniam viam aut faciam*, for
indeed, if she could not find out a way she made one. . . .

(*The chatter rises*)

ODETTE: Well, Charles, what do you think of my guest?

(*Pause*)

SWANN: Revolting!

ODETTE: Oh!

(*The noise continues, dropping abruptly when Mme Verdurin
speaks*)

MME VERDURIN: M. Swann! Attention, if you please. Madame
Cottard was debating which of M. Ohnet's plays was the best,
Le Maître des Forges or *Serge Panine*. Madame de Crécy wor-
ships *Serge Panine*, as we all know. But let's hear your opinion!

SWANN: Pardon me, but I can assure you that my want of admira-
tion is almost equally divided between those two masterpieces.

ODETTE: (*Whispering*) Charles! What *is* the matter with you
to-night? Do try to behave yourself!

FORCHEVILLE: I never seem to run across you these days, do I,
Swann? That's a fact, Madame Verdurin; this creature spends
all his time shut up with the La Trémoïlles, with the Laumes
and all that lot.

MME VERDURIN: Indeed? You'd need to pay *me* a lot of money

before I'd let them into my house. Saniette! Finish your pudding, will you, so they can take your plate away. — So you're always shut up with the bores are you, M. Swann? To think of that, now! What surprises *me* is that they can get anyone to go near them. I'm sure *I* should be afraid. How can people be so common as to go running after them?

VERDURIN: Come, come, my dear, let Swann tell us frankly what he thinks of them himself. We shan't repeat it to them, you may be sure!

SWANN: Why, I'm not afraid of the Duchess — if you're speaking of the La Trémoïlles. I can assure you, everyone likes going to see her. She's not at all 'deep', of course, but she *is* intelligent, and her husband is positively a bookworm. They're charming people.

MME VERDURIN: Saniette! You're keeping the servants back. (*Under cover of chatter: to her husband*) There! You see Swann posing right at our very table? Pretending those Trémoïlles and Laumes are intelligent, just to make himself look less of a snob. . . .

FORCHEVILLE: (*Under chatter*) You know, Doctor, Madame Verdurin can't have been at all bad-looking, though she's getting a bit broad in the beam now. But Madame de Crécy! Now, there's a little woman who knows what's what!

VERDURIN: (*Under chatter*) Sidonie, M. de Forcheville thinks Odette charming. . . .

MME VERDURIN: Do you, indeed, Count? Well, let me tell you, she so wants to meet you again some day at luncheon! We must arrange it, but don't let Swann know, on any account. He spoils everything.

FORCHEVILLE: By Jove, Madame, I'd appreciate that . . . on my word I should. . . .

(*The noise dies down*)

MARCEL: Swann was still unconscious of the disgrace that

threatened him at the Verdurins', rising slowly like a mist, at first imperceptible, from the whitening surface of a marsh. He had heard again that evening the 'Little Phrase', and had turned to it for comfort, as to an old friend who had just told him that he need not worry about this Forcheville, who was nobody at all. In the meantime Odette was agreeable, even permitting him, to his delight, to relieve her from the pressure of her creditors. He had never been able to think of her as a 'kept woman', which strange personification was for him an iridescent mixture of unknown and demoniacal qualities, embroidered as in some fantasy of Gustave Moreau, with poison-dripping flowers interwoven with precious jewels: yet he was coming to the realisation of an idea wholly different — which was, that he must endeavour, in the coming month, to send Odette six or seven thousand franc notes instead of five, simply as a surprise for her and to give her pleasure.

One evening she delighted him by saying in front the 'little clan', in front of Forcheville, and without the slightest attempt at concealment —

ODETTE: Oh yes, I know, you must go to your banquet. I shan't see you, then, till I get home: don't be too late!

MARCEL: It was past eleven when he reached her door.

SWANN: My dear, forgive me for being so long! The speeches were interminable. I assure you, I tried to get away, I did my best.

ODETTE: Yes, it's terribly late and the storm has given me a frightful headache. I shan't let you stay more than half an hour.

SWANN: No cattleya to-night? I've so been looking forward to a nice little cattleya.

ODETTE: No, dear, no cattleya. You can see I'm not well.

SWANN: Oh . . . then I won't bother you. Only it might have done you good, don't you think it might?

MARCEL: But no sooner was he in his own house than a terrible thought struck him: that Odette had only pretended to be tired, that she was expecting someone else, that the moment he had gone she had lit the lamps again and, in one of her wrappers of mauve or pink crêpe-de-chine, had run downstairs to re-open the door to the stranger who was to be her guest for the night. It was an hour and a half since he had left her. He went out, took a cab and left it close by her house. He walked along the dark and deserted street, behind the row of houses in which was Odette's. Amid the glimmering blackness of all the row of windows, the lights in which had long been put out, he saw one, and only one, from which overflowed, between the slats of its shutters, closed like a wine-press over its mysterious golden juice, the light that filled the room within.

SWANN: (*To himself*) She's there with a man. . . .

(*We hear his breathing*)

I can hear them talking. . . .

(*The faint murmur of conversation*)

(*Loudly*) I *will* not endure it!

(*He raps smartly on the shutters*)

(*Pause*)

FIRST VOICE: Who's that?

SWANN: (*Heartily, in a careless tone*) Please don't bother, Odette. I just happened to be passing and saw the light. I wanted to know if you were feeling better.

(*The shutters open*)

SECOND VOICE: (*An old man's, high and irascible*) What the devil, sir, what the devil —

FIRST VOICE: (*An old man's, but more robust*) What do you want, sir, tapping on the shutter like that?

SWANN: Oh, I beg your pardon! I thought — I thought this was Number Five.

FIRST VOICE: Well, it's not. It's Number Six.

SECOND VOICE: And good-night to you, sir.

FIRST VOICE: *Good*-night!

(*The shutters bang to again*)

MARCEL: Swann's jealousy, the complement of his love, was beginning now to bring him to a torment which was almost a bodily pain. A fresh turn was given to the screw when he recalled a sudden expression he had intercepted, a few days earlier, and for the first time, in Odette's eyes. After dinner at the Verdurins', Forcheville, aware that Saniette was not in favour with them, had decided to make a butt of him: and had replied to some tactless utterance with such a volley of abuse that the poor creature, after asking Madame Verdurin whether he should stay, and receiving no answer, had left the house in stammering confusion and with tears in his eyes. It was then that Swann had seen Odette, who had hitherto looked on so impassively, give Forcheville a quick, sly, sparkling glance of complicity, as if to say. . . .

ODETTE: (*In a murmur*) Good for you! That's finished him off, or I'm very much mistaken. Did you see what a fool he looked? Why, he was actually crying!

MARCEL: Swann realised that Odette was lying to him, concocting her depressing untruths, her evasions, in exactly the same sorrowful manner in which she had once apologised to Madame Verdurin for staying away from dinner on a pretext of illness, but really so that she might be alone with Swann. But he, being deafened by one peril to another, as a man in a jungle stricken

by terror of a snake, may fail to hear the rustle of the under-
growth which betrays the leopard, was unaware of the down-
fall planned for him by the Verdurins, until one night a month
later, at a dinner in the Bois. . . .

(*The rustle of leaves: the music of a distant café-concert.
Small talk*)

MME VERDURIN: (*Whispering*) Now don't forget, M. Biche, to-
morrow at Chatou, and our little wretch to play for us. . . .

M. BICHE: There must be no lights of any sort, and he must play
the *Moonlight Sonata* in the dark for us to see by. . . .

MME VERDURIN: (*Whispering*) Eh-h-h! That will do. (*Aloud*) M.
de Forcheville! Don't you like your sorbet? It's not as good as
the one at my house, I know that, but all the same. . . .

(*Music and chatter rise up*)

SWANN: Odette. I want to talk to you.

ODETTE: (*Agitated*) We can't talk now.

SWANN: What's this about Chatou? No one has asked me —

ODETTE: Oh, be quiet! Later! — Later!

MARCEL: Swann anxiously counted the minutes that still separated
him from the point at which, after leaving the restaurant, he
might drive her home; when he could ask for an explanation,
make her promise either that she would not go to Chatou next
day, or else that she would procure an invitation for him also.

(*Music fades again into distance*)

MME VERDURIN: Come, come, no whispering! It's late, and we
don't want to be up all night. Good-bye, M. Swann. We shall
see you soon, I hope. . . .

(*A pause*)

SWANN: Good-bye Madame.

MME VERDURIN: M. de Forcheville, you shall ride with us this evening. Hurry along, now, we don't want to hold up the carriages. — Odette!

ODETTE: Yes, Madame?

MME VERDURIN: We'll take you too. We've kept a little corner specially for you, beside M. de Forcheville. . . .

SWANN: (*Whispering*) But you're coming with *me* —

MME VERDURIN: Odette!

ODETTE: (*Meekly*) Yes, Madame Verdurin.

SWANN: (*Carried away*) I thought I was to take you home!

ODETTE: But, Madame Verdurin has asked me —

MME VERDURIN: That's all right, isn't it? You can quite well go home alone; we've left you like this dozens of times.

SWANN: But I had something important to discuss with Madame de Crécy!

MME VERDURIN: Very well, you can write it to her instead.

ODETTE: Good-bye, Charles.

SWANN: (*Whispering*) This is ridiculous! You simply can't go off like that —

MME VERDURIN: Good-bye, M. Swann! Good-bye!

(*The carriage moves off*)

RÉMI: Is Monsieur all right? He isn't unwell, is he? It's not bad news?

SWANN: No, Rémi, no . . . it's nothing. You take the carriage home, will you? I shall walk.

(*Music comes to an end*)

MARCEL: As he passed, in the intoxication of grief, through the paths and avenues of the Bois. . . .

SWANN: Imagine going to Chatou, of all places! Like a lot of drapers after closing time! Upon my word, these people are sublime in their smugness; they must all have come out of

I

Labiche's plays. ... The painter will be there too, inviting
Forcheville to come with Odette to his studio, the painter who
enjoys match-making. ... The damned pianist playing his
Moonlight Sonata, and Madame Verdurin saying (*He mimics
her brutally*) 'You can make room for M. de Forcheville there,
can't you, Odette?' Playing the sonata in the dark! Codfish!
Pander! Pander! ... Verdurin ... what a name! Oh, there's
something complete about them, they're the most perfect
specimens of their disgusting class. Thank God, it was high
time I stopped condescending to promiscuous intercourse with
such infamy, such dung!

MARCEL: The evening after the dinner at Chatou, Dr Cottard,
who had not seen the Verdurins for some days, looked up and
down the table in bewilderment, even unthinkingly casting a
glance beneath it, so as to leave, as it were, no avenue unex-
plored.

COTTARD: Why, aren't we going to see M. Swann this evening?
He is quite what you might call a personal friend of —

MME VERDURIN: I sincerely hope we shan't! Heaven preserve us
from him; he's too deadly for words, a stupid, ill-bred bore!

COTTARD: (*Stupefied*) A bore, eh? Oh, is he? Oh, I see. (*In a
descending scale*) Oh, oh, oh, oh, oh!

(*Pause*)

MARCEL: After which there was no more talk of Swann at the
Verdurins'.

(*Odette's voice, humming a tune. She breaks off suddenly*)

ODETTE: I'll have to send you away early to-night, I'm afraid.
I'm going to the Opéra Comique with the Verdurins to see
Une Nuit de Cléopâtre.

SWANN: What on earth do you want to see a thing like that for?
Don't go.

ODETTE: Oh, I can't break a promise. Give me that scent-bottle, will you? Oh, clumsy! You've spilled my powder.

SWANN: I ask you not to go. I ask you because I have your welfare in mind. I —

ODETTE: *Will* you look what you're doing? You've got powder on your hands and now you're putting it all over my dress! Oh, go away!... Welfare? What on earth are you talking about?

SWANN: Your *Nuit de Cléopâtre* (what a title!) has no bearing on my plea to you not to go. I only want to know whether you are indeed one of those contemptible creatures incapable of foregoing a pleasure. If you refuse, I shall cease from that moment to love you; but at the same time you will appear less attractive to my eyes when I realise that you are beneath everything in the world and have not the intelligence to raise yourself higher —

ODETTE: (*Placidly*) Yes, darling, but if you go on talking much longer I shall never get there in time for the Overture.

MARCEL: When the Verdurins took her off to Saint-Germain, or to Chatou, or, if it was fine, to Meulan, where they would not infrequently stay overnight, Swann would be tormented by fear and loneliness. He fed upon his doubts and fears as the pelican upon his own flesh. Although she would not allow him, as a rule, to meet her at public gatherings, saying people would talk, it happened occasionally that he found himself in the same room with her. He could see her, but dared not remain for fear of annoying her by seeming to be spying upon the pleasures which she tasted in the company of others. Yet now and then she would offer him, by calling him back just as his hand was on the door, a vivid and mysterious pleasure, a hope that fed and sustained his torment, giving him the strength to endure it and to hang back from the moment that so often seemed within his reach when, by a simple act of will, he might bring it to an end. Once, when she had driven both himself and Forcheville as far as her door, she had allowed both to come in for a little while; but had made Forcheville beg Swann's permission to be present.

ODETTE: I warn you, though, you mustn't stay long. M. Swann just likes to sit and talk quietly with me, and he's not at all pleased if I have visitors while he's here. Oh, if you only knew the creature as I know him; isn't that so, my love? There's no one who really knows you, is there, except me?

MARCEL: After such evenings, Swann's suspicions would be temporarily lulled, and next day, in gratitude, or in a paroxysm of love, he would send her jewels. But at other times grief would take hold of him; he would imagine that Odette was Forcheville's mistress and seem to see once more, in her sly and cunning smile, the horrible complicity he had surprised upon her face on the evening when Forcheville had driven Saniette from the Verdurins'. At such times he hated her.

SWANN: I've been a fool, Mémé. I'm paying for other men's pleasures with my money. All the same, she'd better not pull the string too tight, or I might very well stop giving her anything at all. Do you know, the other day, when she said she wanted to go to Bayreuth for the season, I offered to take one of those jolly little places the King of Bavaria has there, just for the two of us?

CHARLUS: That would have cost you a pretty penny, my dear fellow.

SWANN: Yes: well: let's hope she'll refuse. (*Pause*) Do you know what I believe she's capable of doing?

CHARLUS: The capacity of Odette has always seemed to me infinite.

SWANN: Listen: she's perfectly capable of asking me for money to take the house at Bayreuth and warning me that I'm not to be there myself, so that she can invite Forcheville and the Verdurins.

CHARLUS: Come, come, that's going too far!

SWANN: If only she would! How I'd love the chance to refuse! I should say . . . something of this kind . . . 'My dear, I have not, you will admit, behaved without generosity in the past . . .' . . . er . . . er . . . 'but this new demand seems to me so preposterous and so lacking in taste that my opinion of your intelligence. . . .'

(Scratch of Odette's pen, rustle of paper)

ODETTE: '. . . The Verdurins would so like to be present at the performances of Wagner, so if only you'd be so good and kind as to send me some money so that your little Odette could have the pleasure of entertaining them in her own house. . . .'

(Pause)

SWANN: *(Thunderstruck)* Mémé — I never dreamed she would really do it. . . .

CHARLUS: However, you have your reply composed in advance.

(A pause. Pauvres Fous, a few bars, played by one finger on piano)

SWANN: It would be impossible for me to cause her distress. She trusts me. . . .

MARCEL: As the months went by, Swann's anguish, his suspicions, his dreadful watchfulness, increased, till the disease of love whch had seized upon him had reached that stage at which the boldest of surgeons ask themselves whether to deprive a patient of his vice or to rid him of his malady is still reasonable or, indeed, possible. He sent M. Charlus out with her as often as possible to spy upon her movements; to him, at least, he had the con-

solation of speaking of her openly. Now that her nature was
becoming revealed to him more and more clearly, still less did
he comprehend her. At times she was charming, honest and
affectionate; at others she would terrify him by her indifference,
listlessness and irritability. For all this, he refused to believe,
even to contemplate, the possibility that he could be losing her
love, until one night, he went to a party given by Madame de
Saint-Euverte.

(The chatter of a big party)

BASIN (Prince des Laumes): By Jove, Oriane, isn't that Swann
over there? He doesn't go out and about much these days, does
he?

ORIANE (Princesse des Laumes): Poor Swann, he's always charming. But he does look so dreadfully unhappy, Basin! I do feel
it's really absurd for a man of his intelligence to let himself be
made to suffer by a creature of that kind, who isn't even interesting! For they say she's an absolute idiot.

BASIN: Yes, there he is, talking to old Froberville. What on earth
are they saying, I wonder? Swann looks excited.

SWANN: There was that explorer, now . . . La Pérouse. . . . He
was a fine character and interests me very much, does La
Pérouse.

FROBERVILLE: Oh, yes, of course, La Pérouse. There's a street
called that.

SWANN: *(Eagerly)* Do you know anyone in the Rue La Pérouse?

FROBERVILLE: Only Madame de Chanlivault. She gave a most
amusing party there the other day.

SWANN: Oh, so *she* lives in the Rue La Pérouse. It's a most
attractive street. It's so sombre, the Rue La Pérouse.

FROBERVILLE: Indeed it isn't! You can't have been in it for a long
time. It's not at all sombre now. . . .

(This duologue dies away)

ORIANE: My precious Charles! How nice to see you again!
SWANN: And infinitely delightful to see you, my dear Princess.

(*A sudden silence*)

What, are they starting the music?
ORIANE: Yes, and you shall sit by me.

(*Applause: tuning up*)

I have a special corner all to myself. You're looking rather pale.
Haven't you been well?
SWANN: Oh, yes, perfectly well. But let me look at you! Behold
our charming Princess! Ah, yes, the new headdress — quite
delightful! She has come up on purpose from Guermantes. . . .

(*Vinteuil Sonata begins, arranged for violin and piano*)

. . . to hear St. Francis preaching to the birds, and has only had
time to pick a few little hips and haws from the hedges and put
them in her hair.
ORIANE: Sh-h-h. Be quiet with your nonsense! You'll have us
both turned out —

(*Sonata continues: the 'Little Phrase'*)

. . . for I'm sure old Mother Saint-Euverte wouldn't think twice
about having two footmen drag me from the house, just to
show that music is so much more to her than society. . . .

MARCEL: (*While music continues*) It was suddenly as though
Odette had entered the room; Swann's heart was torn with
sudden anguish. All his memories of the days when Odette
had been in love with him, which he had succeeded, up till that
evening, in stifling in the depths of his being, had dawned
again.

ODETTE: (*Voice faint against the music*) Why did you not leave your heart also?

(*Music rising*)

I'll always be free when you want me.

(*Music rising*)

Just send for me. . . . Will you do that?

(*Music rising and dying away*)

MARCEL: From that evening, Swann understood that the feeling which Odette once had for him would never revive, that his hopes of happiness would never be realised now. He knew that she was free from him, but that he would never be free from her, free to return to his interrupted work, to visit the Hague, Dresden, Brunswick. . . . Odette less and less made any pretence of fidelity. She announced quite casually that she was going for a trip to Egypt in Forcheville's company and, as if in derisive consolation, or out of some audacity the range of which even she herself felt astonishing and pleasurable, promised to send Swann a view of the Pyramids.

One day he received an anonymous letter which told him that she had been the mistress of countless men, and the lover of women also: and that she frequented houses of ill-fame. He recoiled in terror from this vast inferno of new possibilities opening in his mind. He recalled how Odette had once told him of something Madame Verdurin had said to her — 'Take care, now! I know how to melt you all right, you're not made of marble,'— and how Odette herself had remarked carelessly some two years ago. . . .

ODETTE: Oh, Madame Verdurin, she won't hear of anything just now but me. I'm a 'love', if you please, and she kisses me, and wants me to go with her everywhere. . . .

MARCEL: Suddenly Swann made up his mind to question her. It was M. de Charlus to whom she fled in fear and rage after the interrogation, M. de Charlus, Swann's friend and Odette's disinterested pander.

ODETTE: (*Storming*) I will not bear it! I *will* not! Why should I? How dare he torment me like that, Mémé? He wanted to know if I'd ever cared about women — can you believe that? Oh, it was odious! I told him people were telling lies about me, that it wasn't true — and *then* he tried to make me swear on my Laghetto medal that I'd never done anything of the sort!

CHARLUS: I am willing to wager, my dear, that you resisted the test.

ODETTE: You know how sacred my medal's always been to me! I won't use it for swearing to a lot of nonsense.

CHARLUS: Indeed, no. Very wise. Merely wise. Simply as a matter of interest, *was* it true?

ODETTE: Oh, how should I know? Perhaps once or twice, years ago. I've forgotten.

CHARLUS: Poor Swann.

ODETTE: Poor? Don't I devote my whole life to him?

CHARLUS: Has he any idea about Forcheville? Or Bréauté, for instance?

ODETTE: I don't know what he knows, and I don't care! He torments me like a fiend! He's killing me, I tell you. He pretends to be so mild, so gentle, when all the time he's trying to worm things out of me. . . . I'm a liar, he says. That's the trouble, that's what he can't bear. He says he can and does forgive me everything because he loves me, all except my untruthfulness. . . . That's the kind of thing I have to listen to!

CHARLUS: You are a most curious woman, Odette. It is really most unfortunate that any real understanding of your nature should have been vouchsafed only to myself who am, alas, only capable of a bystander's interest.

ODETTE: (*With a giggle*) Go along with you, I know your sort. You're not quite blind to me, are you? Though you won't admit it. Confess, Mémé, tell the truth!

CHARLUS: Odette, my dear; in you, conceit is so highly developed as to be a poetic virtue. I find it quite charming. But tell me, how did Swann take all this in the end?

ODETTE: Oh, he stormed himself to a standstill. He always ends up in tears, or pretty nearly. He started fussing over me and saying it was all over, and he'd never think about it again . . . but I know just what it will be like this time next week!

MARCEL: And her lies, her omissions, Swann could never forget. His spirit carried them along, cast them aside, then cradled them again in its bosom, like corpses in a river. And they poisoned it. On certain evenings she would suddenly resume towards him a kindness of which she would warn him sternly that he must take immediate advantage, or lose the chance of it for years to come. He must instantly come home with her; and the desire she pretended to have for him was so sudden, so inexplicable, that this brutal and unnatural fondness made Swann just as unhappy as any lie or unkind action. . . .

ODETTE: No, no, no, that's not at all nice of you, to sit like a statue. I want you here, by me, in your old place. Look, we'll put the little lamp so that it shines through the flowers — isn't that pretty? Oh, darling, you look so distinguished to-night, you really do, you make me proud of you. Do you know, I was thinking of you all the evening — I had no other thought but you. Oh, my love. . . .

SWANN: No! Don't touch me. Why are you like this to-night? After tormenting me with your coldness, your meaningless, perverse coldness, you turn into quite another woman.

ODETTE: (*With restrained impatience*) I've told you again and again, I can't add myself up as though I were a column of

figures! Sometimes I don't feel like being loved, sometimes I
do. Can I help that? (*Beguilingly*) Now stop being so suspi-
cious, because I feel so happy to-night, in my own little house,
alone with you and no one to spoil things —

SWANN: Why did you refuse to let me take you home from
Madame de Chaussepierre's ball on Wednesday?

ODETTE: Oh, because I wasn't in the mood! I wanted to be by
myself.

SWANN: And were you by yourself?

ODETTE: If you begin questioning me I shall hate you. And I
I want to love you to-night, just as if it were the old times —

SWANN: Why are you looking at me like that? There must be a
reason. Tell me the truth! Why did you make me come here
this evening?

ODETTE: Because I adore my little Charles! Haven't I always said
it? I have my moods, I know, but women *do*, and you, who
understand women so wonderfully, ought to understand *me*!
Come and kiss me ... please. ... Ah, that's better! ... And
again. ... (*Abrupt change of tone*) What's the matter? Where are
you going? What are you doing?

(*Swann's feet across the floor. The opening and closing of doors,
noise of a search*)

I said, *what are you doing?*

SWANN: There's somebody here. I heard someone.

ODETTE: There's nobody at all, silly. Whom should there be?
Come here!

SWANN: You are hiding someone. I know it.

ODETTE: Oh, don't be ridiculous! You're making a fool of yourself. (*Change of tone*) Darling, I adore you, you know I do.
Come here and be friendly to your poor Odette. ...

SWANN: I heard someone.

(*Noise of search renewed*)

ODETTE: (*In a furious rage*) I can never do anything right with you, you're impossible! Oh, go away, I tell you, go away!

(*A smash*)

SWANN: You've cut yourself!

ODETTE: It was worth it! I wish I'd smashed that wretched vase over your head! Oh, you're a devil, a devil, a fiend, that's what you are, a fiend!

MARCEL: Odette began to grow away from Swann's life, at a physical distance now proportionate to the moral, for the Verdurins had bought a yacht, and several of the 'Faithful', Odette among them, were constantly going on cruises of a duration which, on one occasion, stretched almost to a year. During her absence Swann felt that he was beginning to detach himself from her, that the power of detachment no longer lay solely in her hands, but in his also. . . . And, in fact, though he could not resist seeing her whenever he heard she was back in Paris, he felt, during these periods of separation, perfectly at ease and also happy: for there is a point in tormented love when the desire for peace of spirit may conquer the love itself, conquer, even, the desire for suffering which, in itself, may become one of the most strong, abiding and destructive of human addictions. It was near to this point that Swann had come when, one day shortly before the return of the travellers, he encountered in an omnibus the foolish, kindly Madame Cottard, returning from paying a round of calls.

MME COTTARD: Well, Monsieur Swann, what a stranger you are these days! You look well, I must say. Are you going here, there and everywhere?

(*Background of horses' hooves: 'Tickets, please!'*)

Oh, is this your stop? No, of course not! You know, your ears must have been burning lately.

SWANN: My ears? Why? When?

MME COTTARD: When we were on the yacht with Mme Verdurin. We were talking about you all the time.

SWANN: (*Astounded*) About me?

MME COTTARD: Oh, yes! You see, Madame de Crécy was there; need I say more? When Odette is anywhere, it's never long before she begins talking about you. It was 'Monsieur Swann' all the time. She used to say, 'I can see him at this very moment! He's thinking of us, wondering where we are!' Monsieur Verdurin asked her, 'How in the world can you see what he's doing when he's a thousand miles away?' And Odette answered, 'Nothing is impossible to the eye of a friend.' We thought it was so pretty of her!

SWANN: (*Choked with emotion*) Madame Cottard, you're just trying to flatter me —

MME COTTARD: No, no, I assure you I'm not. With Odette, you're the *only* one. Madame Verdurin said to me herself on our last day — 'I don't say Odette isn't fond of us, but anything we may say to her counts for very little beside what Swann might say —' Oh, mercy, here's the conductor stopping for me!

CONDUCTOR: Rue Bonaparte! Anybody for the Rue Bonaparte?

MME COTTARD: M. Swann, would you be so very kind as to tell me whether my plume is straight?

SWANN: Yes, yes, quite straight, perfect — and it's been so delightful to meet you, you can't imagine how delightful — goodbye, Madame. . . .

MARCEL: Madame Cottard, a wiser physician than her husband would have been, had by her desire to please, to console, grafted into the moribund feelings that Swann had for Odette, others more normal, feelings of gratitude and friendship which in his mind were to make her seem again more human; and paradoxically, make it easier for him to face the day that must come when he would cease to be in love with her. For now, to the faintness of his love, there corresponded a simultaneous faintness in his desire to remain her lover.

He believed now that he would never see again the Odette who had once made him suffer so horribly, but in fact he saw her once more in a dream. And awakening from this dream to the summons of the barber who had come to dress his hair for a journey. . . .

SWANN: (*In a great voice of conviction and revelation*) To think that I have wasted years of my life, that I have longed for death, that the greatest love that I have ever known has been for a woman who did not please me, who was not in my style!

(*A pause: then Pauvres Fous, played with one finger. A pause*)

SWANN: A woman not in my style —

(*Two or three bars — Pauvres Fous. Pause*)

MARCEL: (*Quietly*) But at last Charles Swann and Odette de Crécy were married, for the sake of their child, their daughter, Gilberte.

Upon Swann's death, Odette married her old lover, Forcheville, and into her old age was the lover of many men. I had known Swann all my life. As a young man I had become a friend and even, for a short while, a romantic admirer of Odette, with whose daughter I fell in love. I had watched Odette's adroit progress up the ladder of society, had watched her grow old in the drawing-rooms which, in more powerful days, would rigorously have excluded her. But towards the end of the Great War, I had to retire into a sanatorium; and a long time passed before I left it. I saw Odette for the last time at an afternoon party given by the aged Princesse de Guermantes, who had

once been Madame Verdurin. Which was the effect of paint and
which of dye, I could not tell; but Odette seemed to me not to
have changed. With her ruffled chignon, like a doll's, and her
doll-like face, she looked as though she were a young woman
playing a part in a Christmas revue featuring the Exhibition of
1878.

She was the mistress of the aged Duc de Guermantes, who
had been Prince des Laumes, to whom she ministered, and whom
she deceived, without charm, without generosity, without
kindness. She was commonplace in that as in everything else.
Life had given her good parts but she could not play them.
That night she spoke to me of Swann.

ODETTE: (*A tired, ageing, wistful voice*) Come and have tea with
me one day soon, and I'll tell you how I made M. de Forcheville's acquaintance. Really, my life has been a cloistered one,
for I've only had great loves for men who were terribly jealous
of me. I don't speak of M. de Forcheville: he was quite indifferent and I only cared for intelligent men. But it was M. Swann
I loved madly, and one can sacrifice dancing, society and everything to please a man one loves or even to spare him anxiety.
Poor Charles, he was so intelligent, so seductive, exactly the
kind of man I liked.

(*Music: the 'Little Phrase'*)

Oh yes, you may believe me. . . . It was Monsieur Swann I
loved madly.

(*Music rises*)

MARCEL: Because I never knew Swann or Odette in their youth
and so could not create them from my own knowledge, having
to build them in mosaic from the memories of observers of
their own stature in Time, I cannot tell how far, that day, she
spoke the truth.

As far as she could love, Odette may indeed have loved Swann. She was in herself utterly commonplace; but she had aroused in him one of those passions which seem to overflow the vessel which contains it, as too great a light in a bowl of alabaster may spill the blazing edge of its radiance beyond the milky cup and scatter its coals beyond; I found it almost possible to believe, as I listened to this old yet ageless Odette, that some of the fire from Swann's passion may, as it were, have attacked its object, so that she also, unknowing, uncomprehending, had been fretted by some trace of it implanted in her own restless and fugitive spirit.

(The 'Little Phrase')

ODETTE: One can sacrifice dancing, society, anything, to please a man one loves or to spare him anxiety. . . .

(Pause in the music)

SWANN: I can, and do, forgive you everything because I love you, all except your untruthfulness. . . .

(The 'Little Phrase'. Pause)

CHARLUS: *(In a voice of sepulchral resonance)* Hannibal de Bréauté, dead! Antoine de Mouchy, dead! Adalbert de Montmorency, dead! Baron de Talleyrand, dead! Sosthène de Doudeauville, dead! *(His voice falters)* Charles Swann, dead!

(Music restarts)

MARCEL: There is much to conjecture. There is nothing more to know.

(Music rises to the end)

IV

Albertine Regained

NOTE

IF WE knew as little of Proust as we do of Homer, and if the practical circumstances of Albertine's history were not so ambiguous, we should without question accept her as a girl. She is most beautifully a girl, in fact, a schoolgirl: perpetually a schoolgirl, unformed, uneasy, with a strong sense that she is being 'got at'. According to my own tentative chronology for the book, Albertine is in her early twenties when she takes up her life of captivity in Marcel's house: but she *seems* no more than seventeen. Her relations with her girl friends are boarding-school relations; for her, Andrée, who scolds, approves, disapproves, teases, ridicules, supports and betrays, is always the Head Prefect.

Albertine Regained is largely a *jeu d'esprit,* but has one serious critical intention — to make clear the extreme subjectivity of Marcel's picture of those nearest to him. It should be manifest — it is not only a joke — that Marcel's word on Albertine may not be, almost certainly is not, the last one. So I tried to mark the similarity of the Marcel/Albertine and the Swann/Odette stories by protracting the former and therefore bringing each to an end in a marriage of tedium and staleness. It is not impossible (if we examine Marcel's subjective vision) that Albertine's inversion was no more than a transient homosexual impulse of adolescence. Andrée, we know, is jealous and mendacious: Aimé will say, for a good tip, anything he thinks the interrogator wants to hear.

There is a considerable psychological similarity between Aimé and Jupien: they are both pimps: they are both instinct with the spirit of obligation. They are by no means unlike physically (Aimé, *The Guermantes Way*, I, 222, Jupien, *The Guermantes Way*, I, 17); it has not yet been pointed out, so far as I know, that both must have emanated from a common source in the mind of Proust. In any case, it would be a pity to hang a dog on the word of either, still less to hang Albertine.

It should be noted that none of the three objects of love in the three great affairs — Swann/Odette, Marcel/Albertine, Charlus/ Morel, is made unhappy by love itself, but only by exasperation at being hounded by the lover's suspicions. Albertine's temperament is a cool one. She has laid all her plans: like the shrewd girl she is, she has a secondary plan to fall back on if the more important fails. Octave is always in her scheme of things, as Forcheville was in Odette's.

Even though we let Albertine speak for herself, however, we must not expect to get a definite answer: the haze of subjectivity around her is too dense for that. She remains ambiguous to the last, even when we hear her voice, even when we approach her in Marcel's absence. She explains away the syringa, the two intaglio rings: she claims that Andrée lied about her because she wanted Marcel for herself — but it is not obligatory to believe that claim.

In this programme I have also tried to explain away the singular transformation of the dull Octave into the great stage-designer. Proust does not justify this at all. He is often careless about his minor characters, working to death the device of misdirection. This device, we know, he picked up from Dostoievski who 'instead of presenting things in their logical sequence, that is to say, beginning with the cause, shows us first of all the effect, the illusion that strikes us'. (*The Captive*, II, 238.) No novelist ever tried this more often than Proust; and sometimes he produces an illusion that, despite all his efforts, we are unable to shake off. With several characters the misdirection is altogether too strong, and we believe the first impression to the end; it is hardly possible to believe in the transformation of Bloch, that essentially uncreative, critical mind, into a successful playwright; hard to believe in the transformation of the sly, devious, malicious and selfish Gilberte into a kind of married saint; hardest of all to believe in the transmogrification of the cloddish golf-player, Octave, into someone like Bakst.

ALBERTINE REGAINED

(Chord on piano. Girls' voices)

GIRLS SINGING: Il court, il court, le furet,
Le furet du bois, Mesdam',
Il court, il court, le furet,
Le furet du bois joli.
Il a passé par ici,
Il repassera par là, (il dort),
Il court, il court, le furet,
Le furet du bois joli.

(Singing dies away)

ALBERTINE: My name is Albertine Simonet (Simonet with one N).
I think it is quite time I said something for myself: nobody ever
hears my side of it. A nymph, mutable as the sea — that is what
Marcel said about me. (*Working herself up a little*) The *principle*
is that I'm so mysterious! No one ever knows where they are
with me! No one really knows my . . . (*Falters*) well, my *tastes*.
(*Working herself up again*) But I tell you, no girl is ever really
mysterious to herself, and I jolly well don't feel mysterious, but
the things he said about me. . . . Though I know he loved me,
and I did love my little Marcel, I did, even when he was most
impossible . . . that is, I loved him most of the time, but sometimes I could have broken it over him! He was always saying I
told lies, but honestly, with him one *had* to fib a little or there
was the devil to pay. There was all that business of pestering
me about whether I had known Swann's daughter, Gilberte, for
instance. Well, of course I was at school with Gilberte, though
she was older than I was. . . .

GIRLS' VOICES: Il court, il court, le furet,
                   Le furet du bois, Mesdam',
                   Il court, il court, le furet,
                   Le furet du bois joli.
                   Il a passé par ici,
                   Il repassera par là,
                   Il court, il court, le furet,
                   Le furet du bois joli.

MLLE LE CHEMINANT: Bien! Asseyez-vous, mesdemoiselles! Et maintenant, dites moi quelle est l'origine de cette petite chanson que nous avons apprise cette après-midi. Alors . . . Gilberte Swann!

GILBERTE: Le furet est une ronde enfantine, mais surtout un des plus anciens jeux de France, très en faveur à la cour de Marguerite de Valois. (*Dead stop*)

MLLE LE CHEMINANT: Bon. Et alors? (*Pause*) A qui maintenant?

VOICES: Mademoiselle! Mademoiselle!

MLLE LE CHEMINANT: Alors . . . Albertine Simonet. Levez-vous, s'il vous plaît.

ALBERTINE: (*In a small, slightly lubricious voice*) Sous Louis XV, le jeu devint franchement libertin. (*Titters from other girls. Self-righteously*) J'ai lu ça dans l'encyclopédie!

MLLE LE CHEMINANT: (*Hastily*) Ça suffit, Albertine. Décrivez-nous le jeu lui-même.

ALBERTINE: Les joueurs s'asseyant en rond et tiennent en rond et tiennent dans leurs mains une corde qui passe dans un anneau. Ils font courir de mains en mains cet anneau, qu'on appelle le furet, et qu'on ne doit pas voir. Un joueur placé au milieu de cercle doit deviner dans quels mains le furet se trouve. Les joueurs chantent: 'Il court, il court le furet', etcétéra. Lorsque l'un des joueurs s'est laissé prendre le furet dans la main, il change de place avec celui qui était au milieu.

MLLE LE CHAMINANT: Très bien, Albertine! Asseyez-vous donc.

ALBERTINE: (*Sotto voce*) Tout de même, le jeu pouvait vraiment être libertin, n'est-ce pas, Mademoiselle?

MLLE LE CHEMINANT: Cet aspect là ne nous concerne pas. Mes enfants, levez-vous. Nous allons chanter encore une fois notre petite ritournelle. (*Strikes key-note on piano*) Un, deux, trois —

GIRLS' VOICES: Il court, il court, le furet,
                      Le furet, du bois Mesdam'
                      Il court, il court, le furet —

MLLE LE CHEMINANT: (*Rapping on wood of piano*) Silence! Gilberte! Vous avez passé un papier à Albertine. Albertine, apportez le moi.

ALBERTINE: Mais ce n'est rien, Mademoiselle.

MME LE CHEMINANT: Apportez moi ça, tout de suite! Albertine, Gilberte, venez ici!

ALBERTINE: Mais, Mademoiselle, ce n'est qu'une petite esquisse....

MLLE LE CHEMINANT: Gilberte! Qu'est-ce que ces dégoutants personnages?

GILBERTE: (*Meekly*) C'est Louis XV et Madame de Pompadour qui jouent au furet.

MLLE LE CHEMINANT: Et vous avez osé montrer une chose comme ça à une des petites! Vous me faites honte, Gilberte! Albertine, ne gloussez pas comme ça!

ALBERTINE: Pardon, Mademoiselle.

MLLE LE CHEMINANT: Silence! Albertine, Gilberte, vous allez rester jusqu'à l'heure de la sortie, et vous écrirez chacune cinquante fois: 'Je ne ferai pas circuler des dessins ridicules pendant la classe.' Et puis non, Gilberte l'écrira cent fois, puis-que c'est elle qui a pris l'initiative dans cette affaire. La classe est finie! Albertine, Gilberte, vous allez rester ici. Quand vous aurez fini votre pensum, vous me l'apporterez. C'est bien compris?

ALBERTINE: Oui, Mademoiselle.

GILBERTE: Oui, Mademoiselle.

(*A pause*)

ALBERTINE: Eh, bien, on s'en est bien tiré!

GILBERTE: *Tu* t'en es bien tirée.

ALBERTINE: Après tout, ce n'est pas moi qui avais fait le dessin.

GILBERTE: C'est toi cependant qui m'en avais donné l'idée! Tu le sais bien.

ALBERTINE: Oh! mais je l'adore!

GILBERTE: Tu adores qui?

ALBERTINE: Mademoiselle, bien sûr. Son prénom est Rose. Rose le Cheminant! On dirait un poème. Cela me fait penser à Vigny.

GILBERTE: (*Repressively*) Tu es trop jeune pour avoir des idées aussi folles.

ALBERTINE: Mais elle est magnifique, tu ne trouves pas? Ses cheveux, si bruns, si doux, comme le sable de la mer. . . . (*Gives a long sigh*)

JOAN: (*With strong English accent*) Que faites-vous donc ici, vous deux? Vous devriez être en bas, en train de vous changer.

ALBERTINE: Nous avons des lignes à faire, Joan. Nous sommes punies.

JOAN: Vous avez encore des ennuis?

ALBERTINE: (*Sentimentally*) Nous étions en train de dire que nous adorions Mlle le Cheminant.

GILBERTE: Moi je ne l'ai jamais dit.

ALBERTINE: Mais tu l'adores, tu le sais bien! Tu lui as apporté du muguet pas plus tard qu'hier. Toute l'école l'adore, d'ailleurs surtout quand elle se fâche. Tu ne trouves pas qu'elle est absolument merveilleuse, Joan? L'éclat de ses yeux bleus!

JOAN: Je trouve que c'est de la pure bêtise de parler comme ça. Comment pouvez-vous toutes les deux être aussi stupides, cela me dépasse tout simplement.

(*Bangs the door*)

ALBERTINE: Bon débarras.

GILBERTE: (*Mechanically*) Une petite fille comme toi ne doit pas être impolies envers ses ainées.

ALBERTINE: Mais on ne peut pas s'attendre à ce que Joan puisse comprendre, n'est-ce pas? Elle est anglaise, et les anglais ne comprennent jamais rien à tout cela.

GILBERTE: Vrai. C'est comme cela, ils ne peuvent pas. Eh bien, il vaut mieux que nous le fassions ce malheureux pensum. Passe moi l'encre, veux-tu?

(*The scratching of pens on paper. Pause*)

ALBERTINE: But perhaps I had better tell my story in English, because after all, it is the English over whom my poor little Marcel has had the most influence. They believe every word he says. His account of our *affaire* is particularly popular with the people of England. For instance, the first reference he makes to me shows me in an unpleasant light, as if I were very ill-bred and rude. Being an orphan, I lived with my Aunt Bontemps, wife of the Permanent Secretary of the Ministry of Posts, so you will see that we were people of a certain position. This was poor Marcel's story of what happened when the wife of the Under-Secretary for Finance came to tea.

(*Clatter of tea-cups*)

MME BONTEMPS: (*A harsh, strident voice*) You can't imagine, my dear, what trouble I have had with my 'Vatel'! As I said to my husband, 'The creature can't boil a potato.' Indeed, my little niece, who has hardly entered the kitchen in her life, could pre-pare a better dinner. Couldn't you, Albertine?

ALBERTINE: (*Modestly*) Well, I do know that potatoes have to be properly drained and not left *swimming* in water, as they are in that horrid thing the English call 'Irish stew'.

WIFE OF U.S. FOR FINANCE: (*Ill-concealing boredom*) He must be dreadful. I'm sure, Madame Bontemps, that I could find you

someone better if you wanted me to look around for you. Not
that I personally know a thing about cooking —

ALBERTINE: (*Brightly*) But surely, Madame, you ought to know
all about it, after all the dishes your father had to wash?

MME BONTEMPS: *Albertine!!!*

(*A long pause*)

ALBERTINE: But of course it wasn't at all like that. She *did* say she
knew nothing about cooking and then she went home. And I
said to my Aunt, 'What a woman! She ought to know something about it, shouldn't she, since everyone says her father was
a dishwasher at an hotel in Dijon?' That's all I said, but Auntie
— who simply can't help embroidering things — had to go
and tell Madame Swann I said it to the woman's face, and before I knew where I was the story was halfway round the world.

Still, what I want to tell you about is myself and Marcel. I
was staying in Balbec with my governess — most of my best
friends were there at the time, because it was the place where
you met everyone who was anyone — when I first caught sight
of him. I was pushing my bicycle along the front, and I was fed
up, I can tell you, because my mademoiselle said I'd had too
many late nights and she was going to see I had an early
one. . . .

(*Sound of the sea*)

GOVERNESS: It's no use, Albertine. I am responsible to your
Aunt, and I've promised her you'll have plenty of rest and quiet
while you're in my charge.

GISÈLE: (*A light, high voice*) Oh, Mademoiselle, you don't want to
be a spoilsport! A holiday's a holiday, after all!

GOVERNESS: I'm not responsible for *you*, Gisèle. . . .

ANDRÉE: (*A deeper, slower voice*) Mademoiselle, you were young
yourself once, or so we imagine.

GOVERNESS: . . . or for you, Andrée (and please don't be imper-
tinent) — but I am responsible for Albertine.

ALBERTINE: But we were going dancing at the Casino! It's a gala night.

GOVERNESS: There will be no dancing. You must have ridden at least fifteen miles on that machine of yours, and you're looking as white as a sheet.

ALBERTINE: I'm not a child! I want to live my own life!

GOVERNESS: You're a child still, my dear, and you are my responsibility.

ANDRÉE: Now I come to think of it, Albertine still looks like a baby, don't she, Gisèle?

GISÈLE: (*Entering into joke*) She will till she fines down. She's still got her puppy-fat.

ALBERTINE: Oh, be quiet, both of you! Let me tell you, there's a certain somebody who doesn't think I'm a child. (*Sharply*) Mademoiselle, will you *stop* tugging at my handlebars? I'll come, all in good time.

ANDRÉE: Who doesn't think so?

ALBERTINE: That little fellow, dark as a Turk, with the huge black eyes — the one in the straw hat, staring at us. . . . No, don't look now . . . he's just outside the dining-room windows of the hotel.

GISÈLE: Oh, I saw him. He wasn't staring at you in particular, though.

ALBERTINE: Yes, he was!

GISÈLE: No, he wasn't.

GOVERNESS: Will you please try to behave like young ladies? (*In a screech*) Andrée, what do you think you're doing? Come back from that bandstand! Oh . . . !

ALBERTINE: What's she done?

GISÈLE: She's jumped off it on to the sands, right over somebody's head. . . .

OLD LADY BY THE SANDS: How dare you, you rude girl! How dare you? You nearly fell on top of my husband!

ANDRÉE: (*Coolly*) I'm awfully sorry, Madame. I just didn't see him.

GISÈLE: (*Whispering*) Oh, the poor old man, he makes me feel sick, he looks more dead than alive!

OLD LADY: You should watch what you're doing! A young girl like you, behaving like a hooligan!

ANDRÉE: (*Drawling*) I said I'm awfully sorry. But there doesn't seem to be any harm done, does there?

OLD LADY: Such insolence, such utter lack of consideration, all these girls jumping about and screaming, and hitting people in the face with their horrible Diabolo. . . .

ANDRÉE: Well, one doesn't expect to find people lurking *right* under the bandstand. . . .

ALBERTINE: But of course Marcel had to have it that Andrée did it on purpose — you can never trust what he says. All the same, I was taken with him from the very beginning — (*Tenderly*) my Marcel, with his great eyes like some nocturnal creature's, an owl's or a bat's, only his were inky black eyes and owls' eyes are yellow. He fascinated me. I knew he wanted to meet me, but he couldn't pluck up the courage. I had to arrange it with Elstir, the painter, a great friend of mine and a terrible matchmaker, who asked us both to tea on the same afternoon, though Marcel says he arranged it himself. . . .

MARCEL: When, some days after Saint-Loup's departure, I had succeeded in persuading Elstir to give a small tea-party, at which I was to meet Albertine, I regretted my inability to reserve that freshness of appearance, that smartness of attire, which were to be observed in me at the moment of starting out from the Grand Hotel, and were due respectively to a longer rest than usual and to special pains over my toilet, for the captivation of some other, more interesting person; I regretted having to use them up on the simple pleasure of making Albertine's acquaintance.

ALBERTINE: (*Mournfully*) That was him, all over: blow hot,

blow cold. Of course, he came from a smart set and knew everybody, and was very rich; but after all, my aunt and uncle were high up in official circles and we weren't exactly nobodies. . . .

MARCEL: (*Background of other voices*) I've so often seen you with your friends on the beach and wondered about them. May I ask you who that pretty girl is with the green eyes? The one who seems a little older than the rest of you?

ALBERTINE: (*With her pretty manners*) Oh, that's Andrée. She's perfectly mad but very nice for all that. I simply adore her.

MARCEL: And there's a young man you speak to sometimes, the one always playing golf and saying he's 'in the soup'.

ALBERTINE: You mean Octave. He's very rich and smart, but perfectly common and quite a bore: not that he doesn't amuse us occasionally. We've known him for years.

MARCEL: And that red-haired girl you were talking to by the bathing pavilion yesterday? You mustn't think me inquisitive; I just fancied I might know her.

ALBERTINE: Oh, I'm sure you never would ! I know who you mean. We know her a little, but we don't have much to do with her. She's got a bad style.

MARCEL: A bad style?

ALBERTINE: I only mean, not our sort. Our little band likes to keep together, you know. We never encourage outsiders.

MARCEL: All the same, mademoiselle, I hope I shall have the pleasure of meeting you on the front again soon, and perhaps of knowing all your charming friends. . . .

(*The sound of wind and waves*)

ALBERTINE: (*Irritable*) Oh, it's you, monsieur! I didn't see you at first. What weather! Really, the 'perpetual summer' of Balbec is all stuff and nonsense. You don't go in for anything special here, do you?

MARCEL: Special?

ALBERTINE: Oh, play golf, or ride, or dance at the Casino. Aren't you bored stiff? I could never bear just to bask in the sun all day like a lizard, as you do. I just have to race around. I enjoy all sports. We didn't see you at the Sogne races, though we looked out for you.

MARCEL: I seldom go far afield.

ALBERTINE: We went there on the tram. What an old tin-pot it is! It took us two whole hours. I could have gone there and back three times on my bike. . . .

MARCEL: In speaking, Albertine kept her lips motionless, her nostrils closed, allowing only the corners of her lips to move. The result of this was a drawling, nasal sound into the composition of which there entered, perhaps, a provincial descent, a juvenile affection of British phlegm, the teaching of a foreign governess and a congestive hypertrophy of the mucus of the nose. But it was peculiar to herself and delighted me. And I thought then that there could be no one in the world so desirable. . . .

ALBERTINE: He'd have been surprised if he had known how fascinating I found him also. But I didn't want to give him too much encouragement just then. For one thing Octave, 'In the Soup', as we called him, was mad about me, too; and I had to think of the future. For another my aunt, when she came to Balbec to see me, thought I was wasting my time.

MME BONTEMPS: . . . You see, Titine, your uncle and I can't be responsible for you for ever. You'll have to be thinking about making a life for yourself. Young Octave's rich enough even if he is as stupid as a pig, and if you ask my opinion, he'd marry you to-morrow. As for your new acquaintance, he's 'in with the Faubourg'— with Madame de Villeparisis, who's somebody even if she does look like an old pew-opener, even with the Guermantes, or at any rate with that nephew of theirs. He may admire you, but he's not the kind to marry you, even though he's only a nobody by birth himself, and runs around with all sorts of Jews and people. . . .

(Sound of the sea)

MARCEL: Mlle Simonet, may I present to you my friend, Monsieur Bloch?

BLOCH: (*Carelessly*) How d'ye do, mademoiselle? (*Goes straight on*) Excuse me breaking in on you, Marcel, but I wanted to tell you that I'm going to Doncières to-morrow to visit our friend Saint-Loup. I don't know what he'll say if I fail to respond to his courtesy any longer. Are you coming with me?

MARCEL: I'm sorry, Albert; it's quite impossible for me to get away just now.

BLOCH: (*Huffily*) You're quite sure? (*Pause*) Oh, very well then, I shall go alone. If you can't tear yourself away from the wreathèd nymphs of old Triton I shall make my way friendless as our unfortunate acquaintance, that filial mishap, Orestes. Good-afternoon to you. Your servant, mademoiselle.

(Departing footsteps)

ALBERTINE: What an Ostrogoth! I admit he's not a bad-looking boy, but he makes me feel quite sick. Such a sneering air he's got! It's the same with that cousin of his and her precious friend. We simply look the other way when we see them coming.

MARCEL: (*Eagerly*) Why, do you know Mlle Bloch?

ALBERTINE: Only by sight. We don't want to know them. They've got such a bad style. Anyway, we shouldn't be allowed to play with Israelites. . . .

MARCEL: Now what *do* you mean by that, 'a bad style'? I must ask you. You used the phrase before.

ALBERTINE: (*Evasively*) It just means — well, not our kind at all. People like that are just shocking bad form. . . .

(Her voice dies away)

ALBERTINE: So you see, he was questioning me even then. But when one is fascinated by a man one doesn't mind answering questions; it suggests that he is interested. It is only when we are quite *sure* he is interested that questioning gets on our nerves. Of course, he was only a boy in those days, so thin, so frail in his smart flannel suit and his straw hat! And he could talk you around his little finger so that we were all a little in love with him; he was like an enchanter from the Arabian Nights, he had a way of looking at you as though your forehead were made of crystal and he could see all your thoughts going on behind it like the works in a clock. Of course, he was soon part of our little band, going with us everywhere, in the little tram, cycling on the cliffs, playing games like the King of the Castle and 'Ferret', though he was pretty silly at games, really.

GIRLS SINGING: Il court, il court le furet
                 Le furet du bois Mesdam'
                 Il court, il court le furet.
                 Le furet du bois joli.

ALBERTINE: (*Shrilly*) Marcel, wake up! It's no fun playing games with you if you won't keep your mind on what you're doing!

MARCEL: I'm so sorry. I thought. . . .

ALBERTINE: No, no, get back in the centre! You're still Seeker.

SINGING: Il a passé par ici,
                 Il repassera par là,
                 Il court, il court le furet
                 Le furet du bois Mesdam'. . . .

MARCEL: (*Through music*) You've got it, Gisèle!

GISÈLE: (*Laughing*) No, I haven't, so there!

SINGING: Il court, il court le furet,
                 Le furet du bois joli.

MARCEL: Rosemonde!

ALBERTINE: Right at last, thank Heavens! Come on; Rosemonde goes in the middle now.

SINGING: Il a passé par ici,
Il repassera par là. . . . (*Song continues*)

ALBERTINE: (*In a furious whisper*) For pity's *sake*, Marcel! I'm simply pushing the ring at you.

MARCEL: Oh, forgive me! I didn't know. . . .

ALBERTINE: Everybody stop! (*Song ceases*) This is a thoroughly babyish game. I've had enough of it. Let's sit down and talk like sensible people, for Heaven's sake. No, Marcel, you can go and sit next to Andrée. . . .

(*Pause*)

ALBERTINE: And yet, though I got cross with him so easily, I'd already passed him a little note telling him I loved him. Andrée saw me do it and afterwards she made me tell her what was in it. Andrée was a dreadful bully, in her own way.

ANDRÉE . . . How absurd you are! What will he think of you? You should have more pride.

ALBERTINE: I'm tired of his nonsense, pretending to be in love with one after the other of you just to make me jealous.

ANDRÉE: If he asked you, would you marry him?

ALBERTINE: Don't be so silly; we're only children still.

ANDRÉE: Who have you loved best in all your life, Titine?

ALBERTINE: Why?

ANDRÉE: I want to know.

ALBERTINE: Let me think. . . . (*Sentimentally*) Do you know, I don't believe I've ever adored anyone as I adored Mlle le Cheminant at school?

ANDRÉE: (*Scornfully*) That sentimental stick! She looked like a Guido Reni, all enamel with tears of castor oil.

ALBERTINE: You *are* clever! It's you and Marcel who ought to make a match of it, both of you being intellectuals.

ANDRÉE: I don't want him, don't think it. If I were a man. . . .

ALBERTINE: Well?

ANDRÉE: I'd marry you myself and take you away from moping little boys like that. What I say is, he's ruined our summer.

ALBERTINE: I'll tell you one thing. You've got quite an eye for him yourself!

ANDRÉE: (*Loftily*) Really, what nonsense!

ALBERTINE: Anyway, you were furious when he tried to get to know my aunt through Elstir.

ANDRÉE: Well, I dislike sneaks.

ALBERTINE: What's sneaking about that?

ANDRÉE: If you don't know, I certainly shan't tell you.

ALBERTINE: You're riddled with jealousy, that's what it is.

ANDRÉE: And you're making yourself cheap, running after such a poor little fellow for his money.

ALBERTINE: Don't you say that to me!

ANDRÉE: (*Drawling*) I shall say to you exactly what I like.

(*Pause*)

ALBERTINE: Oh, darling, don't let's quarrel! Nobody's worth it.

ANDRÉE: (*Slowly*) No, they're not. Are they?

ALBERTINE: Say you're sorry.

ANDRÉE: No. You say it.

ALBERTINE: Well, then I will if you will! Darling, it's so silly to let silly people come between *us*. . . .

(*Her voice fades: pause*)

ALBERTINE: We were only schoolgirls then. But, you know, people never understand Andrée. You have to understand Iago first. Of course she was a darling, and so, I suppose, was he in his own way; but they were both given to what they call 'motiveless malice', and unless one has met it one never believes in it, though heaven only knows, it's a common enough affliction. But Marcel understood her in the end; he wrote about her in a piece he never published — that was long after we

L

came to know each other really well, which for years, of course, we never did.

MARCEL: Once Andrée had made up her mind to marry Octave, (which she did only in order to cause sorrow to Albertine, though not in certainty that it would really cause sorrow but simply taking a chance that it might; as if we should shoot an arrow at an enemy invisible behind a thicket hoping, if not expecting, to cause him some injury), she became imbued with that strange and noble loyalty which is shown only by the wife who in secret despises her husband and holds her breath when he kisses her, so that she may not be irritated by the odour of his domestic flesh. If she had failed to hurt, she intended to enjoy all the satisfactions that would have come her way had she succeeded. She was one of those brilliant and high-headed women, by nature mendacious and oblique, who never face failure because they cannot; and so turn their public lives into a spectacle of loyalty and success, in the meantime deceiving their own hearts as they have deceived the hearts of others into accepting the manufactured being as the being that was within them from the hour of their birth. It was by no accident that 'In the Soup', that coarse and empty young man the cut of whose trousers I had so much despised and admired as they clipped into successive triangles the sky of Balbec and the blue and smiling sea, became a great stage designer, for to his animal dexterity Andrée added her impeccable taste; it only remained for him to run a line, as a child upon tracing paper, about the precise creation of her intricate and original mind.

ALBERTINE: But that is anticipating history; I mention it now only to explain why Andrée told so many lies about me later and why, if she were my dearest friend, she was also my most false. To return to Marcel: there were two things he never understood at all that first summer at Balbec — to begin with, why, when I was staying the night at the Grand Hotel because I had a cold,

I allowed him to come and see me in my bedroom and then refused to let him kiss me. Next, why I left so soon afterwards, and without a word, for Paris.

You must first understand that, at this time, all we girls were very free and easy. We weren't in the least snobs: we made friends with everyone — the waiters, the lift-boys, the bathing-hut attendant, even with the Manager of the Casino, though he always pretended to be angry with us when we slid on his floor and broke his chairs. I hadn't been in the Grand Hotel half an hour before I made friends with the head-waiter, Aimé.

(Tinkle of a bell)

AIMÉ: (*An unctuous, lubricious voice*) Mademoiselle needs something?

ALBERTINE: (*Her voice slightly distorted by her cold*) The young gentleman staying here with his grandmother; isn't he in?

AIMÉ: Oh, the one with the fine black eyes! He went out half an hour ago, I expect to the bookshops. He's always prowling round them and coming back with such great burdens, you'd think they'd break those thin arms of his. He's sure to be back soon.

ALBERTINE: Thank you. (*Stifling a small sneeze*) If you should happen to see him when he comes in. . . .

AIMÉ: I shall tell him Mademoiselle Simonet is here.

ALBERTINE: (*She has an instant tone of familiarity with servants*) Now, how did *you* know my name?

AIMÉ: A head-waiter knows everything, mademoiselle. Many a time I've seen you about with the other young ladies; I've thought to myself, 'They're lively ones!'

ALBERTINE: (*Laughing*) I see one can't be private here!

AIMÉ: Mademoiselle can't imagine how much I know about her. I know, for example, that she's a friend of Mlle Léa, the actress. . . .

ALBERTINE: What, you remember me from last year?

AIMÉ: Who could forget mademoiselle? I'm sure the young ladies who are her friends never could. And there's a certain very smart young gentleman who admires her too, let me tell you; Monsieur Octave.

ALBERTINE: Oh, him!

AIMÉ: Mademoiselle doesn't fancy Monsieur Octave? Let me tell her that if I were a charming young lady.... (*Albertine laughs*) Well, let us suppose I am, and I have a choice between Monsieur Octave with his horses and his grand swagger, and Monsieur Blackeyes, who is all aches and pains and knocks on the wall at night for his grannie when he can't get his breath....

ALBERTINE: (*Guardedly, feeling he has gone too far*) I don't think there's any question of choosing. I'm far too young to think of such things yet.

AIMÉ: But Monsieur Octave is not. I heard him with some of his friends in the restaurant last night, and if mademoiselle will forgive me, her name came into the conversation. 'There's the lady I'd marry at the drop of a hat,' Monsieur Octave said out loud, so that everyone heard him, 'only she's so take-it-or-leave-it one never knows where to have her.' (*Pause*) It wasn't respectful, perhaps, Mademoiselle, but it was certainly emphatic.

ALBERTINE: Anything else? — Not that it matters in the slightest.

AIMÉ: And then he said he'd have to be back in Paris by the first of September, because his father knew a little filly — his word, not mine, mademoiselle — that he wanted Monsieur Octave to cast an eye on, and who knew? (he said)—she might be his fate.

ALBERTINE: (*Agitated*) September the first?

AIMÉ: That's what he said. But of course mademoiselle would not be in the least interested, since all her blue eyes are for the young gentleman with the grandmother. Hullo, what do *you* want?

PAGE: Excuse me, Monsieur Aimé. There's somebody on the telephone for mademoiselle, a Madame Bontemps. She's calling from Paris.

ALBERTINE: Oh! All, right, I'm coming. (*Sneezes violently*) Oh, dear!

AIMÉ: Mademoiselle should use Rhino-Gomenol. There's nothing like it for colds. . . .

MME BONTEMPS: . . . Hullo! Hullo! Is that you, Titine?

ALBERTINE: Yes, Auntie.

MME BONTEMPS: They told me you were staying here for the night. Have you got a cold?

ALBERTINE: Yes, an awful one.

MME BONTEMPS: Take care of yourself. We don't want you being ill on our hands back in Paris. Is that young Marcel still at the Grand?

ALBERTINE: Yes, Auntie.

MME BONTEMPS: Well, you watch out there, my child, and don't waste any more of your time. I've heard on perfectly good authority that he doesn't really like girls at all, he just pretends to, that he's one of those young men one doesn't talk about. . . .

ALBERTINE: Speak up. I can't hear you.

MME BONTEMPS: (*After certain amount of crackling*) . . . perfectly good authority, so do stop mistaking the shadow for the substance, and stop cold-shouldering young Octave, who is very well-connected and quite clever, it seems, after all, even though he does look a fool.

ALBERTINE: But Auntie, it can't be true. . . .

MME BONTEMPS: Your Marcel has *a very bad style,* I assure you, and if you don't listen to what I say you'll only have yourself to blame. . . .

ALBERTINE: (*Sadly*) So you see what lies people can tell, even about *him*; that is what life is like. Anyway, you see now why I wouldn't let him kiss me and why I rushed back to Paris, because my aunt and uncle were longing to get me off their hands, and I couldn't let Octave slip right away. However the first thing I learned was that my aunt was perfectly mistaken about poor Marcel, and the second thing was that I could still marry Octave any time I chose to lift my little finger. And indeed, for a year or more I was half-engaged to him. Everyone thought we would marry. Then, one Saturday, I went to a café-concert with Octave and things went quite wrong.

(Music: sound of a crowd. A sugary tenor singing Le Biniou)

TENOR: 'De ma bourse un peu pauvrette,
                Où l'ennui m'a fait fouiller,
                Je me suis permis l'emplette
                D'un biniou de cornouiller. . . .'
(As song proceeds, Albertine first hums with the singer, then talks)

ALBERTINE: Oh, I adore that song! I could listen to it all day.
OCTAVE: Ah-ha.
ALBERTINE: He's got quite a distinguished voice, hasn't he?
OCTAVE: It's all right.
ALBERTINE: *(Singing quietly with singer)*
                'Les douleurs sont des folles,
                Et qui les écoute est encor plus fou!
                A nous deux toi qui consoles,
                Biniou, mon biniou, mon cher biniou!'
(Applause, in which she joins) Bravo! Bravo!
OCTAVE: I don't see anything in that chap. He looks like a street musician.
ALBERTINE: But he's got such a way with him! Those sad brown eyes. . . .
OCTAVE: Look here, Titine, I wish you'd take your own eyes off him. You're out with me.
ALBERTINE: I should be in no danger of forgetting it, thank you.
OCTAVE: You needn't snap a fellow's head off!
ALBERTINE: Nor need you be so stupidly jealous because I happen to praise an artiste.

OCTAVE: *Artiste*, my foot.

ALBERTINE: He reminds me of someone — oh, I know! Don't you think he's a tiny bit like Marcel?

OCTAVE: I shouldn't be surprised. Your Marcel did look rather like a street musician.

ALBERTINE: Don't be detestable! And don't call him *my* Marcel!

OCTAVE: (*As music begins again*, Do you want another ice? Because if not, I'd like to get out of this fug.

ALBERTINE: (*Suddenly*) Hullo! Hullo! Andrée! Over here . . . ! (*To Octave*) It's Andrée, all by herself. — How are you, darling? What are you doing here?

ANDRÉE: Hullo, Titine. Hullo, Octave; you don't want me playing gooseberry, I'm sure. Besides, I'm meeting Rosemonde.

ALBERTINE: Oh, do sit down with us! We can always keep a look-out for her.

ANDRÉE: Two's company.

OCTAVE: Not at all. Delighted to see you.

ALBERTINE: Besides, it's time somebody came between us. Octave is being so horrid and disagreeable.

ANDRÉE: (*Her tone is sarcastic throughout this scene*) Were you? And to my poor, defenceless Titine! What creatures you men are!

OCTAVE: 'Pon my word, I do assure you. . . .

ALBERTINE: He's saying Marcel looks like a street singer.

OCTAVE: Well, so he does.

ALBERTINE: You be quiet.

ANDRÉE: Birds in their little nest, my dears! This is truly shocking, Octave. Mind you, I don't say Titine doesn't need a strong hand and I'm sure you're just the man for it. May I take one of these pink cakes? I'm hungry.

OCTAVE: I say, I'll be in the soup with Albertine if you go on like that.

ANDRÉE: Oh, surely not. The poor girl so needs a master.

ALBERTINE: I do, do I? You'll see.

OCTAVE: (*Slowly*) Well, perhaps you do, in a way. I don't know where I am with her, Andrée. First she will and then she won't.

ANDRÉE: (*Sarcasm deepening*) Oh dear, how sad that is! If I were you I should be very, very firm with her. 'Make up your mind,' I should say, 'or else. . . .'

ALBERTINE: (*Really angry*) I won't have you two discussing me! Or if you must, you can do it all by yourselves.

(*She scrapes her chair back*)

OCTAVE: Here, here, look — I say, my dear . . . where are you going?

(*Pause*)

ALBERTINE: Unless you *both* apologise to me at once, I shall go and pay a certain call that I have in mind.

OCTAVE: A call on whom?

ALBERTINE: On someone who doesn't bully and badger me. Someone who is really tender, and only says beautiful things.

ANDRÉE: And whom, if we may ask, might this paragon be?

ALBERTINE: My little Marcel.

ANDRÉE: (*After pause: laughing*) You wouldn't dare!

OCTAVE: I'll say she wouldn't. And besides, how do you know he'd want to see you again? You can't just call on a man like that. It's ages and ages since. . . .

ANDRÉE: (*Quietly*) You wouldn't dare.

ALBERTINE: *Do* you dare me? (*Pause*)

ANDRÉE: Yes.

ALBERTINE: Octave?

OCTAVE: (*Gravely: weighing his words*) I'll tell you what; in my opinion this fellow isn't a man of the world: he's just an upstart. If you were to do anything so foolish as to call upon him he might treat you to some kind of impudence, which I should, of course, bitterly resent and which I should feel obliged to punish. So if you'll just sit down again, Titine, and think about things quietly. . . .

ANDRÉE: I dare you.

ALBERTINE: (*Loudly*) Very well, then!

(*Scrapes her chair again. Pause. Waltz swells up*)

OCTAVE: (*Aghast*) She can't go like that! She simply wouldn't do it!

ANDRÉE: No, of course she wouldn't. She's just trying to tease you. If I were you I should let her go; she'll come running back again, because she can't resist you really. (*Sombrely*) I don't believe anyone could.

OCATAVE: (*Delighted*) I say, do you really mean that? No. You're pulling my leg. . . .

ANDRÉE: Not at all. Would you mind ordering me a grenadine? I'm so thirsty. . . . (*Fade*)

ALBERTINE: If people dare me to do things, I do them. And I knew at once that Marcel was interested in me, even though he was trying to begin an *affaire* with that horrid, thin, blue-faced Alexis de Stermaria, who looked like a Puvis de Chavannes and didn't like men at all, as everybody knew except him. Soon he wanted to see me more and more, and one day he sent me a box for *Phèdre*, telling me I was to go straight to him after the play. But during one of the intervals I ran into Andrée and Octave, who had become quite thick, and we three made up our differences and neither of them would let me go until I had met an old friend again. . . .

ANDRÉE: We're going to meet Léa in Montmartre, at a café. You must come with us! You know how she took to you at Balbec!

ALBERTINE: But I have an appointment. . . .

OCTAVE: Oh come, half an hour will make no difference. I'll see to it myself that you're not late. . . .

(*Music: Noise of glasses, voices, etc.*)

LÉA: (*A rich, exaggerated, sardonic voice*) My little one, you really have grown most enchanting, and so much slimmer! Gilberte Swann — you were at school with her, weren't you? — told me I simply wouldn't know you if I saw you nowadays.

ALBERTINE: (*Rather shy*) That's very nice of you, Madame.

LÉA: Madame? So stiff? You weren't very timid a year or so ago. Andrée, I really think we shall have to make her relax a little! Come nearer, darling, and don't look as though you were going to leap up and fly away!

ALBERTINE: (*After a pause*) I thought you were wonderful in *Les Fourberies de Nérine*, Léa.

OCTAVE: But she hadn't a décor worthy of her. Now if I'd had the designing of that third act. . . .

ALBERTINE: You? *Designing?*

LÉA: Didn't you know? Our Octave has quite a gift! He sketched a costume for me on a menu card — I kept it for ages — Andrée, love, look in my bag and see if it's there, because if I lose hold of this little Albertine she'll vanish in a puff of smoke. . . . Not there? Never mind. Yes. Octave is going to surprise us all.

ANDRÉE: I should never have been in the least surprised.

LÉA: Little Know-all! Albertine, sweet, do you ever see Germaine Vinteuil and her friend these days?

ALBERTINE: Oh, no. But then, I hardly knew them at all really. Only to pass a word with now and then.

LÉA: And they were content with that? . . .

(*Pause: Music*)

ALBERTINE: (*Fading in*) Do tell me the time, somebody . . . oh, it's nearly midnight! I must make a telephone call. Where is the instrument? Where do I go?

ANDRÉE: I'll take you. It's this way. . . .

(*Steps along a passage: background music, woman singing.*
Far off, bicycle, a motor horn)

ANDRÉE: Here you are, it's just inside the door. I suppose it's your little Marcel. What are you going to tell him?

ALBERTINE: Oh, I don't know! Certainly not that I've seen Léa again. You don't know the extraordinary things he suspects. He even questioned me about that stuck-up Gilberte Swann, and I lost my head and said I didn't know her.... (*Lifts receiver*) Hullo ... hullo ... Passy 41.... I said I didn't know her because anyway I don't care for Hebrews, because if you admit anything to him, however innocent, he goes on and on.... Hullo.... Is that you, Marcel? I'm not disturbing you, ringing at this hour?

MARCEL: Not at all. It doesn't matter in the least. (*With false indifference*) Are you coming round?

ALBERTINE: Why ... no, unless you absolutely must see me.

MARCEL: Are you near your home?

ALBERTINE: Yes, dear, and absolutely miles away from you.

MARCEL: You got my note?

ALBERTINE: Yes, but I'm afraid I didn't read it properly. I've just found it again, and I was afraid you might be waiting up for me. (*Pause*)

ANDRÉE: (*Whispering*) What does he say? — It's all right, put your hand over the mouthpiece.

ALBERTINE: Oh, do be quiet! (*To Marcel*) Do you want me to come?

MARCEL: Well, I don't *really* want you to. I'm dropping with sleep and it will be a frightful nuisance at this time of night. By the way, I am bound to say there was no possibility of your misunderstanding my letter. You answered that it was 'all right'. What did you mean by that?

ALBERTINE: I couldn't quite remember what we'd arranged, that's all. And now you're cross with me, and I wish I'd never *gone* to *Phèdre*! If I'd known there would be all this fuss. . . .

MARCEL: Where are you now?

ALBERTINE: At a friend's house.

MARCEL: Oh. I thought I heard music.

ALBERTINE: They're playing a gramophone in the other room.

ANDRÉE: (*Whispering*) Good for you. That was quick.

ALBERTINE: Oh be *quiet*, I tell you. . . . (*To Marcel*) Well, it's a nuisance it's so late now, but I shall call to-morrow or the day after and make it up.

MARCEL: Oh, please, Albertine, having made me waste a whole evening, you might just as well. . . .

ALBERTINE: . . . . But I went to him, late as it was, and that beauty of a Françoise, that old image of a servant of his, let me in grumbling because she'd had to get up and dress, and with her opinion of me written all over her face. And it was really that evening that he fell in love with me, which I think he makes clear in another piece that he never published, although I wanted him to — I mean, the piece he *did* publish about it wasn't even right, because he said it was on that evening that he asked whether I knew Gilberte, when, in fact, it was quite a week earlier. It's only a little thing, but it does show how wrong he could be about others more important. . . .

MARCEL: . . . As she tiptoed into my room, smiling in the shadow of the little flat hat that Françoise had thought so absurd, desire for her left me and I was conscious only of irritation that I had made her come to me when, in fact, I wanted, so much more than to see her, to write a letter I had delayed for over a month, to re-read a half forgotten page from *Les Causeries du Lundi*, to look in a book of reproductions of the portraits in last year's salon to see if I could trace the likeness of the soft and violet-tinted cheeks of a young working-girl I had that day noticed on the corner of a street, waiting for the omnibus to bear her home to her supper. Yet, perhaps, because the hour itself was charming, and also, perhaps, because the disapprobation of Françoise had added a shadow of secrecy to its charm, I found myself watching Albertine with a kind of new wonder as if she, in slipping off her hat and cloak, had slipped like a single distinct blossom from the spray of roses, branching across the sea, which had been the little band of girls, whom I had loved not as single blossoms but as an indistinguishable and cabbalistic unity of gathered flowers.

ALBERTINE: Yet even after that we didn't see each other again until we met at Balbec in the following summer. I called on him at his hotel but he wouldn't see me; and at the time I didn't care, because my friends and I were having a marvellous time and in any case Octave had lost interest in Andrée and it was all *me* again and nobody else. When Marcel did ask me to call I was in a bad temper. I'd heard from other people that his horrible Françoise was saying I was 'fast'; and I honestly felt he was playing with me simply to please himself, not having any really serious intentions towards me. . . . (*Her voice fades*)

ANDRÉE: . . . What a fool you are, Titine! If I were in your place I should write a stiff little note telling him you never proposed to set eyes upon him again.

ALBERTINE: If he asks me to set eyes on him, that's exactly what I shall do. . . . (*Her voice fades*)

MARCEL: Françoise! Why have you come back here alone? Didn't I tell you you were to fetch Mademoiselle Albertine at once?

FRANÇOISE: I've been as quick as I could, but she wouldn't come because she didn't think she was looking smart enough. If she was five minutes painting and powdering herself she was an hour by the clock. You'll be having a regular scentshop in here. She's coming all right. . . .

(*Knocking below*)

There she is. That's her knock.

MARCEL: You may show her in and then leave us.

FRANÇOISE: (*Mumbling*) She'll be the ruin of Monsieur, that one. I know her. I know what kind she is.

MARCEL: (*With elaborate patience*) Françoise, you are a good woman, a loyal woman, but your opinions upon any person or human relationship are of no interest to anyone but yourself. Please let Mademoiselle in.

(*Pause: Opening of a door. Mutter of voices*)

ALBERTINE: (*Gaily*) My dear Marcel! How I've longed to see you again! When Françoise came for me, I though to myself. . . .

MARCEL: She informed me (in contradiction to what she had said the other day) that she would be staying for the whole season, and asked me whether we could not arrange, as in the former year, to meet daily. I told her that at the moment I was too melancholy and that I would send for her from time to time at the last moment as I did in Paris. She told me. . . .

ALBERTINE: . . . If ever you're feeling worried, or feel that you do want me, do not hesitate to send for me. I shall come immediately and, if you are not afraid of it creating a scandal in the hotel, I shall stay as long as you like. . . .

ANDRÉE: . . . Titine, you promised you wouldn't go back to him! How weak-minded you are! Why did you do it?

ALBERTINE: Oh, because of something my aunt wrote to me. She was taking tea with Madame Swann last week, and Madame Swann said. . . .

ODETTE: . . . My dear, I hear your little niece is making a tremendous impression in most unlooked-for quarters! The little Marcel, who was once so in love with my Gilberte!

MME BONTEMPS: How people do talk! I assure you there's nothing in it.

ODETTE: But his mamma thinks there is.

MME BONTEMPS: His mamma? What's that?

ODETTE: You've heard of old Madame Sazerat, who knows the family? Well, *I* hardly know her, but Madame Cottard does, slightly, and she said Madame Sazerat told her that Mamma was worried to death about his passion for Albertine!

MME BONTEMPS: Odette! She can know nothing about it whatsoever!

ODETTE: Mammas know everything, my dear, and any mamma so intent as that one upon keeping her baby in cottonwool would tease out any little romance in next to no time. *She's* wondering if he means to marry her.

MME BONTEMPS: Do you really think so?

ODETTE: My dear, why not? He's a nobody, really — though he's quite enchanting and was quite an admirer of mine at one time. Such a funny little boy, always standing like a page in the Allée des Acacias, waiting to see me go by, and then bothering me afterwards by wanting to know *all* about my clothes! It used to make Charles laugh so much, though he adored Marcel as much as I did.

MME BONTEMPS: Such a *parti*. . . .

ODETTE: Very rich, my dear . . .

MME BONTEMPS: You're sure his mamma is worried?

ODETTE: . . . and quite irresistible. *Mon petit Saxe psychologue*, I used to call him. (*Change of tone*) You tell your Albertine to let *nothing* stand in her way, absolutely nothing. . . .

ALBERTINE: So you will understand that my aunt persuaded me to be agreeable to Marcel again; and of course she was prepared when the crisis came — I mean, when he asked me to go and live with him in his house in Paris. I think he would never have done so at all if it hadn't been for that nasty-minded Cottard, making suggestions about Andrée and me when we were dancing together. It was so silly; we were just girls, playing about a little perhaps, but never thinking for a moment of that sort of thing. But Marcel would be jealous of anything, however absurd. How he thought I should explain matters to my aunt I can't imagine, but in fact it happened like this. . . .

MME BONTEMPS: Well, if the mother consents, starchy as *she* is. . . . I'm sure I don't know what I ought to do.

ALBERTINE: I shouldn't be unchaperoned. There's always Françoise.

MME BONTEMPS: A medieval peasant, half-deaf, half-blind! Oh, I don't know what to say! To think of a young girl in your position, decently brought up, living alone with a man in Paris, in this day and age. . . . Oh, you stupid girl, and you could have married Octave!

ALBERTINE: I don't *like* Octave.

MME BONTEMPS: (*Reflectively*) There is this to be said about it. If you please your Marcel as he wants you to, he will have to marry you in the end — no man of honour could do otherwise, which I'm sure his mother would see. And he is a *parti*. But keep his respect, mind! Always keep his respect!

ALBERTINE: Of course, Auntie. We should simply be friends. . . .

(*Pause*)

Which we were. As Marcel himself writes, we were never lovers in the fullest sense. I think he had certain difficulties. Certainly he made life difficult for *me* as time went on; but at the first all was happiness.

(*Sound of running taps: splashing of water*)

ALBERTINE: (*Humming Le Biniou, breaking into words*)
        Les douleurs sont des folles,
        Et qui les écoute est encor plus fou!

MARCEL: (*Calling out*) My darling!

ALBERTINE: What is it?

MARCEL: Come to me as soon as you've had your bath. I've finished dressing.

ALBERTINE: I won't be long. . . . (*Continues to hum*)

(*Opening of a door*)

There! Wasn't your little Albertine swift to be with you? Good-morning, my love! Oh, what a wonder it looks this morning, with its cheeks all smooth and shaved and sweet, and a glossy black crest like a little parakeet!

MARCEL: Did my dear sleep well?

ALBERTINE: Oh, wonderfully! I dreamed that I was floating out for ever on a blue sea, looking up at the little clouds and there wasn't a shore in sight; yet I wasn't frightened at all.

MARCEL: Why should my mouse be frightened, with the sea of our love all around her? What's she going to do with herself to-day?

ALBERTINE: I believe Andrée wants to take me to the Buttes Chaumont. I should rather like to go there; I've never been before.

MARCEL: Wrap yourself up carefully, then; I don't want you to catch cold. I trust Andrée to take great care of you and not to let you out of her sight.

ALBERTINE: Oh, listen! Street cries! I do so love them! May I open the window just a little bit?

(*Voice of street crier 1: faint, through glass*)

CRIER ONE: À la romaine, à la romaine!
               On ne vend pas, on la promène.

MARCEL: Now, my darling, you know I can't bear an open window in my house. It's so bad for my breathing if I get the least chill.

ALBERTINE: Oh, but do listen! (*Sings with crier 2*)

CRIER TWO: Bon fromage à la cré,
               À la cré, bon fromage. . . .

ALBERTINE: Do tell Françoise to run and buy us some little cream cheeses! Listen to them, they're crying out all the things I want to eat!

M

CRIER THREE: À la crevette, à la bonne crevette,
> J'ai de la raie toute en vie, toute en vie. . . .

FRANÇOISE: Mademoiselle Andrée is here, Monsieur.

MARCEL: Ask her to wait for a few moments, Françoise.

FRANÇOISE: And the journalist has come with the papers.

ALBERTINE: (*In whispered giggle*) She means the newsboy! Oh,
no, Françoise, don't shut the door, not for a minute. . . . I can
hear better. . . .

CRIER FOUR: (*More distinct*)
> Il arrive le maquereau,
> Maquereau frais, maquereau nouveau,
> Voilà le maquereau, mesdames,
> Il est beau le maquereau. . . . (*Fade*)

ANDRÉE: (*Fading in*) What a time you've been! I thought you'd
never come.

ALBERTINE: Françoise was late with my breakfast, and then I
lingered in the bath, and then Marcel kept me.

ANDRÉE: Hurry up now, then, or we'll be late.

(*Noises of open street. The voices of the criers, at first close
at hand, tail into distance*)

> Il arrive le maquereau,
> Maquereau frais, maquereau nouveau. . . .

ANDRÉE: Léa's coming too, and bringing Morel. We're meeting
them there. *He* doesn't guess, does he?

ALBERTINE: Of course not. Not that there's anything *to* guess, I'm
only seeing my friends, and heaven knows I see them seldom
enough! But I adore Morel, he's such a queer sort of boy! I
bet he likes to get off his chain, too; they say Monsieur de
Charlus positively tries to lock him up. How anyone could
stand for that sort of thing!

ANDRÉE: What about your Marcel? Aren't I the only person he
lets you out with?

ALBERTINE: And that beauty, Françoise! He'd have fits if he knew who I was going to meet to-day! Yet it isn't important, though he'd never understand that; I mean, you and I and Léa and Morel, we only have a kind of *amitié amoureuse*, and what's there in that, after all?

ANDRÉE: You're going to have a new chaperon soon.

ALBERTINE: Who?

ANDRÉE: None but Gérard, my dear!

ALBERTINE: Gérard?

ANDRÉE: You remember! The chauffeur your Marcel used to hire at Balbec! You know he went to the Verdurins': well, Madame Verdurin is lending him to Marcel as your driver and Cerberus!

ALBERTINE: (*Choking with laughter*) Not Gérard, oh, not Gérard! A fine Cerberus he'll be! He and I became tremendous friends the first time, we had all sorts of silly secrets. Where did you hear all this?

ANDRÉE: From Morel, of course. He and Gérard have lots of things in common. But mind you, be surprised when Marcel tells you, otherwise. . . .

MARCEL: . . . I have a great surprise for my little Albertine, who deserves so much pleasure and amusement. Madame Verdurin is going to lend me her chauffeur who, you may remember. . . .

ALBERTINE: And so at first I really did have a certain degree of liberty which, after all, a young girl needs, for however good Marcel was to me, and however much I loved him, it was really quite stifling for me in his house. And however nice it is to have Fortuny gowns and gold kid slippers just the same as the ones made for the Duchess of Manchester, it can be very dull having only one person to show them to. Hour after hour I used to sit at the pianola, playing to him while he sat and read his eyes out. . . .

Piano: the 'Little Phrase')

MARCEL: (*Dreamily*) That was the National Anthem of the love of Swann and Odette, my darling, and now it is ours. (*Pause*) By the way, talking of Swann, did I understand you to say you had never known Gilberte? After all, you must have seen her at school. . . .

ALBERTINE: And so he would go on, questioning, questioning; and if I did lie to him, it was not because I really had anything to be guilty about. But you see, I did want to marry him, and I was so afraid that if I upset him in any way he would make up his mind against me then and there. To take a foolish example, there was the business of the two rings. My aunt gave me both, in fact, because she never liked them. Marcel found one and said, where did I get it? and I told him the truth; but you could see he didn't believe it. And then when he asked me about the second I thought, Well, he's never going to believe it a second time, so I said I'd bought the ring myself . . . quite innocent, all of it, you see, but one simply had to lie to him. . . .

MME BONTEMPS: . . . Listen, Titine, this is becoming impossible. Everyone's talking about you, and your uncle tells me it's even all over the Ministry of Posts! Either you bring Marcel to the point or you must leave him. If this ridiculous situation goes on, you'll be so shopsoiled that nobody will want you at all.

ALBERTINE: But Auntie, one simply *can't* hurry Marcel. He's promised me a yacht and a motor-car of my own, which I'm sure he wouldn't do if he weren't serious.

MME BONTEMPS: I doubt very much whether he's in the least serious. But you can still marry Octave, if you want to, and if I were you I'd keep that iron in the fire. He's always raving about you to Andrée, which makes her furious, by the way.

ALBERTINE: I consider that ominous. I adore Andrée, of course, but I never know what she's up to behind my back. Marcel came home unexpectedly the other day when she was with me, and she stopped him on the stairs and wouldn't let him give me some syringa he'd brought for me. I'm sure she was making up some fantastic mystery for her own ends. If you ask me, I believe she wants him for herself. . . .

MARCEL: . . . And indeed, when I began many years later to realise the nature of that double deity, the son of Hermes and Aphrodite and the nymph Salmacis, whom he loved, which was the nature of that crepuscular and smiling Andrée whom I had made my counsellor, I realised also that in love alone man may be modest, unable to see in himself an object of desire, unable to understand that the reason for a lie or a malicious act by a friend whom he trusts may rest in the captive desire of that friend for himself. So I wondered therefore whether, by assuming a passion for Andrée at Balbec simply in order to make Albertine look upon me with eyes freshened by jealousy, I had not inspired in Andrée one of those affections not in themselves profound, but having a tenacity a more profound love may be too arrogant to express; and whether the key to every so-called 'revelation' she had made to me after Albertine's disappearance, may not have been the expression of love for myself and, as its complement, the desire to deprive and to destroy that Albertine whom I had loved in her stead. . . .

ALBERTINE: . . . He would not publish this because, he said, he had only touched the surface of his own meaning; and besides, it was written like a pig. (*Hastily*) He didn't put it like that, of course; that was my slang. I wish he had published it, though, because it would have been better for me. Some of the English complain that too much was written about me; I say, not half enough! But as there has been this criticism, I shall pass over the way in which our happiness faded, and my hopes died as he tormented me more and more, till one night I had to rush upstairs and fling open a window to get some air into that stifling house and into my own heart. . . .

(*Pause: violent banging up of window*)

ALBERTINE: (*Her voice shaking*) Oh God, oh God! It's unbear-
able! I won't bear it! I won't, I won't. . . . To be bothered and
badgered from pillar to post, treated like a criminal, taken up
and dropped again as he pleases, promised yachts that are never
ordered, smeared with affection as a criminal is smeared with
honey so that the ants can come and eat him to death. . . . Why
can't people be happy and quiet? Why can't it be as it used to
be? . . . But not long after that I had a note from my aunt, which
gave me an idea.

MME BONTEMPS: '. . . If you are sensible you will leave him at
once and join us for the summer in Touraine. If he does mean
to marry you he'll come running after you like a little dog; if he
doesn't you'll be able to think seriously again about Octave,
who will be staying near us at Châtellerault. . . .'

(*Ring of a bell. Pause. A door opens*)

MARCEL: (*Yawning*) Good-morning, Françoise!

FRANÇOISE: Oh, Monsieur, I don't know what to say to Monsieur. . . .

MARCEL: Why, what's the matter? Give me my slippers, Françoise.

FRANÇOISE: It's been most awkward, Monsieur being so late in
ringing this morning. I didn't know what I ought to do. This
morning at eight o'clock Mademoiselle Albertine asked me for
her trunks. . . .

MARCEL: (*Aghast*) Her trunks?

FRANÇOISE: Yes, Monsieur, and I dared not refuse her, I was
afraid of Monsieur's scolding me if I came and waked him. . . .

MARCEL: Didn't you try to stop her?

FRANÇOISE: Oh, it was no use my putting her through her
catechism, telling her to wait an hour because I expected all the
time that Monsieur would ring. She wouldn't have it, she left
this letter with me for Monsieur, and at nine o'clock, off she
went.

MARCEL: Albertine. . . . Gone? (*Pause. With an effort*) Very good, Françoise, you did right not to wake me. Leave me for a little now, I'll ring for you presently. . . .

ALBERTINE: . . . And of course he did come running after me, as my aunt Bontemps said he would. But she was so eager that I shouldn't make myself cheap any longer — I could afford not to, she said, with Marcel sending his friend Saint-Loup down actually to *offer her money* if she'd make me return — did you ever hear of such a thing? Really, he could act like a madman sometimes. . . . Where was I . . . ? She was so eager for me not to make myself cheap, and besides, Octave had asked me to marry him again and I was thinking about that, and anyway all my friends were in Touraine and I was having such a splendid time.
(*Sings*) 'Les douleurs sont des folles
        Et qui les écoute est encor plus fous!'
But I did love him really, and I couldn't keep it up. At last I wrote to him promising to return — but on the same day I met with a riding accident.

(*Pause*)

MARCEL: For the death of Albertine to be able to suppress my suffering, the shock of the fall would have had to kill her not only in Touraine but in myself. There, never had she been more alive. In order to enter into us, another person must first have assumed the form, have entered into the surroundings of the moment; appearing to us only in a succession of momentary flashes, he has never been able to furnish us with more than one single aspect of himself at a time, to present us with more than a single photograph of himself. A great weakness, no doubt, for a person to consist merely in a collection of moments; a great strength also. It is depending upon memory, and our memory of a moment . . . (*'Little Phrase' begins*) . . . is not informed of everything which has happened since; this moment which it has registered endures still, lives still, and with it the person whose form is outlined in it. . . .

ALBERTINE: (*Sadly*) Talk, talk, talk. . . .

MARCEL: When I had reached the stage of enduring the grief of losing this Albertine, I must begin afresh with another, with a hundred others. So then (*His voice and the music die away*) my life was entirely altered.

ALBERTINE: He made his autopsy upon my memory. He wouldn't let me be. He sent for his experts, to help him in his horrible investigation . . . Aimé, the headwaiter, my friend of Balbec — Marcel offered him money to find out whether I had done this, that or the other . . . and of course Aimé would have told him just what he wanted to know; for Marcel never wanted the truth, he wanted only to be tormented, as poor old Monsieur de Charlus needed to be tormented, when all other pleasures failed. Marcel questioned Andrée, and because she half-loved him and was jealous of me — Oh, it's so simple, really, once you understand the Iagos of this world! — She also told him what he wanted to know. At last he grew tired of it all and went at last to his beloved Venice. And there, a few days before he returned to Paris, he received a telegram. . . .

(*Sound of departing train: whistle, cry of guard, etc.*)

MOTHER OF MARCEL: Oh, it's unheard of, Marcel! Listen; at my age one has ceased to be astonished by anything, but I assure you there could be nothing more unexpected than I find in this letter.

MARCEL: First listen to me, Mamma. I don't know what it is, but however astonishing it may be, it can't be quite so astonishing as what I have found in *my* letter. It is a marriage. It is Robert de Saint-Loup who is marrying Gilberte Swann.

MOTHER: Oh! Then that, no doubt, is what is in my other letter, which I have not opened, for I recognise your friend's hand.

MARCEL: But Mamma, something is even odder than that. I didn't tell you before, because I didn't want to worry you: but a few days ago I received a most mysterious telegram.

MOTHER: A telegram? From whom?

MARCEL: It read: 'My dear, you think me dead, forgive me, I am quite alive, should like to see you, talk about marriage, when do you return? Love . . . Albertine.'

MOTHER: (*Horrified*) Oh, no, no! That can't be! That's impossible!

MARCEL: Yes, quite impossible. But Mamma, even when I fancied it might be true, I no longer *cared*. For me, Albertine was dead at last. Having ceased to see her I had ceased to love her. . . .

MOTHER: Thank God for that! She was *never* the right girl for my little wolf.

MARCEL: Of course, I've just realised that the telegram wasn't from Albertine at all; it was from Gilberte. The clerk who sent the telegram had simply misread her name.

MOTHER: What amazing things do happen! It must have been a shock to you, my dear, all the same.

MARCEL: I think I am sad because it was not a shock, Mamma.

MOTHER: My little boy, my little wolf, you have always been too tender-hearted! (*Excitedly*) But Marcel, what do you think of the news? How proud poor Swann would have felt, to know his daughter was marrying into the Guermantes family!

MARCEL: Who would never receive her when he was alive, and when it would have given him such infinite pleasure. I shall telephone Gilberte when we get home. . . .

(*Sound of telephone bell ringing, heard through receiver*)

MARCEL: Hullo, hullo. . . .

GILBERTE: Who is calling?

MARCEL: May I speak to Mademoiselle de Forcheville?

GILBERTE: It is she speaking.

MARCEL: Gilberte! This is Marcel!

GILBERTE: Marcel! Oh, my dear friend, how delightful to hear your voice! We had no idea you were back again.

MARCEL: I only arrived to-day.

GILBERTE: Was Venice as ravishing as ever?

MARCEL: For the first week a dream, for all the other weeks a home. Last night there was the same sky as there is over Paris this evening, lavender and periwinkle thinned with rosewater and clear as the Vivonne. If you look out of your window you can see it now. I want to share it with you, in this moment of wishing joy to you and Robert.

GILBERTE: My dear, I hope you approve! I feel as though some miracle had happened, that I must have turned from a crossing-sweeper into a princess, for how would he have looked at me otherwise? Marcel, I am so happy! You do approve, don't you? Robert was so much to you.

MARCEL: And you so much to me.

GILBERTE: That's all a long time ago. I'm afraid I teased you dreadfully.

MARCEL: Abominably.

GILBERTE: But you've forgiven me now? For I'm going to be good always, and make Robert a good wife. Do come and see me!

MARCEL: Of course I shall. I would have answered your telegram, only. . . .

GILBERTE: My telegram?

MARCEL: (*Puzzled*) Why, the one you sent me to Venice, telling me you wanted to talk to me about your marriage!

GILBERTE: But I have never sent you any such telegram!

(*Pause. Whispering in a passage*)

ALBERTINE: Be quiet, Françoise! I shall announce myself. No, I don't care if he's on a hundred telephones.

MARCEL: You never . . . sent me . . . a telegram?

(*The door opens*)

ALBERTINE: (*Softly, her voice full of laughter*) My dear, you thought me dead. I assure you, I am quite alive. My little Marcel!

MARCEL: (*Stupefied*) Albertine!!

(*Drops receiver: Pause*)

GILBERTE: (*Her voice faint*) Hullo! Hullo! Marcel! Marcel! Hullo, hullo, are you there? Operator! . . . You've cut us off, Operator! . . .

(*Pause*)

ALBERTINE: I am afraid it was rather a shock to my poor Marcel to find we had played such a trick on him. But after my accident I lay in bed for days with a severe concussion, and when I was properly able to talk, my aunt and I planned to tell Marcel that the accident had been fatal. For she had made me promise to marry Octave, anyway, and thought Marcel needed a lesson. I don't think I should have consented to such a thing had I been in my right mind — and indeed, the moment I *was* in my right mind I took a really good look at Octave and decided to let Andrée have him after all. I was sure I could manage Marcel if I played my cards properly. He used to spy on me; but as you know, two can play at the same game. I had news of him all the time he was in Venice from one of the servants of the Danieli, a nice fellow who used to be lift-boy at Rivebelle; and he told me Marcel wasn't going about with anyone else, and that the time would soon be ripe for me to reappear. So I reappeared, as you see.

(*Pause*)

And we were married.

(*Pause*)

Of course, he did not write about *that* in his book! As he said, his book was not meant to be autobiographical; and perhaps it is better so, as I am not sure that this fragment I found crumpled on his desk, and took away with me to keep among my very private possessions, shows me in any better light. . . .

MARCEL: Just as Swann married Odette after he had long ceased to love her, so at last I made up my mind, in face of my mother's tears, to marry Albertine. It is a mistake to think that we are the most bound only by those who are our present torment and joy, who, because we can see and touch them, whom we can regulate by the hours they will be away from us, the hours at which, smiling and mysterious, they will return to appease us by the mere fact of their corporeality, are momentarily part of ourselves. As the past binds us by the multiplicity of its essences, so we are bound by the innumerable pasts existing in those whom we have long ceased to love. If Albertine herself had failed to interest me, I was nevertheless bound to her by the seas of my youth that yet lay, blue and slanting, behind the blue slits of her eyes, by the sands that rippled even now in the marvellous rippling of her hair; and if she often bored me, which she did, I could still feel in her presence the comfort of those memories that poured from within her, a sacred oil, like the light we see emanating from a Madonna by Caravaggio or from Elstir's portrait of his cook. Now that I no longer watched her comings or goings, Albertine was no longer interested in escape, and, indeed, loved above all things to sit beside me like a great, comfortable cat who edges nearer and nearer to the knee or to the lap, drawing life from the warmth and odour of its master, without desires of its own and without further intention than the prolongation of the minute.

ALBERTINE: I must say there are times when I wish my little Marcel showed a little more interest in me, as he did in the old days. But we get along as nicely as most people — indeed, as I don't ask him what he does and he never asks me (though I don't do anything, as a matter of fact) we are often spoken of as one of the most devoted *ménages* in Paris. I have my yacht, now, which is quite delightful. I am taking Madame Verdurin and a party on a cruise next spring, so really everything has turned out quite nicely after all.

(*Sings*)   'Les douleurs sont des folles,
                 Et qui les écoute est encor plus fou!
                 À nous deux toi qui consoles,
                 Biniou, mon biniou, mon cher biniou!'

V

Saint-Loup

SAINT-LOUP is Proust's one serious attempt at the study of sexual ambivalence. It seems to me unlikely that when he first conceived Saint-Loup and introduced him to the reader on the blazing esplanade at Balbec, he had the conscious intention of making him homosexual. Yet there is no doubt that the oddity of Saint-Loup's behaviour towards the timid and dazzled Marcel is by no means inconsistent with his behaviour in *Le Temps Retrouvé*: it is conceivable that Saint-Loup's latent obsession, hinted at in the introductory scene, became obvious to Proust himself only *after* the character had been conceived and presented. He saw in Saint-Loup potentialities that had not been realised even by himself (Proust) at the beginning; and he developed them.

It is possible to argue on certain premises that the homosexuality of Saint-Loup really does come as a surprise to the reader and is a serious artistic mistake: but to argue this simply on the grounds that Saint-Loup was for years passionately in love with the actress Rachel is to ignore the complexity of sexual behaviour in some types of men.

It is characteristic of a certain kind of homosexual love for jealousy to assume forms far more overt, far less controlled and *far more enjoyed* than is common in heterosexual relationships: and Robert's jealousy of Rachel has the histrionic stamp notable in Marcel's jealousy of Albertine, in Charlus's jealousy of Morel, but absent from Swann's jealousy of Odette. In such homosexual relationships there is often a marked tendency to 'carry on the affair in public'; to make one's friends onlookers, participants, referees. The quarrel is more enjoyable if witnessed by a third party; the reconciliation more satisfying if friends are brought in to make a party of it. It is significant that Saint-Loup likes to quarrel with Rachel and be reconciled with her under Marcel's gaze: this seems to me a genuine psychological observation on Proust's part, and I do not for a moment believe that Marcel takes part in the restaurant and theatre scenes simply because he has to be there in order to tell the reader about them.

Proust's narrative method lands him in real difficulties only when he is forced to let Marcel 'eavesdrop' upon scenes he could never otherwise have witnessed and would, in real life, have been extremely unlikely to witness — as when he spies on the Lesbians from the hillside at Montjouvain (here even architectural and topographical possibilities are somewhat stretched for the narrator's convenience) and sees from his window in the Hôtel de Guermantes the first meeting between Charlus and Jupien: but it is not by accident, nor by the author stretching a point, that Marcel becomes involved in the affairs of Charlus and Morel. Charlus actually wants him to be present: in accordance with his peculiar sexual temperament, he needs the stimulation of an audience.

Proust, probably intending Saint-Loup to be heterosexual but having towards his creation an ambiguous personal emotion, instinctively gave him certain characteristics not uncommonly associated with certain homosexual types; and because he did this, and later, perhaps, perceived that he had done so, the *whole character* of Saint-Loup assumes an air of consistency. It is certainly true that Proust overdid the final denigration of his hero. Because love is largely unreasonable and is not to be explained by analysis of the qualities of the object, there is no reason why we should be surprised at the liaison with Morel: but it is certainly astonishing to find Saint-Loup, a highly fastidious man and still a young one (not a man who has ragged every sensation to pieces, like the senile Charlus, who is pathetically groping for new stimuli, however absurd, to comfort his old age) losing his *croix de guerre* in the messy and ridiculous squalor of Jupien's male brothel. We may have felt before this that Saint-Loup was losing moral integrity, that his splendour was rapidly fading; but we were not given to understand that he was going downhill at the rate of a played-out valetudinarian Charlus.*

The aim of this programme is to reconcile the young and the middle-aged Saint-Loup, using Bloch as a catalyst. There is some justification for the intrusion of Bloch. It is odd to find him, in the novel, so much in Saint-Loup's company. No two men could have been more antipathetic; yet we hear of their continuing friendship, their occasional meetings, right up to 1914, where Bloch, meeting Saint-Loup in Paris, is jeering at him for not rejoining his regiment, and vulgarly deriding his references to 'The Emperor William'.

'Can't you say simply "William"? That's it, you're in a funk, even here you're ready to crawl on your stomach to him. Pshaw! They'll make nice soldiers at the front, they'll lick the boots of the Boches. You red-tabs are fit to parade in a circus, that's all.'

(*Time Regained*, p. 56)

Something must have kept these two incompatible men together. I have made the suggestion that it might have been a kind of self-protection on Saint-Loup's part. I do not pretend, of course, to believe this, any more than I pretend to believe all the excuses I have made for Albertine: but there is a curious lacuna in the book between the two Roberts. My programme is meant to emphasise this rather than to put forth a theory; but without the theory I could not have made the emphasis.

* The first five paragraphs of this Note are extracted from my essay, 'A Single Saint-Loup,' in The London Magazine, July 1955, and are reprinted here by the permission of the Editor.

N

SAINT-LOUP

(The noises of a Paris street)

SAINT-LOUP: (*Whistling*) 'Les amours sont des folles,
                Et qui les écoute
                Est encore plus fou. . . .'
MARCEL: (*Joining in*)   'Ta-ta-ta, ta ta ta tatatatata,
                Biniou, mon biniou, mon cher biniou.'
SAINT-LOUP: Catchy little thing, isn't it? I can't get it out of my head.
MARCEL: I have a little friend who sings it from morn till night.
SAINT-LOUP: My dear fellow, when Rachel heard me singing it, she broke sticks over me, as they say. 'Robert,' she said, 'how you can sing those revolting cheap ballads. . . .' She's absolutely above popular taste, you know. When she does sing — she wouldn't whistle, mind you, she's always trying to get me out of the habit — it's always Fauré or Duparc.

She took a great fancy to you, the other day. In fact . . . you know, Marcel, old boy, if it were anyone but you I wouldn't pass the message on.
MARCEL: Message? For me?
SAINT-LOUP: Well, she has an idea that it might be amusing for you to see the understudy rehearsal to-morrow. They're doing Regnard, you know — *Le Légataire Universel* — frightful out-of-date stuff, she's quite fed up with it. But she's understudying Lisette; it might give you an idea of how marvellous she is if you heard her. That is, if you could spare the time.
MARCEL: My dear chap! Nothing I'd like better. We'll go along together, shall we? May I come and pick you up?
SAINT-LOUP: Well . . . er . . . that's rather the point; I mean, the difficult part. You see, she's so sensitive, she feels we shall only

be really close to each other if she understands just what my
friends mean to me. And knowing how I adore you and worship your intellect, she felt that . . . well, she thought it would
be easier to get to know you properly if you had a tête-à-tête,
as it were. In fact, she said positively that you were to go alone.

MARCEL: Well, I . . . I'm flattered; but surely you. . . .

SAINT-LOUP: Oh, I'd be jealous of anyone but you, old boy, I'd
be murderous, in fact; but I'm sure you could speak well of me
to her, you might perhaps give her the idea that I'm not such a
Philistine as she makes out . . . that I'm not responsible for my
family, as it were.

MARCEL: She objects to your family?

SAINT-LOUP: Well, you heard her outburst about my mother's
attitude towards Dreyfus. She thinks the aristocracy are a lot
of bone-heads, without the slightest idea of art, music and so
forth. Which on the whole is pretty true, mind you! You
remember how my good Aunt Oriane and her crowd insulted
her when she came to recite *Les Sept Princesses?* I tell her she
might have a better opinion if only she knew my uncle Charlus,
who at least has the rudiments of culture. But I'd never dare
introduce them, even if she'd permit it; she'd never be safe with
an old womaniser like that. No, you go, will you? She'll adore
you as I do; she'll tell you more of her sublime ideas about Ibsen
and Tolstoi. (*Whistles 'Les amours sont des folles. . . .'*) What a
splendid morning it is! It makes one glad to be alive.

(*Whistling continues: then dies away*)

MARCEL: The reader may remember that at this time Robert de
Saint-Loup was at the height of his passion for the young actress
Rachel, who, with her small and narrow face framed in short
curls of black hair, irregular as if outlined in pen-strokes upon
a wash-drawing in Indian ink, I had found it so hard to admire:
for her lover, her price, if not above rubies, was equal at least
to that of those rubies displayed upon velvet the colour of

ancient papyrus in the windows of Boucheron or Cartier; but
her price for me was merely the 'present' she had once been
accustomed to demand in the disorderly house into which,
some years ago, I had been introduced by my friend Bloch. It
is true that I had never attempted to make an assignation with
her there, and that she had known me only as one client among
the many whom she herself did not oblige; yet, when Robert
presented to me, a few days before, the intellectual and advanced young woman who was driving him to despair, I felt I
had failed to keep from my countenance my stupefaction at
setting eyes once more upon the sharp-tongued and saleable
girl once known to me as 'Rachel quand du Seigneur'; nor,
morover, could I suppose that she had failed to recognise myself, and I interpreted her anxiety to see me alone as a desire to
find out whether or not I intended to hold my tongue. My inter-
pretation was by no means incorrect. I was just about to enter
the theatre by the stage-door, as Rachel had instructed me, when
I was hailed by Bloch himself.

BLOCH: Great Gods, what groundling do I see about to enter the
dubious pastures of Thalia? For we are on our way to the most
fustian of comedies, in case you didn't know it. Have you got
your pass? Are your papers in order?

MARCEL: Bloch! It's good to see you. What's been keeping you
from your old friends?

BLOCH: I might ask what had been keeping you from yours, if I
hadn't seen you only a day or so ago walking in the illustrious
company of de Saint-Loup-en-Bray, golden lads both of you,
for all the world like Damon and Pythias. A bit of a snob, eh?
Aren't you? Confess it? Poor Helots of the pen like myself
can't hope to compete with a marquis.

MARCEL: Oh, nonsense. Saint-Loup's on leave, and I like to see as
much of him as I can.

BLOCH: And you've an assignation with him here, eh? What? Oh,

I know about his fair charmer, you can be sure. Rachel of the
lofty brow. As a matter of fact, I'm writing a little piece for her,
something I hope she can perform, if not at old mother Villeparisis's, at least in some other not-too-Boeotian drawing-
room.

MARCEL: No, I'm not meeting Saint-Loup to-day. In fact, it's
Rachel I've come to see. She sent me a summons.

BLOCH: I take it that this is not the first time of meeting her, eh?
I mean, de Saint-Loup-en-Bray would already have made you
acquainted with his cultivated Aphrodite?

MARCEL: Well — yes. He has.

BLOCH: (*With a shout of laughter*) Then you know who she is!
You must have recognised her — didn't you?

MARCEL: (*Laughing*) I could hardly help it.

BLOCH: She's become the most noble of Hetairae nowadays, with
pure eyes, fair as Hera's. She likes to forget there was a time
when she only cost your humble servant twenty francs for
delights brief, but so immeasurable, that Villon himself would
have found it hard to sing them adequately.

STAGE-DOORKEEPER: Yes? What do you young gentlemen want?
If you don't want nothing, don't hang about here.

MARCEL: I have an appointment with Mademoiselle Rachel.

STAGE-DOORKEEPER: She's on stage right now. But if you like
to creep round in front, quiet-like, you can wait till she's
finished.

MARCEL: Thank you, but I . . . I'm not quite sure of the way. . . .

BLOCH: I shall be Virgil to your Dante. I am well acquainted with
the insalubrious shades of this particular limbo of the Drama.

STAGE-DOORKEEPER: Oh, it's Monsieur Bloch, is it? Didn't
recognise you at first, sir. But the moment you began to talk,
of course, I'd know your gift of the gab among a million. . . .

(*Bloch and Marcel make their way round stage to front of
house. Noise of someone tripping over some heavy object*)

BLOCH: (*Whispering*) Watch your step, dear Master, or we shall have the wrath of Jove poured down upon us. . . .

MARCEL: (*Whispering*) I'm sorry. Ouch! I've barked my shin.

BLOCH: No, no, not that way — to your left! You'd better let me go ahead.

STAGE DIRECTOR: (*From stage*) That's all right. Go on. From Lisette's speech. . . . Quiet now, everybody, please. . . .

RACHEL: (*As Lisette, reciting from stage, end of Act I, Le Légataire Universel*) 'Madame, you see the power of your glances; one look from you (of an easy motion) moves more humours, agitates more bile, works more in him the very first time than all the medicines he has taken in six months. Oh, the power of love!'

DIRECTOR: (*From stalls*) Mademoiselle Rachel! You are not playing *Phèdre*. 'Oh, the power of love!' is a cry of complete cynicism; it is an emotion in which you do not believe. Take it again, please: from —'works more in him. . . .'

RACHEL: '. . . works more in him the very first time than all the medicines he has taken in six months. Oh, the power of love!'

DIRECTOR: That's better. Carry straight on.

ACTRESS: (*As Madame Argante*) Farewell, I must go.

ACTOR: (*As Eraste*) Madame, permit me the honour of accompanying you.

RACHEL: (*After pause: as Lisette*) 'And I must go in and look to my work: the old man is waiting and he can do nothing without me. For the beginning of an arranged marriage, I must confess this was a pretty interview!'

DIRECTOR: (*After pause*) All right! Break now, everyone. Be here again at four o'clock.

(*Noise and chatter of actors leaving stage*)

RACHEL: (*Calling over footlights*) Someone's out there — who is it? Is that you, Bloch? I can't talk about your piece to-day. I'm expecting someone.

BLOCH: I have him with me. Are you coming down?

RACHEL: Robert's friend? Wait a minute. I'll be with you. . . .

BLOCH: She's superb, don't you agree? A footling play, but what bite she gives to it! I assure you, dear Master — by the way, you might pay me the compliment of addressing me in the same fashion sometimes, as we agreed . . . er . . . what was I saying? — Oh yes; I assure you, our little Rachel is going to outclass Lecouvreur, Réjane, Berma herself!

RACHEL: (*Close at hand; she is out of temper*) Oh, there you both are. Why didn't you wait for me behind?

MARCEL: But Mademoiselle, we had no idea how long the re-hearsal would last.

RACHEL: It's been lasting for ever, the out-of-date rubbish. And they rehearse us in such an 'anyhow' sort of fashion — they know that none of us will ever get a chance to play, so long as the leading actors can manage to hobble in on crutches. I tell you, when I think how I waste my time here among all these dirty corner-boys who only want to squeeze my foot. . . .

BLOCH: (*Cutting in*) Fair votaress of the art of Thalia and Mel-pomene! I have brought you golden words to comfort your sad heart. A new speech, thirty lines long, as fitted to the celes-tial arc of your lips as the feathers to the heels of Hermes. . . .

RACHEL: Oh Bloch, I can't stand here listening to your babble! I told you I couldn't see you to-day. I have business with this gentleman and it's private.

BLOCH: Oh, well, if you're in that sort of mood. . . .

(*A silence*)

MARCEL: Rachel, saying she had little time to spare, refused my invitation to take tea at Wéber's and insisted that we should walk in the Champs Elysées. Silent as a Pythoness, her dark thoughts like a fillet upon her curiously protuberant brow, to conceal which she had trained the flat dark curls inwards after the fashion of a Caesar, would not open her lips until we were walking beneath the chestnut trees which, beautiful and tragic as women just past their prime who are not yet prepared to acknowledge the end of youth, were casting upon the earth an oriental tapestry of tindery petals that were partly of rose and partly of a melancholy brown, pale as the sands of a lake shore at the opening of a clouded day.

RACHEL: All right, out with it. Don't pretend we never met each other before Robert introduced us.

MARCEL: Mademoiselle, I shall remember nothing that is not pleasing to you.

RACHEL: It's not easy for a woman of my sort to make her way. By cheapening myself a little, I made myself rich enough to buy the things that would give me a start in my profession — smart clothes, a few furs, a little jewellery. . . . If you're going to tell him, you'd better get it over and done with.

MARCEL: I assure you that nothing was further from my thoughts.

RACHEL: No? And what about the thoughts of your friend, Bloch? Oh, he won't betray me at the moment. He knows I'm going to the top of the ladder and he hopes I'll act in his plays when I get there. These Jews always have an eye to the main chance. But he . . . he may get there first.

MARCEL: Oh, surely you're exaggerating! He's clever enough, I know, but. . . .

RACHEL: As a man, he's a fool. But he will be a successful playwright. I know. I'm never wrong. I can tell the best when it's so new it's scarcely got a voice at all, let alone a form. You may take my word for that. . . . What about Robert? Shall you tell him?

MARCEL: I had no such intention.

RACHEL: I wish I could believe it. But you two are so thick that if I didn't know him, I might think his tastes weren't far removed from those of some of his precious relations. . . .

MARCEL: Why, what do you mean?

RACHEL: (*Laughing*) Do you know, I really believe you're as

innocent as a daisy? It makes me laugh to see those great big
eyes of yours. Oh, my poor boy! What the years have in store
for you! — But seriously — I can trust you?

MARCEL: I give you my word.

(Pause)

RACHEL: Do you find me attractive, by the way? Most men do.

MARCEL: Well . . . of course. No one could help it. But. . . .

RACHEL: I could do you a little favour perhaps, now and then if I
really thought you were my friend. . . .

(A silence)

MARCEL: I told Rachel that she might have my promise of silence
(for it was not really my friendship in which she was interested)
without recompense, for however much she might appeal to
me — which in fact she did not, since I had not sought her
favours even when they had been available for a few francs but
had taken as my favourite a little girl from the Dordogne,
whose cheeks, in moments of ecstasy, assumed the silvery-
mauve patina of a plum — I could not accept such recompense
without disloyalty to Saint-Loup.

From that moment she trusted me, though for years she
continued to dislike and often to vilify me: for people who are
once assured of our confidence not infrequently abuse it just as
we may abuse a lover of whose constancy we are entirely convinced.

Saint-Loup was happy that summer, for although she teased
him and quarrelled with him, and though her exorbitant de-
mands for money kept him perpetually in debt, she was not yet
prepared to accept fully the assurances of her friends among the
younger writers and actors that he was stupid, that by living
with him she was spoiling her future as an artist. Saint-Loup
often took me with him to visit her in the little house she had
taken near Versailles, and though it puzzled me that he should

wish an onlooker to intrude upon their intimacy, I was agreeable to anything that might please him.

*(Barking of dogs: whistling of canaries: chatter of a monkey
and a parakeet)*

SAINT-LOUP: Really, my darling, I can't make myself heard above
this menagerie and I'm sure Marcel's getting a headache! Do
throw something over that bird's cage, at least.

RACHEL: I'll do nothing of the sort! Don't you suppose he enjoys
this beautiful afternoon light just as much as you do? How
would you like it if I threw a cloth over *you?*

MARCEL: (*Agitated*) No, get down, you really must get down!
(*A monkey chattering*) I love you, I am charmed by your African
graces, but I really can't have you eating my collar!

RACHEL: Oh, my poor little monkey! Are they cross with you,
my love? Just keep quiet, Marcel, and I'll disentangle him. He
wouldn't cling on to you unless he adored you.

SAINT-LOUP: Then you'll have to be as sorry for me, darling,
when you find me clinging to your neck and chattering piteously
in your ear.

RACHEL: Wait a minute — since you're both making such a fuss,
I'll put him in the other room and the birds too. Come on, my
sweet, come to your Mamma, come to your dear little cage fit
for a king. . . . (*A clatter, and concerted noise of the animals as
she gathers them up and retires*)

SAINT-LOUP: You must admit, old boy, she's enchanting! Of
course, she's in a frivolous mood to-day, but if you could have
heard her yesterday on Emerson — I assure you, there was
something sidereal about her, something hieratic — half-poet,
half-priest.

RACHEL: (*As she re-enters the room*) There! Now I've exchanged
one kind of chattering for another. The Lord knows if I'm any
better off. If we knew what the monkey was saying we'd probably find he was far more intelligent than you are.

SAINT-LOUP: Oh, I say! Is that fair?

RACHEL: Well, there's no denying — is there, Marcel — that people like Robert are born enemies of the intellect? With centuries of pure *bone* behind them, how can they hope to *think*? His aunt Guermantes, for example, she imagines she's tremendously advanced because she admires the latest Hugo; but as for Mallarmé, Rimbaud, Laforgue — she'd only think they were dressmakers. (*With sudden, fatuous affection*) Hullo, *you!*

SAINT-LOUP: (*In same tone*) Hullo, *you!*

RACHEL: What a delicious chin he's got, hasn't he, Marcel? I don't feel I could endure him if it weren't for that chin. No, Robert, I won't sit on your knee. Not just now. I want Marcel to play to us, while the sunset fades beyond that window into the apple-green of the Hesperides. . . . Go on, Marcel, what are you waiting for? You're not too bad for an amateur.

MARCEL: I'll do my best.

SAINT-LOUP: Hullo, *you!*

RACHEL: Hullo, *you!* Oh, you!

(*Marcel begins to play the 'Little Phrase'*)

SAINT-LOUP: I adore you.

RACHEL: You should show it better.

SAINT-LOUP: How can I?

RACHEL: There was a little trinket you've been promising me for ages. I haven't had it yet.

SAINT-LOUP: My dear darling girl, I told you, you'll have to wait a bit; my broker will have to sell out something first.

RACHEL: I know somebody quite nice who would give it to me if I'd let him. He adores me, too. Don't imagine you're the only one.

SAINT-LOUP: Just be patient, please, I beg you.

RACHEL: Marcel! Do stop playing that old-fashioned stuff!

(*He stops playing*)

It's so sentimental. It makes me feel I'm painted with honey and staked out on an anthill. Don't you know any Debussy?

MARCEL: I'm sorry, I'm afraid I don't.

RACHEL: Let me go, Robert! — No, don't be silly, I want to go. *I'll* play for you now.

(*The sound of a scuffle as she pushes Marcel from stool*)

(*She begins to play: Debussy's Sarabande from Pour le Piano. She plays splashily, but is not too bad*)

RACHEL: Now listen! Isn't that divine? Can't you hear a new world unfolding like a waterlily, cooler and cooler, till suddenly you come to the fires burning at the heart of it? For pure, plastic beauty Debussy's sublime. But none of Robert's precious relations would think so. They haven't got past Meyerbeer yet, any of them. . . .

(*Music fades away with her voice*)

MARCEL: Sometimes, when she was acting in Paris, she would invite Bloch and myself to meet her artist friends in an apartment she had rented near the Place de l'Odéon; but on these occasions would make me swear to say nothing to Robert.

(*Noise of party*)

RACHEL: . . . It's no use asking him, these people aren't his sort and he isn't theirs. Oh, he thinks he's a socialist, he spouts Proudhon at them, but you can see the aristocrat beneath. He makes them uneasy.

BLOCH: Why, is Saint-Loup, tamer of horses, charioteer of the sun, not proposing to honour us with his presence to-night?

RACHEL: Oh, you know he isn't, Bloch! He wasn't invited. Last time we had him here he was falling over himself to show he didn't think he was better than we were.

(*During these last two speeches, an actress Coralie and an actor Edmond have been talking together: these speeches should synchronise faintly, emerging at asterisk)*

CORALIE: If they produce the Richepin I may get a small part, anyway he promised, so we'll just have to see what happens.

EDMOND: I wouldn't count on it. My dear girl, you'd better find yourself a protector like our hostess. Not that it seems to advance her career — quite the opposite. You'd think her Marquis would put a little money behind her in that way. . . .   *

RACHEL: What's that, Edmond? Are you talking about Robert?

EDMOND: I was only saying that your tremendously smart friends don't seem to help you on the stage.

CORALIE: Not that he isn't charming, Rachel, and handsome — oh! I could swoon. But if people know you're going around with that type, then they soon start to think you must be as démodée as he is.

RACHEL: You're jealous, Coralie. I'm well aware of that.

EDMOND: No, but what use *are* these swells? They try to follow the new movements, but really, the smell of the past they carry with them is quite suffocating. Like old lace, or thigh-boots.

BLOCH: Thigh-boots, eh? That's a good one. They would be a bit fetid, eh?

CORALIE: Now if only you were one of his set and could *marry* him, that would be different. Then you could forget about all us artists raising feeble voices in our garrets. . . .

RACHEL: (*In a quiet, violent tone*) You fool! Is that what you think of me? If I could marry him a hundred times over I'd never give up my art to queen it in a lot of stuffy drawing-rooms with a mob of uneducated bitches in coronets!

BLOCH: Oh, I say, you know! It's said that chance is a fine thing.

RACHEL: Hold your tongue, Bloch. You know I mean what I say. When they're dead and forgotten, my name will still be known all over the world. I say it shall!

BLOCH: Bravo! You know, you looked quite like Pallas Athene

of the grey eyes when you said that; your faith is your shield and Marcel here, with his big eyes, is your faithful owl.

RACHEL: (*Working herself up into a rage*) Oh, I'm sick of the lot of you! You can all clear out — yes, Marcel, you as well. And you, Coralie! Edmond! You eat and drink at Robert's expense and then chatter your mean little souls out about him. Clear out, I say, go on! (*She bursts into tears*) Sometimes I think he's worth six of you! Go home! Go home! Can't I even have my own room to myself?

(*A silence*)

MARCEL: It was by no means uncommon for Rachel to terminate such evenings with mass dismissal, nor was she at all consistent in her choice of reason for so doing. Sometimes she would drive her friends away for not singing Robert's praises, defending him with the passion, almost, of a young girl in love for the first time who dreads criticism of the beloved lest it should awaken criticism in her own heart; sometimes she joined with them in abusing him savagely and drove them away because, perhaps out of perversity, perhaps out of some genuine stirring of shame that they should mock such a generous, if unwitting, host, they tried to put in a good word for him. Yet in one thing she was genuine, and that was in her devotion to her art. If it had been possible for her to marry Robert, had some inspired genealogist brought it to light that she was a Mortemart or (perhaps more plausibly) a Mirepoix-Lévy, she would have refused to do so.

What puzzled me more than the behaviour of Rachel, however, was the curious attraction Bloch appeared to have for Saint-Loup, for Bloch, though clever and imaginative, was extremely vulgar and could scarcely open his mouth without uttering a solecism that brought a flush to Robert's cheeks.

At last the idea occurred to me, though not until many years later, that the attraction was, perhaps, that malign one we feel towards those who alone, we suspect, could give us information

we dread to receive; information we crave for, but which must
be for us a thing of horror, the mere thought of it heating our
cheeks, making the blood halt in our veins; information concerning some mystery lying in the past of one we love.

*(A party at the Duchesse de Guermantes'. Tuning of violin
and 'cello. Party chatter. The laugh of Oriane)*

(1st movement of Suite)

ORIANE: You really must not tell us that creature can *act*! When
I was idiot enough to let her appear in my drawing-room, she
lay down on her stomach with a lily in her hand, and recited the
most improbable nonsense at the rate — I am not exaggerating
— of twelve words to the minute!

MARCEL: Madame, she's really very gifted. I saw her myself at a
rehearsal. . . .

ORIANE: There! You've been encouraging the monster, when
you know we're all dying to prise her claws out of Robert's
throat. I call it most unfriendly of you. Eh, Palamède? Isn't
our little friend extremely treacherous?

CHARLUS: My dear Oriane, you speak of treachery; what duty he
may own to our family it is hard for me to assess — any more
than I can for the life of me see that Dreyfus is a traitor.

ORAINE: What's that? You too, Mémé?

CHARLUS: Why, if the fellow were a Frenchman he'd be a traitor.
But as a Jew, is he guilty of anything more venal than a breach
of the laws of hospitality? You, young man!

MARCEL: Sir?

CHARLUS: I gather that my nephew still disports himself with his
disagreeable and ridiculous young woman, who encourages
him to set himself against his family by espousing the cause of
another equally disagreeable and ridiculous Jew. By Gad,
Madame de Surgis looks splendid to-night! Like a figurehead of
alabaster.

ORIANE: Don't be silly, Mémé! Figureheads aren't made of alabaster. If they were, I'm sure the ships would tumble on to their noses and look like ducks diving for worms, with their behinds in the air.

DUC DE GUERMANTES: What's Oriane saying? Gad, there are times when my wife sounds just like a peasant. Well, little brother, how wags the world?

CHARLUS: Like the behinds of Oriane's preposterous ducks: that is, vigorously. But I was addressing our young friend here. Now then: is my nephew coming to-night? — Oh, how d'ye do, Marie-Aynard.

MME DE MARSANTES: Did I hear you speaking of my little son? I hope he is coming. He has two days' leave, and I did implore him not to forget his kinsmen altogether.

FOOTMAN: Monsieur le Marquis de Saint-Loup-en-Bray!

MARCEL: (*Narrating*) He came into the room with his quick soft glide, his monocle flying out before him like a butterfly as he walked, his blue and piercing gaze fixed upon the far wall as though he meant to pass through all impediments including that of the wall itself; but in fact he changed course suddenly, came to his mother and kissed her hand.

MME DE MARSANTES: My dear boy! How good it is of you to spare even an hour for us!

ORIANE: Well, Robert: we'd almost given you up!

DUC DE GUERMANTES: Now you *are* here, you'd better stay to dinner. You'll have to take pot-luck, you know.

SAINT-LOUP: I'm sorry, mother, but I must be off again almost at once. Someone is waiting for me. Will you be going my way, Marcel?

MME DE MARSANTES: Oh, no, it is too bad, too bad! You have time for everyone but myself, who love you best. . . .

SAINT-LOUP: (*Impatiently*) Well, it simply can't be helped. I'm late as it is.

ORIANE: None but the punctual deserve the fair. . . . Oh, wasn't that funny? I do think people might laugh when I attempt my humble witticisms.

SAINT-LOUP: It's not that at all, my dear aunt. It's military business.

MME DE MARS: When you're on leave?

SAINT-LOUP: (*Shortly*) Yes.

(*Quartet begins 2nd movement: lightish composition reminiscent of central phrase of Mon Biniou*)

CHARLUS: If by 'military business' you mean that you are proposing to assist in organising another petition for that wretched Dreyfus, let me tell you that you're asking to be blackballed when you put up for the Jockey.

ORIANE: (*In a whisper*) Oh, don't be so obtuse, Mémé! His 'military business' is undoubtedly an appointment with *la Fille du Régiment*.

SAINT-LOUP: I don't care about that, Uncle Palamède. Why I should want to sit in a club with a crowd of bone-headed Nationalists without a trace of common humanity between them, let alone of culture, I can't imagine.

CHARLUS: In that case, you'd better withdraw your candidature.

SAINT-LOUP: (*After a slight pause*) Oh, may as well let it stand.

CHARLUS: Oriane, why the devil is your quartet playing such gutter-music? I expect better in your house.

ORIANE: Gutter-music? Oh? Are they? They're new; I haven't had them here before. . . . What are they playing?

CHARLUS: God alone knows. Don't have them here again; I forbid it absolutely. Not that it matters so much tonight, with the Princesse de Parme here. Her whole family's tone deaf.

SAINT-LOUP: Marcel, I want a word with you. Come on.

MME DE MARS: Oh Robert, you're not going to disappear right at this very moment! Please be nice to me, my darling boy. . . .

SAINT-LOUP: Yes, yes, yes, Mother. In a minute. I'll see you before I go. . . .

(*Quartet playing louder*)

O

SAINT-LOUP: ... I say, Marcel, do listen to what they're playing. ... It sounds like a bit of a crib, doesn't it? It's like that little
tune ... (*Hums Mon Biniou against the quartet*) ... it always
makes me think of my girl. God knows why ... she detests it.
I suppose it's because I couldn't stop whistling it one day when
I was happy just because of her.

MARCEL: You look far from happy now.

SAINT-LOUP: They're sending me to Algiers. Oriane could quite
well stop it if she wanted to: she's hand in glove with old
General de Monserfeuil. But she won't. The family want to part
me from Rachel.

(2nd movement comes to an end)

Listen, while I'm gone I want you to look after her. I know I
can trust you.

MARCEL: I'll do my best. This is wretched luck for you!

(3rd movement)

SAINT-LOUP: I could hardly bring myself to speak to my mother
at all, if only she knew it. She's been working to exile me as
hard as the rest of them. As for my uncle Charlus, I often suspect he'd like me out of the way so as to make just one man less
in Paris; in his view, it ought to be a vast harem with himself as
Pasha. Damnable old skirt-chaser! He's got an eye on Madame
de Surgis now, but I think my uncle Basin will be quicker off
the mark.

MARCEL: Robert, you should try to be more kind to your mother.
She had tears in her eyes.

SAINT-LOUP: She has only herself to blame. How shall I be able
to bear it without my girl? (*Moodily*) The worst of it is, we're
quarrelling at the moment.

MARCEL: What's the matter?

SAINT-LOUP: I can't find out. But of course I've sent her a telegram telling her I acknowledge my fault, I'll abase myself, I'll

do anything if only she'll forgive me. That's what I wanted to
see you about, too. Do go and plead my cause, like a good chap!

MARCEL: When?

SAINT-LOUP: To-night. Straight away.

MARCEL: But my cousin is calling upon me. . . .

SAINT-LOUP: You can put your cousin off, can't you? After all,
what on earth are relatives for? . . .

ALBERTINE: (*Fading in*) Oh, my dear Marcel, I was hoping we'd
have a nice time to ourselves for once! But of course, if it's for
your friend's sake you must help him. Saint-Loup has been so
kind to you that your little Albertine must always owe him
gratitude!

MARCEL: But what will my little mouse do while I'm away? I shall
want to know where she is, you know, just so that I can imagine
what she is saying and doing during every moment of my
absence.

ALBERTINE: Why, it wouldn't be a bad idea if I went to call upon
Andrée!

MARCEL: That would be capital. Do you promise to do that?

ALBERTINE: If it makes my darling happy. Remember me to your
friend, won't you? I think he's such a nice friend for you.
Better than that horrid Bloch, with his huge nose and his great
showy laugh. I really wonder Saint-Loup has so much to do
with him, especially as. . . .

MARCEL: Especially as what?

ALBERTINE: Well, I oughtn't really to mention it, only people do
say that Rachel hasn't been disobliging to *him,* on more than
one occasion. . . .

(*Pause*)

MARCEL: Although I rebutted this suggestion I did so without
sincerity, knowing that Rachel, who was used to giving her
person as freely to men as she gave coins to beggars (for in fact
she was not mean, dispensing the money Robert gave her with

prodigal liberality to her seedier acquaintances and to those street mendicants who aroused her pity) would not withhold herself from the embraces of Bloch, if she felt any tactical advantage was gained by so doing. I found her alone that night, walking up and down before the fire with a kind of deliberate sinuosity that was foreign to her, since off the stage her natural movements were abrupt and even a trifle awkward. I guessed Saint-Loup had prepared her for my coming and that she had carefully considered the mood in which she should greet me. She pulled the coat from my shoulders rather in the fashion of a tigress clawing at her keeper through the bars out of idleness and without animosity, and she concentrated upon me like bullseye lanterns the light of her too-full, too-aqueous eyes. . . .

RACHEL: Oh, so he's sent *you* to crawl for him, has he? Tell him I want proof of good behaviour, not a franc's worth of paper from the telegraph office.

MARCEL: But my dear, what has he done? I assure you that despite his admissions of guilt, he hasn't the slightest idea!

RACHEL: Done? He's tried to keep me caged up, so that my life isn't my own. It makes me sick to come out of the theatre, dog-tired, and see him waiting for me, rain, hail or snow. He sends me an absurd quantity of flowers, enough for a hot-house, and my friends all say it's revolting to spend so much on roses when there are people dying of starvation! He's so insensitive it's enough to drive one mad! As for what he *can* do. . . . (*Pause*) He needn't go prancing off to Algiers, if he doesn't want to.

MARCEL: But he's a soldier. His duty. . . .

RACHEL: He can resign his commission, can't he? He can have me or not have me — he can take his choice. But it's no use for him to suppose he can go running off in his wonderful uniform, just like Lohengrin, to enjoy himself out there and expect me to live like a nun in Paris. Oh God, how he fawns on me! He loves

people to trample on him — haven't you noticed that? But
when it comes to doing just *one* thing that might upset those
precious Guermantes of his, especially that dirty old swine of a
Charlus, whom all Paris knows about. . . .

MARCEL: Rachel's references to M. de Charlus were not, however,
comprehensible to me until, in the following year, my eyes
were opened to the tastes that were his, and which, as mani-
fested among the Guermantes family, had almost the appearance of an hereditary taint. But by that time Saint-Loup had
ceased to love Rachel, awakening suddenly from the grinding
pressure of his love, as Swann had once awoken from his love
for Odette; and though she usually visited him when he was in
Paris and would sometimes spend the night at his side for reasons
that were almost therapeutic, since to lie in the shape formed
by his familiar body conquered her tendency to insomnia in the
same way that one's sleeplessness may be conquered by lying
in some familiar bed of childhood, it was evident that his passion would never revive. I saw little of him now, for he seemed
always to be busy, 'on the go', as he phrased it, devoted to his
regimental duties. Since the end of his liaison with Rachel he
had become less interested in the arts, and though a trace of his
former radicalism remained, he seldom gave voice to it for fear
of upsetting his military superiors.

One day, however, he asked me if I would care to spend a
day or so with him at Doncières, where he proposed to visit a
former comrade now in charge of training, saying with a touch
of irony that it might be amusing to revisit the scenes of our
youth.

SAINT-LOUP: (*His attitude now has a touch of cynicism, even when
he genuinely feels affection for Marcel. He is less extravagant in
his enthusiasms and gives the impression of a certain reserve, even
of coldness.*)

... After all, you know, it's eight years since I was a young man in barracks, and eight years at the pace one lives nowadays would make anyone grow old.

MARCEL: You're very kind to me, Robert, very good, but I do feel it is fatal to revisit the places where we were happy, because it makes us superimpose upon a golden memory a mere memory of bricks and mortar.

SAINT-LOUP: I don't know that any memories of mine are worth preserving. But look, you mustn't hang back; the air's fresh there; it'll put the colour back in your cheeks in less than no time. And I'm sure your pretty cousin can spare you for once, if you tell her it's for my sake. . . .

MARCEL: And so, leaving Albertine behind in Andrée's charge, not without trepidation, since she was causing me the greatest pain by her smiling evasions and her scarcely-less disturbing bursts of apparent frankness, I set off with Saint-Loup for Doncières.

(Sound of drilling in a barracks square: trampling of feet, horses' hooves, bugle calls)

MARCEL: . . . Do you remember the day you returned my salute as though I were a mere acquaintance? The thought of it wounded me for years.

SAINT-LOUP: What day was that? How you do treasure things up in that memory of yours! It reminds me of my Aunt Villeparisis's junk-room. She has everything up there, from the Emperor's nightshirt to a ball made out of a thousand bits of string all knotted together in the hope that nobody will ever need to buy a new one. You should get her to show you.

MARCEL: Look! Do you see who's coming towards us?

SAINT-LOUP: Yes, of course. Our friend Bloch. I asked him down for the day.

MARCEL: *(Disappointed)* But I thought we were to have the day alone!

SAINT-LOUP: So did I, but at the last moment I had a note from somebody I've simply got to dine with to-night — he's rushing down here on purpose to see me, it's a frightful bore, I do assure you. I thought if Bloch came he could keep you company.

BLOCH: Saint-Loup, great captain, restored to the terrain of Mars, I salute you! And you, O scribe, whose half-baked but indefinably talented lucubrations I con with professional eye from time to time. Hail to you both!

(Noise of drilling becomes louder, the bugle piercing)

SAINT-LOUP: We can't hear ourselves speak out here. My God, I don't know how I ever managed to endure it. Let's go into a café shall we? — here, this one's as good as the next. . . .

MARCEL: . . . But we had barely sat down at a table before Saint-Loup jumped to his feet, and with an air of agitation asked us to excuse him, on the grounds that his friend had obviously mistaken the train and arrived too early. He begged us to stay until he returned, promising us that he would not be gone for more than a quarter of an hour. I watched him through the distorting glass of the window that seemed to turn him into some slim exotic fish swimming through emerald weeds which were, in fact, only the leaves of the plane-trees merged, melted, dispersed and merged again by the irregularities of the crystal, watched him break into his light and graceful run and, by the railings of the parade ground, catch up with another young man in whom, to my astonishment, I recognised the violinist Morel, son of my uncle's former valet and protégé of Saint-Loup's uncle, the Baron de Charlus.

When I turned away, I found Bloch regarding me with a broad and oafish grin. . . .

BLOCH: . . . You seem surprised, dear Master. Has no one ever told you anything? Does your mother know you're out?

MARCEL: Is *that* the friend who is depriving us of Saint-Loup's company this evening?

BLOCH: A change from our worthy Rachel, isn't it? Yet there's a sort of resemblance, I always fancy. A head taller — perhaps half a nose longer. Rachel says she can't imagine what His Highness the Baron would say if only he knew. Ts-ts-ts-ts-ts! Truly, the ways of this wicked world shock the simple sages like myself, the innocent denizens of Helicon. Well, we needn't expect to see Monsieur le Marquis back with *us* to-night. . . .

MARCEL: But in fact Robert did return, within ten minutes, his face white as marble, to inform us abruptly that his friend would not be staying in Doncières after all, and that he was now at our complete disposal. I guessed that Morel had provoked some brief but violent quarrel, and was at first glad of it; but as Robert's gloom deepened our companionship became the more and more constrained, until I even began to wish that I were alone with Bloch, especially as it seemed to me that there was between Bloch and Saint-Loup some distasteful understanding from which I was deliberately excluded. It was hard for me to credit the insinuations Bloch had made, far harder to discount them; and I felt a weariness and disillusion beyond expression when I looked back upon the affection that had existed between Saint-Loup and myself, and which was now, for me, irretrievably tainted.

I should have liked, that cold and brilliant day of martial springtime, the harness brass shining no less brightly than the citrous sun, the noise of the bugle piercing the ear like the aurist's delicate and finical probe, to make my last farewells to Robert, now utterly transformed for me, by some coupling between the two parts of his being, into a creature as dreadful and no less lovely than the being formed by the fusion of Hermaphroditus and the fountain nymph. I should have liked, also, to turn my back for ever upon Bloch, who had opened my eyes to these disturbing mysteries, but in fact I was doomed to bear both of them with me throughout my life until the death of one, the worldly success of the other. On my return to Paris I expressed a little of my sorrow to Albertine.

ALBERTINE: (*Sadly*) . . . But my poor boy, I could have told you myself, I wouldn't for the world have let it come as a shock to you! If only you would confide in your poor, stupid Albertine, she might save you so much!

MARCEL: You knew? About Saint-Loup? How could you know?

ALBERTINE: There! I have my spies. There are little birds who tell me.

MARCEL: Listen: this time I must have the truth. I insist.

ALBERTINE: Oh, what a thunderous brow he has when he is angry! He mustn't be angry with his dear, for she won't tease him a moment longer. Saint-Loup's friend — Morel, that is — knows Andrée just a little, and Andrée told me that Saint-Loup was trying to steal him from poor M. de Charlus. I think it's horrid. (*Virtuously*) I don't know how people can do such things.

MARCEL: Robert! How could he! He was not. . . not at all like that. People used to say he looked effeminate because he was so beautiful, but everyone knew he had no thought in his head except for Rachel. . . .

ALBERTINE: They do say, my darling, that it runs in families. After all, look at the poor Baron! And rumour had it — Oh yes, I hear all sorts of rumours even in my adorable little cage, my love — that the Prince de Guermantes is the same.

MARCEL: Not Robert! Something must have happened. I'm sure of it.

ALBERTINE: Don't be too sure, dear, because it is dreadful to be sure about things we can never establish for ourselves. And if anything *did* happen to change Saint-Loup — apart from what Bloch said to him in a dreadful temper — we shall never know.

MARCEL: (*Sharply*) What Bloch said to him? What's that? I haven't heard about it.

ALBERTINE: Well, as a matter of fact I had that from Andrée, too, who had it from Bloch's absurd little friend, the actress Coralie. It seems that Bloch thought Saint-Loup was trying to snub him.

(*Faint noises from the street*)

SAINT-LOUP: ... My dear fellow I wouldn't hurt your feelings for the world! If you'd just given me the least hint or sign that you wanted an introduction. ...

BLOCH: You put me off before! There was Sir Rufus Israels, under your nose, and there was I, and you just spoke to him and left me standing. And to-day, when he walked past us in the Avenue Foch, you simply raised your hat and didn't even stop!

SAINT-LOUP: But my good Bloch, I simply can't see that Israels is anything to stop *for*! He merely happens to know my mother slightly, through the Lévis. ...

BLOCH: Oh, I know what you thought! 'Here am I, the great Marquis de Saint-Loup-en-Bray, out with a bourgeois, a clever fellow to be sure, but not our sort, lah-di-dah, I mustn't give Sir Rufus the idea that he's a *friend* of mine!'

SAINT-LOUP: Now listen, this is very embarrassing. And quite untrue. To me Israels is a nobody — you can meet the entire Faubourg, if you like, Trémoïlles, Molés, anybody — it's up to you. But Israels is nothing at all to me. ...

BLOCH: Well, he is to *me*! I'm just about fed up with this! You patronise us intellectuals, you spout about equality — (*He is near to tears*) but when it comes to acknowledging us before your smart friends — (*He sobs audibly*)

SAINT-LOUP: Bloch, Bloch, I beg you, don't upset yourself like this! I'll chase after Israels now, I'll send him a *petit bleu*, I'll do anything. ...

BLOCH: Thanks, but you can keep your favours! Here have I been, year in, year out, acting as a spy on that jumped-up tart you used to worship. ... (*Sobs again and stops, frightened*)

SAINT-LOUP: (*Icily*) Go on.

BLOCH: Nothing. I wasn't saying anything.

SAINT-LOUP: (*In a terrifying voice*) You were speaking of Rachel. Finish what you were saying . . . or I shall cane you, here in the street.

BLOCH: You wouldn't dare.

SAINT-LOUP: You see this cane I carry. I have used it before.

(*Pause*)

BLOCH: (*Blurting out*) All right, then! Didn't you know what she was? Didn't you? Thinking her so wonderful she was worth a king's ransom! Well, Marcel and I knew her years ago when she was on call at a bawdy-house — fifty thousand francs at a go you've coughed up for her; I've had her time and time again for twenty francs! That's one in the eye for you, Monsieur le Marquis. That's what she's like. . . .

SAINT-LOUP: (*Quietly*) Go away.

BLOCH: I tell you, that's what half these damned women are like. . . . No! Don't you dare touch me! You promised, you promised. . . .

(*A silence*)

MARCEL: But Albertine, Robert is still friendly with Bloch. He often dines with him when he's in Paris.

ALBERTINE: Well, men *do* love to pry. They can't resist it. Even when they've quite ceased to love a girl, even if she's dead, they still go on poking around in her past. It's like a drug. I think it's so silly. . . . If you behaved like that about me, I really think I should come back and haunt you! Not that you'd find anything, of course, my darling, even if you did pry, because I've done absolutely nothing at all. My life is an open book. . . .

MARCEL: Although I reflected for a long while upon the possibility that Bloch's betrayal of Rachel had turned Robert overnight, as it were, into a most virulent hater of women, yet it seemed to me that there is not a single question of the human heart, no matter how simple, which can be answered completely, once and for all, in terms that are themselves simple. I did not, I could not, believe that he, the glorious young man who, on the beach at Balbec, had absorbed into his eyes, his flesh, his clothing, into the very handkerchief set with such exquisite negligence in his breast-pocket, the barley-coloured rays of the sun, had even then been an inhabitant of the accursed City; that his love for Rachel had been a mockery, an elaborate mask to conceal his true features, that his friendship, his love for me had not been as plain, as untainted, as mine for him. Yet I knew that there must have been in him from his birth some dark seed, germinating in a place of cold and dark, from the flower and fruit of which he might never hope to be delivered; and I wondered what it was, the thing that had brought him finally to the knowledge of this implacable efflorescence.

I had believed Albertine when she explained Robert's reason for his continued friendship with Bloch, since there was already in myself, at that time, the impulse that would one day cause me to excavate her own remorseless dust; but I felt that this explanation was not the whole of the truth. Perhaps Saint-Loup could not let Bloch go because he could not escape the thought that even yet, behind this coarse and knowing face, these liquid, exopthalmic eyes that could so soon fill with tears of self-pity, there lay another secret he must learn, and which he dreaded to learn.

I remembered an evening in Paris several years ago; Robert's love for Rachel appeared at the time to be a happy love, and we were dining at one of those small firelit restaurants that attempt to preserve the atmosphere of a Breton farm, dining comfortably by firelight while, from the next room, there came to us the sound of a girl singing. The daughter of the proprietor was entertaining friends of her own. . . .

(*A girl is singing: she can just be heard through the wall*)

MARCEL: He had been gay at the beginning of the meal, but as it grew later, his mood seemed to darken. . . .

(A pause)

MARCEL: I must say you're to be envied, old boy. Rich, good-looking, born to the purple — which even in these republican days gives one a certain advantage, to put the matter at its lowest. . . .

SAINT-LOUP: Oh, I don't know about that.

MARCEL: And with someone you adore who seems (at the moment, at least, for I know she's given you trouble in the past) to adore you in return — she's being kind to you, isn't she?

SAINT-LOUP: Oh, she's a good girl, when she takes the trouble to be. And anyway, I never know why she should take the trouble, since I'm not nearly good enough for her. But sometimes it seems to me. . . . Look, we're snug in here, aren't we, with this jolly fire and superb wine — I must say it's a good bottle, my uncle Charlus would approve — it's pleasant, eh? Just ourselves, shut in and warm together.

MARCEL: My dear Robert, it couldn't be nicer!

SAINT-LOUP: But outside this place it's freezing and dark, and we can't stay for ever. That's what I feel it's like for me . . . all right now, with the fire blazing and Jeanne next door giving us a concert — but I've got to go out where it's bitter and black, it's my fate . . . it's inescapable.

MARCEL: My dear old chap, why on earth should you feel like that?

SAINT-LOUP: Even fellows like Bloch have more hope ahead of them than I have.

MARCEL: But you, with your youth and health, and all the most beautiful women only waiting for you to smile at them . . . you should have a marvellous life!

SAINT-LOUP: Oh, don't let's talk about my life. I am doomed in advance.

MARCEL: What on earth can you mean? Something's happened to upset you. Tell me what it is.

SAINT-LOUP: Nothing's happened. It's only that.... (*Music stops*) Oh, the devil take it, old boy, I'm becoming the death's head at the feast! Let's have another bottle of this stuff, shall we? Or would you rather have a change? ...

MARCEL: One evening four or five years later, shortly after Saint-Loup's marriage to Mademoiselle de Forcheville, who had been my old friend Gilberte Swann, I went to a reception at the house of Madame de Montmorency, where Morel was to perform. I arrived after the violinist had begun to play and so, in order to disturb nobody, I waited in the outer hall among the vases filled with cinerarias, and studied the little statue said to be by Falconnet, that represented a spring, and which did, in fact, exude a perpetual moisture.

(Morel's playing comes through the doors: footsteps across the flagstones)

CHARLUS: Well, you little rascal? Late again, eh? If only you had the sense to be a little later you would find the party over and Eliane tucked into bed, which is the proper place for women of her age and tediousness. Still, I suppose her crushes are worth the trouble, if one can hear Morel play.

MARCEL: Yes, indeed, Monsieur; he's as marvellous as ever.

CHARLUS: You may ask me — if you have the impudence, that is, for the years may perhaps have chastened you — why I should come here like a thief in the night to hear Morel at all, seeing that I have forever cast him out of my bosom like the viper he is? For you know that we no longer speak, that he fears me, avoids me, and with good reason. ...

MARCEL: I was, indeed, astonished to find M. de Charlus, now so sadly changed, so old, so exposed to his enemies, the rice powder flaking upon his cheeks, the dye starting out like shoe-blacking upon his hair and his moustaches, at any house in the Faubourg where Morel was likely to be encountered; but I made no comment.

(*The music comes to an end: an outburst of applause*)

CHARLUS: . . . if you had the temerity to ask me, my reply would be that I see no reason why I should be driven from the homes of all my kinsmen because they have the bad taste to harbour this ungrateful dog. I should not be present to-night if this were not one of Eliane's most enormous crushes, but here I shall manage to avoid him, to avoid even catching his eye. . . .

DUCHESSE DE MONTMORENCY: (*Almost inaudible, from within*) And now I have the pride, the honour to present to you the greatest actress of our day, who is to recite for us, as only she can — Mademoiselle Rachel!

(*Renewed and thunderous applause, also distant*)

CHARLUS: But I loved him, you know. You, who have yourself so charitable a heart, will not misunderstand me if I open my heart to you. Let us go in.

(*Sound of their feet on the flagstones. Inner door opens: full sound of clapping and applause*)

CHARLUS: (*Whispering*) By God, they've got Rachel! She's going to recite. That's fame for you, eh? I remember when she was laughed out of Oriane's drawing-room, it must be ten years ago, or is it more? . . .

MARCEL: And indeed, it was Rachel who, in her black dress, stood upon the low dais garlanded with rosy and green hydrangeas, stood silent, one might have said scornful, waiting for the ovation to die down. She was at that time rising to the height of her fame, the fame that would some day eclipse that of Berma.

She was now so thin that one would have said her bones were constructed of ply-wood, her face was lined, there were violet pouches beneath her eyes: but she still wore her dark curls in the style of the Caesars and as she surveyed the guests, seemed like a sibyl about to open her lips upon a prophecy of plague, or war, or the depreciation of the franc.

RACHEL: 'Les deux Pigeons': Fable de la Fontaine.

> (*She begins to recite, according to her own maxim — that a poem should be spoken as if the speaker were actually in the process of composing it*)

Deux pigeons . . . s'aimaient . . . d'amour tendre:
. . . L'un deux . . . s'ennuyant au logis,
Fut assez fou . . . pour entreprendre
Un voyage . . . en lointain pays.

(Pause)

L'autre lui dit . . . (*Rapidly*) 'Qu'allez vous faire?
Voulez-vous quitter votre frère?
. . . L'absence . . . est le plus grand des maux:
. . . Non pas pour vous, cruel! . . . Au moins . . . que les
    travaux,
Les dangers . . . (*More rapidly*) les soins du voyage,
Changent un peu votre courage.

(Pause)

Encor . . . si la saison s'avançait davantage!
Attendez les zephyrs: . . . qui vous presse? Un corbeau
Tout à l'heure annonçait malheur . . . à quelque oiseau . . .

(Her voice fades away)

(Rising applause, chatter)

IST FEMALE VOICE: Isn't Rachel marvellous? One would never

know she was reciting La Fontaine. Fancy choosing a school-book piece like that!

2ND FEMALE VOICE: Well, you know, if she hadn't told us what it was going to be, I should have thought it was Ibsen, or something tremendously deep. . . .

RACHEL: My old friend, Marcel! Tell me, my dear, did you like me to-night?

MARCEL: You were magnificent. I was at your feet.

RACHEL: Let's go into a corner, away from all these overdressed bores. God, the diamonds! God, the dowdiness!

1ST VOICE: Mademoiselle Rachel, may I have the honour to tell you how deeply moved. . . .

RACHEL: (*Brusquely*) Delighted. But some other time. . . .

(*Rachel and Marcel move away over the flagstones*)

It's chilly out here in the hall, but at least we shan't be disturbed. What a repellent fountain that is! It looks like a cold in the head. You must come and see my new house. I've got the most sublime statue of myself, by Maillol. Now *that* is sculpture!

MARCEL: You seem happy.

RACHEL: Oh, my dear, I am, I am! Supremely. (*Sings gently*)
  'Les amours sont des folles
  Et qui les écoute
  Est encore plus fou. . . .'
(*She laughs*) Do you remember how angry I used to be with poor Robert de Saint-Loup when he whistled that nonsense? I was rather a prig in those days. I hear he's making his wife miserable.

MARCEL: I'm afraid so.

RACHEL: By pretending to run after other women! Isn't it *ludicrous*? You know, those men would make the best husbands in the world if they didn't constantly pretend to deceive their wives with women, just to conceal their real tastes.

P

MARCEL: Poor Gilberte.

RACHEL: And they say he's always making scenes, crawling on the floor to her, and begging her to forgive him. But they do *love* scenes you know, that sort. Don't you remember how he loved to have you with us when *we* quarrelled? They just pine for an audience; it's typical. They must make love in public.

MARCEL: It's still strange to me, what has happened to him. For he adored you, all those years. . . .

RACHEL: *I've* always thought it began when his eyes were opened to that precious family of his. . . . Sh — keep quiet a moment. There's that absurd screech-owl, his aunt Oriane, looking just like a salmon but smart, I admit. . . . I don't want her to see us. . . . All right, she's gone. . . . Oh yes, about Robert. I'm sure he always had it in him to go that way, and when he suddenly found he wasn't the only one of them in the world, or even the only one among his nearest and dearest, as it were. . . .

MARCEL: Who was it that opened his eyes?

RACHEL: Oh, Bloch, of course. I remember him telling me about it. It was when everything had been over for some time between Robert and me, and Robert was running after that empty-headed little Daisy d'Ambresac. . . .

(*Saint-Loup whistling: 'Les Amours sont des folles. . .'*)

BLOCH: Hullo, hullo, old boy! Stop a minute. What are you trying to do, avoid me?

SAINT-LOUP: I assure you, no. I didn't see you coming.

BLOCH: De Saint-Loup-en-Bray, strolling along the Bois by moonlight, twirling his stick with his head in the clouds; by Zeus, a sight for sore eyes! Shall we dine together, what? I know a little place off the Boul' Mich, full of the most delectable Hebes, a low eating-house to your lordship, perhaps, but a bit of all right for your humble servant.

SAINT-LOUP: I'm sorry, I've an engagement.

BLOCH: Oh-ho-ho! With the lovely d'Ambresac, eh? You see, I

have my spies. And they say the Thespian Muse is green-eyed with jealousy. . . .

SAINT-LOUP: (*Sharply*) We won't speak of that again. I warned you.

BLOCH: (*Cringing*) Oh, sorry, sorry, a thousand pardons. My master must forgive me. But when I blurted it out about — oh, you know, my old acquaintance with the lady — I thought you were past caring.

SAINT-LOUP: I said, we won't speak of that.

BLOCH: Well, you needn't talk to me as if I were a flunkey! My people may not have been swells, but I've had my plays performed in two continents, which is more than most men can say!

SAINT-LOUP: Yes, yes, I know. Look here, it's getting late. I must be going.

BLOCH: So you've no time for me, eh? The lady's impatient.

SAINT-LOUP: If you must know, I'm dining with my Uncle Charlus.

BLOCH: (*Vindictively*) Well, watch out for your virtue, that's all I say.

SAINT-LOUP: (*Laughing*) What on earth do you mean? I shan't profit from his example to prowl the Faubourg like a satyr. In fact, I'm thinking of settling down.

BLOCH: Ye Gods, I really believe the man doesn't know!

(*He begins to whistle, with false airiness, through his teeth*)

SAINT-LOUP: (*With sharp apprehension*) Know what? I don't like your tone.

BLOCH: What everyone else in Paris knows. That he's the chief of the maiden aunts.

SAINT-LOUP: (*Slowly*) What are you saying?

BLOCH: Don't take it to heart, old boy, we can't help our families, we didn't ask to be born. It seems to run in yours, you know: first your uncle Charlus, and then the Prince de Guermantes and of course that little Châtellerault, who just keeps himself shot of the police. . . .

SAINT-LOUP: (*Stonily*) Get away from me. Don't ever let me set eyes on you again.

BLOCH: Now look here, look here, I'm only trying to stop you from being hoodwinked! Marcel could have told you all this, if he wasn't a snob. . . .

SAINT-LOUP: Get away from me, I say.

BLOCH: All aristocrats are sacred to him. But I'm an intellectual — all men are the same to me. I'm doing you a good turn, I tell you — as I'd do it for the duke or a roadsweeper. . . .

SAINT-LOUP: If you were a gentleman, if you were in any way my equal, I should call you out!

BLOCH: (*Working up into a tearful rage*) So that's it, eh? That's the great egalitarian nob! Ye Gods, one has to laugh! And what are you? What do you think your are? Don't tell me *you* hadn't a fancy for Marcel, eh? It was always him, never me, and his family's no better than mine! Just take a look at *yourself*, will you?

SAINT-LOUP: It's a lie. It's a lie. It is all lies. . . . Don't touch me, I say! Take your hands away! Oh, God, it's all lies. . . .

(A silence)

MARCEL: But even after that, he refused to break with Bloch.

RACHEL: Oh, naturally! Don't you understand? When somebody tells us some horror about ourselves we abominate them . . . until we come to terms with that horror, my dear, until we begin to like it, until it seems delicious to us! Then we're grateful to the informant. He becomes our accomplice. Poor Robert can always trust Bloch, you see . . . because Bloch knows. Ugh, it's cold out here! Oh, that fountain . . . it's only fit for a water-closet.

(Footsteps)

DUCHESSE DE MONTMORENCY: My dear Mademoiselle Rachel! I was wondering where you were. All my guests were so entranced by your recitation they're longing to meet you! Won't you join us for a while?

RACHEL: Forgive me, Duchesse. I was just admiring your delightful fountain. . . .

DUCHESSE DE MONTMORENCY: My little Falconnet? Isn't it adorable? I don't wonder it catches your artist's eye.

RACHEL: Madame, if I am to make my appearance again, I must do so at once. I have to leave by ten o'clock. . . .

DUCHESSE DE MONTMORENCY: Of course, of course! As if it's not delightful of you to honour us at all. . . .

RACHEL: (*Whispering*) Goodbye, Marcel. Remember what I said — Robert will continue to see Bloch till the day he dies . . . he can't resist him. . . .

(*Her voice dies away*)

MARCEL: Combray. Nineteen hundred and sixteen.

PRIEST: *Requiescat in pace.*

ALL: Amen.

PRIEST: *Anima ejus, et animae omnium fidelium defunctorum per misericordiam Dei requiescant in pace.*

ALL: Amen.

(*Bugle: The Last Post*)

SAINT-LOUP: (*Sadly, far away, from the past*) Oh, don't let's talk about my life. I am doomed in advance. . . .

MARCEL: How many times, with sadness, he had said that to me! Was he then alluding to the vice which he had until then succeeded in hiding from the world, the gravity of which he perhaps exaggerated as young people do who make love for the first time or who even earlier seek solitary gratification and imagine themselves like plants which cannot disseminate their pollen without dying? Or had he, owing to his father's early death, the presentiment of his premature end?

For he died in France, protecting the retreat of his men, on the day following his return to the front; and his body was at last brought back to Combray to lie with the bones of his ancestors. He was himself once more in death — he was one of his breed, a Guermantes and nothing more, and this was symbolised at his funeral in the Church of Saint-Hilaire-de-Combray where the 'G' under the closed coronet divested of initials and titles, betokened the race of Guermantes which he personified in death.

I left the cemetery on foot, since I could not bear to talk with others who had known him. It was a clear, chilly day of dying summer, the sky of that cobalt and crystalline blue which seemed to me peculiar to Norman skies and to the eyes of the Guermantes. There were still some poppies strewn about the wheat and a few frail cornflowers also, like lean and unfed schoolgirls straggling home from mass in ones and twos to a breakfast they knew was scarcely worth the eating. On the field-path ahead of me I saw a woman in black, walking as slowly as myself, strange in her veiled and cityfied elegance. She turned suddenly and came towards me, her hands outstretched.

MARCEL: Rachel!

RACHEL: Oh, don't worry, they didn't see me. I slipped in at the back when the service had begun. I am slipping away again as quietly. I have my carriage in the road over there.

MARCEL: Why did you come?

RACHEL: Curiosity. Old times' sake. I don't know. I was quite fond of him, once upon a time. Besides, I wanted to see his daughter. (*Pause*) Not that I could; too much black. She was veiled like an old woman, poor child. (*Pause*) But she ought to be a beauty, if she takes after her mamma — and after him, of course. It's a pity he couldn't see her grow up.

(*Pause*)

MARCEL: What can we say of him, you and I?

RACHEL: That he was beautiful and brave. And far too anxious to be happy.

MARCEL: What do you mean?

RACHEL: He reminded me so much of Joachim du Bellay —

'Je crois qu'enfin l'esclave est jaloux de ses fers,
Je crois que le vautour est doux à Prométhée
Et que les Ixion se plaisent aux enfers. . . .'

Devil take it! These thorns . . . my dress is caught. Thank you. . . . Thank you, my dear. It's a long time since I took a country walk. Oh, Robert! I led him a terrible life, but how alive he *was* with me! Ixion enjoyed himself in hell, he adored his wheel! But the moment I unbound him he started looking for happiness with creatures like Morel. He'd grown tired of the tumult, you know; he wanted to be domestic. A little room by lamplight — all so secret — a nice tame boy to welcome him . . . a *billet doux* . . . a promise of fidelity. . . . He had it all. Morel could give him that. And he was quite wretched. His poor wife never understood, she thought he was yearning for some great passion, like his passion for me. She even tried to look like me, ridiculous woman! So sad . . . so sad. . . .

MARCEL: We had come to the borders of the field. Beyond, in the rutted lane, her carriage was waiting, already filmed a little with the white dust blown from the hedges by one of those sudden breezes which, coming at the end of summer, torment us by their inexplicable scent of spring.

(A church bell chimes the quarters)

As I opened the gate to let Rachel pass through, the chimes came faintly over the corn, disseminated by the wind from the steeple of Saint-Hilaire as the seeds of the poppy from her heart of velvet and of charcoal.

Somebody was waiting by the carriage, hat in hand, the

Mahomet of Giovanni Bellini with a nose incorporated by time into the general softening of the face, so that it was less the nose of my old friend Bloch than of some Grecian warrior who had put on weight with middle age..

BLOCH: .... I was willing to escort the illustrious Rachel to the obsequies of our heroic warrior beloved by the gods and therefore young in death, but alas, could not bring myself to enter the sacred building, not merely out of respect for the faith of my fathers, worthy men noble in their orthodoxy, but because I feared I should be unable to restrain my tears. For Saint-Loup to me was my brother, he thought the world of me. (*Pause*) Also, it was remiss of the family not to send me an announcement.

RACHEL: (*At a distance*) Oh, come along, Bloch, the horses are tired with waiting. And I have a new idea for your second act — we can talk about it on the way back. Can I drive you anywhere, Marcel?

MARCEL: Thank you, no. I am staying in Combray to-night.

(*Bloch mounts*)

BLOCH: We shall see each other in Paris, I hope, before they call me up? Really, it's the most sublime idiocy to send all our intellectuals to the front, robbing the country of its best brains, more especially when they know I'm short-sighted.

COACHMAN: Come up!

(*Whip*)

BLOCH: You really must admit. ....

(*The carriage is driven away*)

MARCEL: All night there burned for him white candles whose flames were shaped like the lilies of France, their radiant pollen sprinkled ardently upon the dark as if to fertilise new lilies and new stars; while at Guermantes his daughter, Mademoiselle de Saint-Loup, tired out by the sorrow and strangeness of death, slept with the silver pollen of tears upon her cheeks, without knowledge that in her being she had brought all the ways of my life into one: and in the morning she would awaken, still sad, but not so sad as before, encouraged by the thought that in yet another day she would be able to think of her grief as belonging to the mysterious 'day-before-yesterday', which must always be the furthest point of our past, and in the algebra of Time the equal of a thousand years.

a new sense while at Guermantes his daughter, Mademoiselle de
Saint-Loup, tired out by the sorrow and strangeness of death,
slept with the silver pollen of tears upon her cheeks, whom
knowledge that in her being she had brought all the ways of my
life into one; and in the morning she would awaken, still sad,
but not so sad as before, encouraged by the thought that in yet
another day she would be able to think of her grief as belonging
to the mysterious 'day-before-yesterday', which must always
be the furthest point of our past, and in the algebra of Time the
equal of a thousand years.

VI

A Window at Montjouvain

NOTE

PROUST finally conceived his great work in seven volumes. Vinteuil composed a septet. The novel was the triumph of 'Marcel', who had believed that his was a wasted life, a squandering of precious time for no reward but the mechanical, unilluminated review of voluntary memory. Vinteuil, betrayed by his daughter, his work virtually unknown, had gone in sadness and poverty to his grave.

The intention of this programme is to equate the triumph of Marcel with the triumph of Vinteuil. In literature, in music, both regained Time Past and engraved it for ever into their art; both succeeded, where Swann failed, in leaving a memorial. Yet Swann did leave the memorial of himself, since he was a part of that Time which Proust recovered: 'Marcel' and Vinteuil triumphed in an act of creation: Swann triumphed through his mere existence.

In this 'reconstruction', there was no chance of restating fully the nature of Proust's discovery. The best I could hope to do was to contract, to scamp, to make a lame précis, and to be content to get what effect I could through the re-echoing of voices heard before.

Like *Swann in Love*, *A Window at Montjouvain* is dependent for its effect upon the ear. It was my hope, and the hope of the producer and the composer, that we could make the Septet *grow* slowly out of the programme, as Rubek's sculpture, in *When We Dead Awaken*, grows slowly out of the play. The music is so important that *A Window at Montjouvain* can be very little without it.

This programme is designed as a climax to the other five, as a summing-up; it is the only one that cannot stand more or less on its own, which cannot be listened to as a separate entity.

I have taken one textual liberty: I have represented Oriane as being present at the first performance of Vinteuil's *Septuor*, whereas, in fact, she was not. But this programme is my own gathering-together of all the themes, and all the people, whom I had been able to protract into other scenes and other times; and there would have been a gap in it if she had not been there.

A WINDOW AT MONTJOUVAIN

(*Theme of Vinteuil Sonata, played by Vinteuil on piano at a distance*)

MARCEL: Sometimes, when I was returning with my parents from a walk and it was a warm spring evening with all the windows open to admit the smell of lime and lilac, I would hear the music of M. Vinteuil's piano sprinkled upon the air like moonstone drops from a watering-can, so that my throat would dry up and I would long for a glass of strawberry-juice or of orangeade. I should have liked to hurry home in order to savour this delight, but was rooted to the little lane that ran alongside his house, Montjouvain, by the equal delight that the music gave me. 'Oh come along,' said my father, 'you've heard the old boy playing a hundred times, I really wonder he doesn't get tired of it himself.' But my mother said, 'How extraordinary it is that he will never play for me when I visit him. . . .'

MOTHER OF MARCEL: . . . how extraordinary it is that he will never play for me when I visit him! He composes, I believe, and I should so like to hear his compositions, but no: the moment I come into the room he snatches up any piece of music that may be lying on the rack and says, 'I wonder who could have put that there? I *tell* them not to. . . .'

(*Music fades*)

VINTEUIL: I wonder who could have put that there? I tell them not to, but they never take any notice — Oh, do please be seated, dear Madame, so good of you to call upon me, so neighbourly —

MOTHER: But it's a pleasure for me, of course.

VINTEUIL: Now you must tell me, how is the little one, the little

Marcel? He's growing so quickly, he's all eyes and legs, that's what I say to my daughter. Does he love music like his mother, I wonder?

MOTHER: Indeed he does! I was thinking of having him taught to play the piano soon, he's nearly nine. I wondered perhaps if you . . . ?

VINTEUIL: I? Oh, no, no, oh dear no, he needs a far better master. I'm getting old, my present pupils are used to me, they're very kind, very patient, but a beginner —

MOTHER: But I'm perfectly sure my little boy —

GERMAINE: (*Breaking in*) Father! I'm just off. I'll be taking the pony-trap — you don't want it, do you? — Oh, I beg your pardon, Madame, I didn't see you. How do you do?

MOTHER: How do you do, Mademoiselle?

VINTEUIL: But Germaine, you aren't going out like that? The glass is falling, it's going to rain. Do just take your shawl —

GERMAINE: It's boiling hot! — No, I don't want my shawl. Anyway, it's upstairs.

VINTEUIL: Then let me fetch it for you, my darling, I'm sure Madame will excuse me for just a moment —

GERMAINE: I can't *wait*, Father! I'm late already, and Liliane hates hanging about for me.

VINTEUIL: Oh, I know you mustn't keep your friend waiting, that wouldn't do at all, but all the same your throat's so delicate, you really should take care —

GERMAINE: Listen, I must go, I tell you. Liliane will be furious. . . .

(Vinteuil Sonata on piano, distant)

MOTHER OF MARCEL: . . . My dear, I can't tell you how absurd it is, poor Vinteuil worrying himself to death about that great strong girl, with her sandy hair all rough like a boy's and her ginger freckles.

FATHER OF MARCEL: If he worried about that friend of hers

there might be some sense in it. Doctor Percepied was throwing out some pretty hints, I can tell you —

MOTHER: Hush, dear, *not* in front of someone we know!

FATHER: Poor old boy, he's always cared so much about what the neighbours think of him. Now he can't hold up his head. There wasn't much else in his life but being respectable, and now — Here, Marcel, stop scraping your feet, you're not a convict! Come along, or we won't be home till midnight. . . .

(*Music fades. Clock of Saint-Hilaire chimes the half-hour*)

There you are, what did I say? We'll be late for supper.

MOTHER: They're so poor, the Vinteuils. He can't make much with his piano lessons nowadays, and I'm sure his compositions are never published. M. Swann was saying only the other day that he'd like to help him, but of course, the old man's so proud. . . .

(*Chink of china, glasses, etc.*)

ODETTE: . . . What a rusty old figure he looks, Charles! Anyone would take him for a tramp. If only that daughter of his weren't so taken up with her precious friend, she'd look after him better. When I see him going about Combray with those two, looking so crushed, I always cross over if I've got the time. I simply don't know what to say to them. (*Change of tone*) Charles, this woman can't cook. I gave her the most wonderful English recipe, and what a mess she's made of it!

SWANN: You know, Odette, I did stop the old boy in the street to-day — he was just coming out of Saint-Hilaire — but 'pon my word, he was so timid I could hardly get a word out of him. I've often thought he must be some connection of our Vinteuil — you remember, the one who wrote our 'little phrase', the one we used to be so fond of?

ODETTE: That old thing! It's getting so hackneyed nowadays, one expects to hear the errand-boys singing it. Really, if she can't follow a simple recipe she'll have to go!

SWANN: — Because if he is, he ought to help financially. You'd really think it would be a reproach to him.

ODETTE: (*Impatiently*) Reproach to whom?

SWANN: Why, to the composer Vinteuil, of course. He must have made a pretty penny.

ODETTE: Well, I don't suppose he's any relation at all. — Charles! Isn't this pudding horrible?

SWANN: I don't think it's so bad. — You look charming in that dress. The little flowers are admirable, like Lippo Lippi's. Did Madame Bontemps notice it?

ODETTE: Oh, yes, she thought it was Redfern. I told her it was my own little woman, and I could see she was dying to get the name out of me. As if I'd have told her!

SWANN: Do you remember the dress I designed for you, like the Primavera?

ODETTE: You know perfectly well I never could stand it! It made me look like an actress. — Charles, the woman *can't* cook! I don't know why we put up with her.

SWANN: Get rid of her if you like. That's your province.

ODETTE: Oh, you make me tired with your indifference! Anything does for you. (*Pushes chair back*) I'd better go and say good-night to Gilberte, otherwise she'll read her eyes out.

SWANN: Don't bother yourself, I'll go up to her. Did you notice her, this afternoon, picking that great bunch of iris? She looked delicious. I wanted to tell her to stand still — just as she was — for ever.

ODETTE: Let me tell you, our delicious child has ruined some of the finest plants, the gardener's furious. She doesn't pick flowers, she just wrenches them up by the roots. If you weren't so soft you'd speak to her. . . .

(*Fade*)

(*Swann, going upstairs, hums the 'Little Phrase'. Knocks at a door*)

SWANN: Darling? May I come in?

GILBERTE: (*Behind door*) Come in, Pappa.

SWANN: (*Opening door*) I've come to tuck you in. You've been reading far too long.

GILBERTE: Oh, please, just five more minutes!

SWANN: Not a minute more. What have you been doing to-day?

GILBERTE: Just playing.

SWANN: Your Mamma says you must be more careful in the garden. She says you're spoiling the flowers.

GILBERTE: No, I'm not.

SWANN: Now, darling, you mustn't contradict. The flowers are so beautiful, we like to look at them; if you trample them all over and pull them up as you do, the place will be a wilderness —

GILBERTE: Pappa, I'm *reading*.

SWANN: Put that book down, and give me a kiss.

GILBERTE: Oh, all right — (*Kisses him*) There you are!

SWANN: Sleep well. Good-night, my little Gilberte.

GILBERTE: Oh, Pappa — I saw that funny little Marcel staring over our hedge to-day. Why can't he come and play here?

SWANN: Oh, because — your Mamma doesn't know his Mamma.

GILBERTE: Why can't she? . . . I think his Mamma's fat and hasn't got much style.

SWANN: No one is as beautiful as yours. If you'd seen her when she was young —

GILBERTE: Was she prettier than me?

SWANN: Now, young vanity, you're not to talk like that. You're both as pretty as the lilacs just by our gate, the mauve and white ones.

(*Door opens*)

ODETTE: Charles! Will you make that child go to sleep? What's the use of you coming up here, if you only keep her up talking to you?

GILBERTE: Oh, all *right*, Mamma. Anyway, I'm not tired.

Q

ODETTE: Put her candle out and leave her. It's high time she was asleep, and besides, I don't want to spend the whole evening with my own company. Good-night, Gilberte; sweet dreams.

SWANN: Good-night, my darling. Kiss me again —

ODETTE: (*Impatiently*) Charles! It's after nine.

SWANN: All right, I'm coming.

(*Swann hums the 'Little Phrase'. His voice dies away*)

MARCEL: . . . . If my dear Charles Swann had married a woman not in his style, when his love for her had faded, yet there came to him still, now and then, a reflection of that love, indistinguishable from the reflection of her beauty that would never cease to cast, upon the glass of his imagination, a shadow touched with rose, like the rounded, blood-tinged shadow of the tassel of roses which used to hang just beyond the frosted door of an obscure, seldom-trodden passage in his own house at Tansonville. He could never free himself utterly, even though he no longer cared for her, from that young, mysterious Odette with whom, in the drawing-room of Madame Verdurin, he had first listened to the music of Vinteuil; he had only to remember the 'little phrase' for the years to return to him, years still lovely in their own tide of time, though meaningless in that tide which had now risen coldly above his heart.

(*Madame Verdurin's drawing-room. Ski at the piano, bringing the Sonata of Vinteuil to a close. A moment's silence. A sprinkle of applause, breaking out of conversation*)

MME VERDURIN: (*Voice rising above the rest*) No, no, no, it is too much! Ski, you must never do that again. You know how it makes me weep, and you don't care, none of you care for your poor Mistress!

COTTARD: My dear Madame, if you would only use your Rhino-Gomenol faithfully, as I prescribed —

VERDURIN: It's no use, Cottard, there's no specific ever invented by man that will soothe my wife when she hears Vinteuil's masterpiece. She is too sensitive: as her medical man you should forbid her music, as you would forbid any over-indulgence!

SWANN: But then Madame would only live longer, and know less of delight. I'm sure she's not cowardly enough to accept such a solution.

MME VERDURIN: There! M. Swann understands me, haven't I always said it? He has a sensitive heart. The first day he came to my house I thought, 'Ah, here is one of us! He will understand!' Odette, my love, we are all in your debt.

ODETTE: In mine, Madame?

MME VERDURIN: For luring him here, like the delicious little siren that you are. Yes, we are all in your debt. And we all love you — eh? Don't we, M. Swann?

ODETTE: Oh, Madame, you're making me blush.

MME VERDURIN: We love to see you blush, don't we, gentlemen? Eh, Brichot? Don't we?

BRICHOT: Ah, you mustn't ask such things of an old pedagogue, *moult Sorbonagre, Sorbonicole,* as myself. You don't want to turn me into a Faustus, with the devil to pay for a dubious renaissance of misspent youth!

(*Laughter*)

MME VERDURIN: What about you, Saniette? Has the cat got your tongue?

SANIETTE: Oh, no. . . . I am sure . . . quite sure . . . Madame de Crécy is charming, blushing or — or — unblushing —

MME VERDURIN: Unblushing? Is that the sort of thing you say about a lady beneath our roof? By God, the man gets clumsier and clumsier. Now it's we who are blushing for you.

SANIETTE: I only meant —

MME VERDURIN: Oh, never mind what you meant, we haven't got all day. Well, my children, how would you like to spend the rest of the evening? A hand of whist, Brichot? Cottard, how about you?

COTTARD: Splendid! I think I shall have my revenge for last Wednesday, though I'd decided to forswear it.

BRICHOT: *Après l'Abandon de la Revanche,* eh? As the literary lady would have it.

MME VERDURIN: Oh, those bluestockings! I wouldn't have had them in my house. Wit, yes: brilliance, yes: but with beauty, gaiety, youth! Oh, how I adore youth! It knows how to *co-operate!* M. Swann, the lilac is charming by moonlight. As I know you are no card-player, I suppose you'd prefer to show Madame de Crécy the garden. I'm sure she won't be disappointed.

ODETTE: The lilacs are so enchanting this year.

MME VERDURIN: I shall leave the window open and ask Ski to play for you. You shall hear him in the moonlight. Ski! You may do your worst now. These young people lack our heart, nothing moves them, they're stone, stone all through. They don't know what it is to shed tears. . . .

(Ski playing Vinteuil Sonata)

MARCEL: They had listened together, then, so many years ago, to the notes of Ski's music watering the night; the same music, played timidly, almost secretively, by Vinteuil himself, that watered the leafy dusk which lay in the lane behind Montjouvain, when I walked there with my parents, and Swann and Odette, now married, wearied of each other, united only in love for their child, sat a mile away behind the orange-golden windows of Tansonville, those windows of night which seem to promise us that behind them lies some enormous felicity, some quietude of joy, that we ourselves shall never attain.

(Music dies away)

Yet behind most of the lighted windows of our lives, as behind the lighted eyes of most of us, there is, at the worst, boredom; at the best there may be fear or sorrow, or those beautiful and monstrous medusas of that love which is sterile and without comprehension of itself.

LILIANE: (*Fading in*) Oh look what a mess he's made! The place looks like a *bistrot*, all litter and cigarette-ends.

GERMAINE: But Liliane —

LILIANE: Oh, I know he's your father, no need to tell me. But he's a silly old fool, for all that. What's all this rubbish lying on the piano? Scraps here, scribbles there — God knows what he's up to.

GERMAINE: He told me he was writing a septet.

LILIANE: And how does he suppose anyone's going to read it? Mess! Mess! Muddle! It makes me sick. I've a good mind to scoop it up and throw it in the waste-paper basket. That's all it's good for.

GERMAINE: No, no, you mustn't! Please, please —

LILIANE: Let go of my arm. Do you hear? I won't have you pawing me. Now what *is* all this?

(*She uncrumples paper. Sings the music written on it: the first theme of Septet.* Breaks off suddenly*)

GERMAINE: What are you going to do? (*Fearfully*) Do be careful with it, do —

LILIANE: (*Slowly, mockingly*) Well, I could do as the spies do when they're captured. I could make it into a pellet and swallow it. But perhaps I'll only set light to it this time —

GERMAINE: Liliane! Oh, darling! Come away from the lamp, please, you must —

LILIANE: (*Steely*) Let me go, do you hear? Take your hands off me — take them off . . . that's better. Stand back — there, by the sofa. And don't move. Don't move, I said! Not a muscle!

GERMAINE: But what —

LILIANE: He's an old fool, isn't he?

GERMAINE: Oh, don't! We mustn't —

* See Appendix C for the phrases of the Septet.

LILIANE: Say it. You know you love saying it. He's a silly, muddling, messy old fool. Say that.

GERMAINE: I can't.

LILIANE: If you don't all this is going into the grate, and we'll have a real blaze — (*Strikes a match*)

GERMAINE: No! It would kill him, I know it would —

LILIANE: Say it, then. Let's hear his frail, delicate little daughter with her ploughboy's wrists say it. . . .

GERMAINE: Oh, yes, oh yes, I will . . . I'll do anything. . . .

LILIANE: For me.

GERMAINE: For you.

LILIANE: (*Laughing*) Then this time I'll let you off. (*Caressingly*) Come here, silly, you're forgiven. Come. Don't be shy. You know you're not a bit shy really, you're as bold as brass. Aren't you? Aren't you as bold as brass? Did I frighten you?

GERMAINE: Yes, you did. You always do.

LILIANE: There, there, I won't again. Though you know you adore being frightened, don't you — ? Don't you know it? . . .

MARCEL: . . . When M. Vinteuil died Mamma attended his funeral, and I, too young for participation in the obsequies of Combray, watched from behind the window blinds as the cortège wound through the streets to the church of Saint-Hilaire.

(*Tolling of bell*)

It was a wintry day, though the leaves had barely yellowed and the chrysanthemums in our garden were still as stiff and sparkling against the darkness of the hedge as the whites of eggs whipped up by Françoise. The sunlight, flickering up and down as if someone were turning the wick of a lamp, showed me the sullen, freckled face of Mademoiselle Vinteuil as she passed in the first carriage, the black veil pushed back from her forehead as though she needed the air, across her shoulders the little rusty shawl I had so often seen her father carefully arrange for her, when he thought the wind was cold. She had the obstinate look of a child driven to visit a relation who bores her, who lives, perhaps, in a stuffy room and whose body exudes the sickly floral odour of decay or of those liquorice sweets whose blackness is concealed beneath a tesselation of violet sugar. Her friend did not seem to be with her, or at least, I did not see her; but behind the cortège walked M. Swann, his tall hat in his hand, the bitter light slanting on to his stiff reddish hair, now touched with grey, his head bowed in respect for the passing of a neighbour with whom he had scarcely exchanged a word from one year's end to another.

(*The bell fades*)

It was perhaps a month after the funeral that Mamma came to us with news.

MOTHER OF MARCEL: (*Fading in*) It really is most surprising, one can live almost next door to somebody for years and not know anything about them at all!

FATHER OF MARCEL: Come along, what's all this? What revelations have you had from the local sibyls? For I see you're carrying your new sunshade, you must have been paying calls.

MOTHER: Oh, my dear, I didn't hear this on my rounds! I was just coming home when I saw Monsieur and Madame Swann coming in the opposite direction, so I crossed over and pretended I hadn't seen them, because really it is impossible to countenance such a marriage, even though their little girl is getting very pretty —

FATHER: To the point, to the point! Marcel here will never learn to order his thoughts unless you set him a better example.

MOTHER: My dear, I wish you would let me tell things in my own way. Well, then: I'd just passed them and was going into Galopin's for some cakes when M. Swann caught up with me, and told me he'd just discovered that *our* Vinteuil was the very man who wrote the famous sonata we've heard so much about!

What do you think of that? Talk of hiding one's light under a bushel!

FATHER: Was Swann sure of this?

MOTHER: Oh, perfectly— and so excited! It seems that we've had a great man in our midst all this time without knowing it —

FATHER: Now, my dear girl, 'great's' a great word!

MOTHER: — and when I think of him, always looking so shabby, so distressed about his daughter and that dreadful girl —

FATHER: Hush! Little pitchers —

MOTHER: I only meant . . . well, so boisterous, such a tomboy, M. Vinteuil was always so quiet. . . .

MARCEL: M. Vinteuil, living and dying in his quietness and disappointment, flouted by his beloved daughter, knowing too well, perhaps, the charitable and exculpatory contempt with which he was regarded by his neighbours in Combray, might well have considered his life a failure, have considered his single work, known only, even at that time, to an esoteric few, too frail a thing to weigh against the sorrows that had hung about him, umbrageous, lightless and as parasitical as the ivy upon his own walls which, as time went by, was slowly crumbling the masonry as the grief of love despised was crumbling the old man's life away. It was not until many years later, when, as a young man, I spent a few days with Madame Verdurin at her country house, La Raspelière, that I first heard of the possibility that the sonata might not be the composer's sole memorial.

I was sitting with Albertine in the drawing-room, where poppies and grasses arranged in vases along the window-ledges by the tasteful hand of the Mistress made a brilliant frieze against the strong, hypnotic blue of the summer sea, and were echoed, as by the double exposure of an inexpert photographer, in the glazing of a youthful painting by Elstir of poppies and cornflowers in a meadow stroked downward by a strong breeze. . . .

(*The noise of general conversation*)

MME VERDURIN: (*Breaking in*) Well? Well? Aren't the young ladies down yet?

COTTARD: Young ladies? Who? What? Has anyone else arrived? No one ever told me.

MME VERDURIN: Really, Doctor, for a Prince of Science you can be a perfect booby! I meant His Majesty and Charlie, of course!

COTTARD: Oh, oh, oh, the Baron and Morel! I see. Yes, they are late! It must be nearly mid-day.

MME VERDURIN: Well, young man? I hope you slept well? And our little Albertine, who looks this morning exactly like a Persian kitten?

ALBERTINE: I slept marvellously, thank you, Madame!

MME VERDURIN: I was so afraid you wouldn't, being next door to Morel and Charlus. The noise might have disturbed you. I know they often like to have a little music when we're all in bed.

COTTARD: Music? Hah! (*Snorts with mirth*) That's a good one!

BRICHOT: Well, didn't the illustrious Bard of Avon, the inexhaustible Shakespeare — or Shagsper, he never seemed to know his own name — remark that music was the food of — (*With mock embarrassment*) Excuse me.

MME VERDURIN: No, no, Professor, if you are going to be so mischievous we shan't excuse you at all! You shall stand with your face to the wall and have no luncheon. A pity, because we are to enjoy some superb little *bouchées à la reine* —

(*The door opens*)

Oh, good-morning, my friends! I was really beginning to think you'd made a suicide pact up there. I nearly sent for the police.

(*Others murmur 'Good-morning'*)

CHARLUS: One might perhaps consider suicide on being compelled to leave your delightful home, Madame, but surely never with the prospect before one of remaining there, if only for a single day.

MME VERDURIN: Why, Charlus, you're becoming quite a courtier!

MOREL: Good-morning, Madame — Mademoiselle — Dr Cottard —'morning, Marcel, I didn't see you. Sorry, I'm sure. (*Yawns*)

CHARLUS: Well, young slugabed! Don't stand there yawning like that! If you must yawn, Charlie, have the decency to put your hand over your mouth.

MOREL: Honestly, Mémé, I'm worn out, I didn't have much of a night.

COTTARD: Practising your music, eh? Ha, ha! I bet that's what it was.

ALBERTINE: I'm sure M. Morel should have no need to practise, after playing so wonderfully to us last night.

MOREL: Oh, but it wasn't first-rate, Mademoiselle. As a matter of fact, Mémé kept me up for hours going on and on about my faults.

CHARLUS: I was just like an old governess with him, you may believe it or not! I felt like Madame de Warens, I nearly had this young Rousseau across my knee. It was quite preposterous, I do assure you.

COTTARD: To make him 'rue so', eh? Ha! That's not a bad one, I must remember to tell my wife that.

ALBERTINE: But M. Morel seemed to me perfect, especially in the Vinteuil! I do so adore it.

MOREL: I'm sick of playing it these days, I can tell you. People always want it, and I'm beginning to think it's on the syrupy side.

MME VERDURIN: So that's what you were thinking, were you, that appalling heresy? And you stood there looking as though you were thinking about God!

CHARLUS: (*Eagerly*) Yes, didn't he? When he tossed his head back and gazed up to Heaven, one could have sworn he was Verrocchio's Tobias, gazing at the angel.

BRICHOT: (*Boringly*) You mention Verrocchio; now it's an extraordinary thing about Verrocchio. When one contrasts the power, one might even say the brutality, of a piece of statuary like his Bartolommeo Colleoni with the almost motherly sentiment of the paintings —

MME VERDURIN: Nobody wants to talk about painting this morning, Professor. It's a beautiful day and we're all going to be quite simple, like peasants. We shall probably go for a picnic on the cliffs and Charlie Morel shall play for us again, just to show us he's profited by the Baron's instruction.

ALBERTINE: What a pity it is Vinteuil wrote so little! There's only the sonata, isn't there?

CHARLUS: Well, I did hear it rumoured that his daughter and a certain friend of hers — *honi soit qui mal y pense* — are trying to decipher a manuscript he left behind him. If so, it would be an event.

ALBERTINE: (*Breaking in*) Oh, then she must have told M. Morel —

CHARLUS: I beg your pardon? You were saying . . . ?

ALBERTINE: Nothing. I don't know what I was going to say.

MME VERDURIN: If it's true, Morel shall be the first to play it, at my house! And you shall all be invited, all my little clan, all my children —

CHARLUS: A moment, please.

MME VERDURIN: I beg your pardon?

CHARLUS: One moment. You should think before you speak, Madame. Worthy as your 'little clan' undoubtedly is, a new work by Vinteuil would be, perhaps, too overwhelming for so intimate — I might say so domestic — an audience. No! You must let *me* arrange such an evening and permit me to issue my *ukase* against the tedious, the tone-deaf, and the merely ridiculous. You shall lend your house, Madame — that will be your privilege. We shall have the cream of the Faubourg to listen to Charlie — in itself an honour for which they should crawl along the gutters on their hands and knees — to listen to Charlie playing sublimely a work so sublime that even my patron, the glorious Archangel Michael, would give his wing-feathers for a card of invitation.

MME VERDURIN: But Baron — surely as hostess I should have the right —

CHARLUS: Nonsense. You'll have people fighting to enter your house who would otherwise never set foot there, not in a million years — surely that's enough for you? Let's see, now: not the Molé. She's a fool.

MME VERDURIN: But surely the Comtesse Molé —

CHARLUS: (*Going straight on*) My cousin Oriane, if you will — she's a fool too, but she has a certain *instinct*. The Queen of Naples certainly — now there's a good little woman if you like, simple but cultivated — the Duchesse de Duras, yes . . . conceivably the Princesse de Parme, at least she won't fidget or applaud in all the wrong places, she'll have the decency to watch what the others do —

COTTARD: Present company accepted? A — double C — epted? Ha! That's not bad! Shall we be accepted? I hope so.

MME VERDURIN: But you are the Faithful, my own disciples — could there be any question?

CHARLUS: I think we had better make no hard and fast promises until the time comes. If it does come.

MOREL: If there is a new work; it may all be a *canard*. By George, I'd like to be on to it, though!

CHARLUS: If, as you say, there is. We must wait and see. . . .

(*Pause. Rustling of paper. Liliane humming beginning of Septet. She goes to piano, tries it out, stumbles, mutters, 'Muddle-headed idiot'. The door opens*)

GERMAINE: Liliane! You really must come to bed, you'll be good for nothing in the morning. Do you know it's past one o'clock?

LILIANE: Oh, leave me alone! This is difficult enough, without you creeping around and interfering. Why the old fool couldn't have written his stuff decently *I* don't know.

GERMAINE: Darling, you're looking as white as death. You can't go on like this.

LILIANE: We said we'd do it, didn't we? We'll rescue his damned septet if it kills us. Besides, I've just found something. You know the passage we couldn't place, the one on the loose half-sheet? Well, I've placed it now. He's quoted the sonata — only a few bars — and this is how he leads it in. Listen.

(*Goes to piano. Germaine gives a shriek. Liliane stops playing*)

LILIANE: *Now* what's the matter?

GERMAINE: Oh, there's a huge moth — you know I can't bear them — oh, do kill it, please!

LILIANE: Don't be a fool. It'll beat itself to death on the lamp if you wait long enough.

GERMAINE: (*Hysterically*) Oh, no, no, no — it will fly in my face — keep it away, I hate it! Don't let it near me!

LILIANE: What's the fuss about? Do you think it's the old man's ghost?

GERMAINE: Oh, please, oh darling, I can't bear it!

LILIANE: It may be his ghost, of course. . . . Well, Vinteuil, there's no need for you to haunt us! We're both working like slaves as it is, trying to salvage your miserable wreck. . . . *Got you!*

GERMAINE: Where?

LILIANE: In my hand, fluttering like fury. Can you imagine a moth's heart beating? A great, grey, thudding, furry heart?

GERMAINE: How can you! I don't know how you can!

LILIANE: Open the window wide, will you?

GERMAINE: Oh, do be careful, don't let it go again —

(*Sound of the window opening*)

LILIANE: Be off with you! There he flies. Good-bye, ghost. Look

at him, flying right into the moon. He thinks it's another lamp.
— You can take your hands from your eyes now, my chicken,
Liliane has saved you. Diddums, diddums, what a coward it is!

GERMAINE: Well, they make me shudder. Do come to bed now.

LILIANE: Oh, all right. (*Yawns*) And don't stand there looking so
pretty or I shall smack you.

GERMAINE: Don't think I don't realise — all you're doing for me.
I am grateful, darling, I am indeed.

LILIANE: Not for you, for him. (*Slowly and coldly*) What do you
suppose *you* matter?

GERMAINE: (*Bewildered*) But darling — darling — you just
said —

LILIANE: Oh, I adore you, you can be sure of that. But that
doesn't make you *matter*. *He* — yes, your fool of a papa, with
ash and dottle strewn all over him and half his food on his disgusting waistcoat — *he* was a genius.

GERMAINE: Yet the things you said — you made me do — even
after he was dead. . . .

LILIANE: Just to show you whom you belonged to. To me. But
I admit we owe him something. And if we've shown any dis-
respect for the immortal memory — aren't we making up for
it now? Do you understand?

GERMAINE: Yes, yes, I do. I think I do. But you must sleep late
in the morning. I'll get up and try to make a fair copy of all this.

LILIANE: I'm sticking at it till it's done. We shall both stick at it.
(*With an exhausted, almost-hysterical laugh*) 'Danton, no weakness!'

GERMAINE: But leave it *now*. I can hardly prop my eyes open —

LILIANE: In a minute, in a minute. There's something I want you
to hear first. Listen. . . .

(*Liliane at the piano: plays the 7 note phrase: she repeats
latter several times. Music continues till the end of first
paragraph below*)

MARCEL: Through the aching hours of the summer evenings, of the stock-scented nights, the lamps burned in a window at Montjouvain where Mademoiselle Vinteuil and her friend, painfully, with a devotion as rough and stubborn as that of a medical saint towards his bone-white isle of lepers, were building from the scraps, the jottings, the scribblings, the doubtful erasures, the scarcely-legible emendations left by the dead man, a work seeded from the sorrow they had caused him and from the scattered joys his daughter had casually bestowed upon him; a work which, because the slightest joy had been for him sufficient compensation for the most loaded, the most marmoreal of griefs, was to assume the lustre and lineaments of a triumph.

After the revelation of M. de Charlus that morning at La Raspelière my thoughts turned throughout the day upon Vinteuil's daughter as I had known her in my childhood, driving with her friend through Combray, her cheeks stung by the air to scarlet beneath the hawthorn powdering of freckles, her large clean hands holding the reins with the casualness and control of a milk-boy, her hair fired like October bracken by the morning sun. I fell asleep imagining that she had stopped to speak to me — which she had never done, beyond the barest salutation — and suddenly awoke to find that dawn was breaking,

(The crowing of a cock, the noise of birds)

that Mademoiselle Vinteuil was still leaning down to me, the fragrance of her breath upon my face. For a moment I stared at her in bewilderment; then I realised that it was not she, but Albertine, who was now drawing a tentative finger along my cheek, and realised also that the dream had put into my mind a certain question which I must not fail to ask her.

ALBERTINE: Is my little Marcel awake?

MARCEL: Only just awake.

ALBERTINE: You were looking at me as though I were quite a stranger! Really, you can't guess how funny you looked!

MARCEL: I was dreaming.

ALBERTINE: Well, wake up now, because it's such a lovely morning! I adore being early in the country. What shall we do today? Unless Madame Verdurin has plans for us; I must say I wish she hadn't quite so many. Oh dear, I suppose I'd better go back to my own room, it would be dreadful if she caught us.

MARCEL: Extremely, my darling. — Don't move for a minute.

ALBERTINE: Why shouldn't I?

MARCEL: Close your eyes. I love to look at you when your eyes are shut.

ALBERTINE: How absurd you are! Well, then. (*Pause*) What do you see?

MARCEL: An innocent Albertine, with her plump cheeks smooth and pink in the innocent light and her throat made up of grains of golden corn.

(*Cock crows again*)

You hear that? Your throat is making the farmyard hungry for its breakfast.

ALBERTINE: Ugh! You are horrible. And I don't know why you should be so surprised if I look innocent. I really don't know what else you expect.

MARCEL: By the way — not that it matters in the least — what does Madame Verdurin say to you when she keeps you upstairs so long?

ALBERTINE: There you go again! Oh, we say all the things women do say, about our dresses, and the way we do our hair, and how stupid Madame Cottard can be —'

MARCEL: Does she tell you you are beautiful?

ALBERTINE: Well, you know she adores young people.

MARCEL: Of course. (*Pause*) I shouldn't be in the least surprised if she kissed you sometimes. I should think it quite natural.

ALBERTINE: (*Crossly*) Well, she doesn't. And a good thing, too, as she's always got a running cold from crying too much at her precious music. I'm going to get up.

MARCEL: But my darling, there would be no need to pretend, even if she did kiss you. I should think nothing of it at all —

ALBERTINE: Oh, wouldn't you? I know you better. You'd be jealous of a cat that sat on my lap. Oh, dear, I really *should* get up, but it's so nice here. . . .

MARCEL: It was now that I meant to put my question to Albertine, while she lay luxuriantly at my side, the early sun tipping with sparks of orange her long lashes and slipping like a goldfish into the undulations of her marvellous hair. . . .

ALBERTINE: (*Fading in*) . . . it was a day just like this when we played 'Ferret' on the cliffs at Combray, and you were so stupid — I never knew anyone more silly at games. Do you remember? (*Singing drowsily*)

> 'Il court, il court, le furet,
> Le furet du bois, mesdam,
> Il court, il court, le furet. . . .'

MARCEL: By the way, my darling —

ALBERTINE: (*Stops singing*) By the way, *what?* You really must make me get up, if I can't make myself do it.

MARCEL: Yesterday, when M. de Charlus was telling us about Vinteuil's new work, you started to say something and stopped.

ALBERTINE: Did I? Well, whatever it was, I don't remember now.

MARCEL: About Morel.

ALBERTINE: About Morel? Did I?

MARCEL: Now, my love, you must try to remember what it was, not that I imagine it's of the slightest importance, but because it is very bad for people not to organise their thoughts properly. Come now, think!

ALBERTINE: (*After a pause*) Oh, it wasn't anything. I was only

R

going to say it must have been Morel who found out about the new work.

MARCEL: But how? How could he? He never knew Mademoiselle Vinteuil, did he?

ALBERTINE: Well, you know I told you that *I* used to know her when I was quite a child — she and her friend used to play with me, and I called them my big sisters —

MARCEL: Go on.

ALBERTINE: I don't see why I should. You made such a silly fuss about it at the time, and you'll only start being stupid again, just when we're happy and enjoying ourselves.

MARCEL: I implore you to go on. Don't you see how your indecisions torment me? I know they mean nothing in themselves, but —

ALBERTINE: Well, you remember the actress Léa, whom I told you I'd met once? She was quite intimate — at one time, anyway — with Mademoiselle Vinteuil and her friend, and of course Léa and Morel know each other *very* well, and so — (*Lamely*) so I was only thinking that the news must have come to him through her.

MARCEL: Do you only suppose . . . or do you know?

ALBERTINE: Of course it was only a guess! I'd never heard of any new work before yesterday. I was as surprised as the rest of you.

MARCEL: (*After a pause*) Tell me, my darling, and don't be in the least alarmed, because I am not at all angry, in fact I never even think nowadays about your friendship with Mademoiselle Vinteuil — (*Pouncing*) Do you still see her?

ALBERTINE: (*Sorrowfully*) Oh, how on earth am I to see anybody, when you keep me all to yourself?

MARCEL: I thought *she* might have told you about the new work.

ALBERTINE: I tell you, I never set eyes on her!

MARCEL: Or Léa? You went to the theatre with Andrée last month. Did you meet her then?

ALBERTINE: You know it was *Tartuffe*. Léa doesn't play Molière!

MARCEL: And you were at the theatre again, just before that —

ALBERTINE: Oh, stop, stop, stop! I won't have you driving me mad and upsetting yourself. What you ought to do is to try and write something. A little work would do you good, and keep you from being so silly.

MARCEL: (*Sadly*) I shall never write again. I know it. I've wasted my life.

ALBERTINE: What nonsense! It will all come back again, you'll see. I'm going to put you to shame by taking out my sketch-book.

(*Cock crows, farther off*)

MARCEL: I have wasted my life.

SWANN: (*An echo*) To think that I have wasted my life, that I have longed for death, that the greatest love I have ever known has been for a woman who did not please me, who was not in my style!

MARCEL: Like Vinteuil, like myself, Swann had been filled with a sense of utter failure, of utter loss. As we shall see later, only he, perhaps, was right in that instinct, since he left behind him nothing but the essence of himself; yet that was indeed immortal, in so far as those who loved him were immortal and were able to preserve his fragrance and his beauty for those to come, who had never known him; as I myself, because I loved you, dear Charles Swann, was able to fetter you in Time, to endure as long as my work shall endure, or that painting by Tissot in which you stand, tall, graceful and urbane, in a moment of your unblemished springtime, the Swann I never knew, still young, still beautiful, in the adrenal torments and delights of love. . . .

(*Odette playing and singing Pauvres Fous*)

ODETTE: 'And I whisper, Poor Fools!
                           O whither away?
                           For death comes all too swiftly.'

SWANN: You sing that charmingly, Odette. But you never seem to sing anything else these days. I wonder why?

ODETTE: Why shouldn't I? I adore it. Anyway, it's all the rage.

SWANN: It would be quite natural for you to sing it so often, of course, if it had sentimental associations for you. (*Pause*) Has it, by any chance?

ODETTE: There you go again.

SWANN: What do you mean, my darling?

ODETTE: You know. Imagining things.

SWANN: But I only asked a natural question. I was simply interested to know why you should like such a trivial little thing. It's only that I'm interested to know *why* people do things — it's of academic interest, that's all.

ODETTE: You can take your academic questions to Brichot, he's the one for that sort of thing. Now stop frowning, and be nice to me. Do you like my fuchsias? They're like tiny little cardinals, don't you think, in their purple and red? — Oh, that reminds me.

SWANN: What reminds you?

ODETTE: Talking of Brichot. Listen, my darling, I really must entertain Madame Verdurin this summer, she's been so good to me. I thought if you'd let me take a little house, something quite modest, not too far away, say Rambouillet —

SWANN: Ah!

ODETTE: *Now* what is it?

SWANN: I suppose you don't intend that I shall join you there?

(*Pause*)

ODETTE: Well, you haven't been very nice to her, and it might be embarrassing —

SWANN: Listen to me, Odette. I am not going to establish you, without me, at Rambouillet or anywhere else!

ODETTE: Don't then. I know somebody who will help me with pleasure, and without any scowling or glowering or swearing.

SWANN: Who's that?

(Odette hums Pauvres Fous)

SWANN: Who's that, I say? Will you stop that singing and look at me! *(Change of tone)* . . . Odette.

ODETTE: *(Demurely)* Yes?

SWANN: The way you are looking at me —

ODETTE: How is that?

SWANN: You take my heart and twist it until I can't refuse you anything. *(Passionately)* My own darling — there's nobody else really? Is there?

ODETTE: No, no, I was only teasing because you were being so disagreeable. . . . Now you are crushing my fuchsias quite to death. As if you haven't already terrified them —

SWANN: Let me unpin them. . . . There. . . . I haven't hurt you, have I? Tell me if I'm hurting you?

(Odette gives a gasp of laughter)

What's the matter?

ODETTE: So like our cattleyas. Do you remember?

SWANN: *(Thickly)* Do you think I could forget? Just kiss me, and then look at me again like that, and you shall have your wretched house and anything else you want in the world.

(Long kiss)

ODETTE: Now you are being nice to me, more like my own little Charles. You know you won't miss me, you've got your work to do, I should only be in the way. You can stay quietly here and finish your precious book on Vermeer.

SWANN: We have an extraordinary love, you and I — isn't that so, my darling? And it makes us extraordinary too. We shall never be like other people, stale or tired or bored: but always as we are now — close your eyes, I shall drown in those great eyes — always as we are now. . . .

(The Vinteuil Sonata: piano)

ODETTE: *(An echo)* That old thing! It's so hackneyed nowadays. Really, if she can't follow a simple recipe she'll have to go.

SWANN: *(Echo)* Because if he is, he ought to help financially.

ODETTE: *(Echo)* Who?

SWANN: *(Echo)* The composer Vinteuil, of course.

ODETTE: *(Echo)* Well, I don't suppose he's any relation at all. Isn't this pudding horrible? . . .

(Their voices fade. Music comes to an end)

MARCEL: It is commonplace to reflect that even the most passionate love must, with time and with propinquity, be drained of its radiance as the radiance is drained from a painted wall when a cloud passes over the sun and the sun itself drops into the crumbling cinders of the night: less commonplace to reflect that there may be, as precious exceptions, loves that fall, not into darkness, but into a glow gentle and steadfast as the eternal lamp behind the unattainable windows of the past. There were moments when, indeed, I felt that such a miracle might be achieved by Albertine and myself; when I was filled with joy to think that a useless, an uncreative life, such as I recognised my own to be, was a trivial price to pay for so godlike a felicity; but alas, such moments were few, and with their passing I felt a wretched astonishment that they could ever have entered into my experience, or into the experience of any man. They were not, however, by any means outside the experience of M. de Charlus, who for many years nourished the illusion that he was truly loved and that the adoration of Morel would burn with a sacred oil to warm the bones of his old age. . . .

(Noises of the street. Footsteps)

CHARLUS: . . . You, my young Marcel, who are so sensitive for a man of your years, who have the soul of the artist, which is of necessity, one would say axiomatically, the soul of a man rather than that of a brute, you are sure to have observed how affectionate Charlie has become these days, how grateful for any little favours I am able to bestow upon him, how truly like a son!

MARCEL: It's pleasant to see, sir.

CHARLUS: Pleasant, you little rascal? Is that all you can say? If I drew your attention to the *Tempesta* of Giorgione, the *Adoration of the Lamb* by the great Van Eyck, would you merely observe that it was pleasant? (*Chuckles*) I must withdraw my commendation of your artistic soul.

MARCEL: I'm glad to see you so cheerful.

CHARLUS: Well, well, even to an old fellow like myself, no longer a beauty, I assure you they won't make me Queen of the May — there are moments when life is good. Here is a majestic sunset above the most noble of rivers, here is all the perfume of every spring evening since the world began, and here we are on the way to Madame Verdurin's to meet Charlie and to discuss the most magnificent musical project since *Tristan*.

MARCEL: (*Eagerly*) It's true, then? About the septet?

CHARLUS: Mademoiselle Vinteuil herself put the score into Charlie's hands last night. Her work of filial piety is complete, and you and I, my boy, are on the eve of musical history. By the way —

MARCEL: Yes, sir?

CHARLUS: Mother Verdurin will be furious. By Jove, we shall see a sight! *Donner und blitzen!* The eruption of Mont Pélé will be a popped champagne cork beside it. I've cut her list of guests in half. You must stand by me, now, when I make the announcement. Such rag-tag-and-bobtail! Imagine whom she wanted to invite! Poor Swann's widow, that absurd whore who married Forcheville; we might as soon invite La Goulue! And some nobodies from the Civil Service called Bontemps, and a draggle-tailed old trot with an implausible foreign title — faugh! We should have to fumigate. Charlie would have to drop his fiddle and run around spraying sulphur — that would be a fine thing, eh? It's bad enough to have the Mistress herself present, it'll send Oriane's eyebrows up into her hair — but to invite demireps and Hottentots and the Tribes of Israel and the lavatory woman from the Champs Elysées —

MARCEL: (*Laughs aloud*)

CHARLUS: That amuses you, eh? But then, you have no social responsibility, no traditions. You may perhaps fail to comprehend the enormity of the Verdurin presumption. I myself shall make it clear to her. But here we are: Quai Conti: and here is Charlie, a perfect Bronzino, one would say, waiting impatiently for my coming!

MOREL: (*Off-hand*) Oh, hullo, Mémé, hullo Marcel. I say, I shan't be able to stay long to-night. I've got an algebra lesson.

CHARLUS: You have a — a what?

MOREL: An algebra lesson. . . . Well, what's queer about that? A man like me wants to improve his intellect. After all, mathematics and music are pretty closely allied.

CHARLUS: But — but — an *algebra* lesson? At half-past nine at night?

MOREL: It's the only time I can get the tuition. I'll be going three nights a week, so don't count on me too much, Mémé.

CHARLUS: If I'd known you wanted to learn algebra, I could have arranged for a tutor at my house — it would be far more convenient! You must allow me to arrange it for you —

MOREL: (*Impatiently*) Oh, it's too late now, everything's settled. Anyway, I hate being bothered once I've made my own plans. . . . (*Fade*)

MARCEL: It was pitiable to see M. Charlus torn between his frantic desire not to be deprived of Charlie's company and his self-protective desire to believe in the obvious fiction of the algebra lesson, a fiction almost insulting in its crudity, as though Morel had not even paid his patron the compliment of inventing a plausible excuse for escape. The Baron was silent as we entered Madame Verdurin's house, as he gave up his hat and stick to the footman, as he bowed to his host and hostess; but in a few moments his irrepressible desire to tease and to frustrate the Mistress had restored some of his spirits. . . .

(A hubbub of protest from Monsieur and Madame Verdurin)

M. VERDURIN: ⎫ But how shall we explain it to our friends?
MME VERDURIN: ⎭ What will they say when they read the newspapers?

M. VERDURIN: You really can't expect us, Baron, much as we respect you and bow to your opinion —

CHARLUS: I expect you to do nothing but to observe my wishes. You are — this is a simple matter of fact, and no reflection upon yourselves personally — not in society: it is hardly conceivable that you would have either the experience or the range of acquaintanceship needed for the organising of so important an occasion —

MME VERDURIN: But surely nobody would object to Madame de Saint-Euverte? Why, she goes everywhere —

CHARLUS: Do you wish to turn your house into a cloaca for the reception of such pitiful chronics as the Marquise? If you do, you'll have all the guests holding their noses and struggling to get out into God's pure and uncontaminated air. Besides, she's a mental defective. No, no, certainly not! If she is invited, I shall not attend; and Morel will certainly refuse to play. His olfactory system is of the most delicate.

MME VERDURIN: Oh, very well, then. But —

CHARLUS: No 'buts', if you please! We are here to discuss the first performance of a divine masterpiece, and you prattle of Saint-Euvertes!

M. VERDURIN: I am sure that music comes first with my wife. Nevertheless —

CHARLUS: 'But', 'but', 'even so', 'nevertheless'— shall we never make an end of it? Let us, the privileged, sit in silence while Morel gives us a taste of the heavenly joys in store for us. And as we listen, let us humbly thank the Almighty for the honour He is bestowing upon us, and beseech Him to pardon us for the littleness of our mortal minds which, in the presence of genius, can contemplate sharing that genius with ennobled drabs who would be hard put to it to gain admission even to the short-time houses of the Batignolles.

(Morel at the piano sketches out fragments of Septet, and 'Bell' motif

MARCEL: As Morel, seated at the piano, admitted me still further into the strange land that Mademoiselle Vinteuil and her friend had reclaimed from the Dead Sea of the past, a land half-terrestrial, half-marine, where the fauna of a new earth struggled to free itself from the innocent and tenacious efflorescence of coral and anemone, I found it as hard to adjust myself to its strangeness as I had found it to adjust myself to the strangeness of Berma, a little Phèdre made of the purest coral on the floor of an ocean of emerald and chrysoprase. A cold atmosphere, soaked in rain, electric, changed at every moment, obliterating the empurpled promise of the Dawn. At noon, however, beneath a scorching though transitory sun, it appeared to fulfil itself in a dull, almost rustic bliss in which the peal of clanging, racing bells seemed to materialise the coarsest joy.

(Marcel stops speaking while Morel plays)

MARCEL: To be honest, this joyous motive did not appeal to me, I found it almost ugly, its rhythm dragged so laboriously along the ground that one might have succeeded in imitating almost everything that was essential to it merely by making a noise, sounds, by the tapping of drumsticks upon a table. . . .

(Morel plays for a few seconds more: stops abruptly)

MOREL: Well, that's the core of it. But I can't give you much. The orchestration's sublime, like nothing you've ever heard. You want to hear a certain little passage for flute and violin — you've no idea how fine it is.

CHARLUS: You gave us your impression marvellously, my dear boy, marvellously. One can't speak, yet. This is no time for words.

(High, moaning sobs)

Madame? Are you not feeling well?

MME VERDURIN: *(Between sobs)* Oh, how can I feel well, when he's made me weep so? You might all have known how it would torment me, that it would make me ill for weeks — *(Continues to sob)*

M. VERDURIN: There, there, Sidonie, we are all here to console you. Take my handkerchief. Really, Baron, I almost think we should have forbidden my wife to be present. We have been kind only to be cruel.

MME VERDURIN: *(Still snuffling)* I must see Cottard, I must tell him that Rhino-Gomenol is no use, he must *personally* come and grease my nose for me if I am ever again to be submitted to such an experience. Oh, Vinteuil, Vinteuil, if you knew what you had done to your discoverer, to your loyal patron, you would weep beyond the grave! I shall go and lie down.

M. VERDURIN: In a darkened room, my dear. And no one shall disturb you. If you will permit me, gentlemen, I shall escort my wife and return to you later, when perhaps she herself will be sufficiently recovered to take a further part in our deliberations.

MME VERDURIN: Yes, yes, help me away. . . .

(Her snufflings fade as the Verdurins go to the door. The door opens and closes. Pause)

CHARLUS: What an egregious fool that woman is! But never mind, Charlie. You shall have a superb triumph before the entire nobility of France and Navarre, and I shall see that you obtain your Legion of Honour. What do you say to that, young Chevalier? Will he be grateful to his old friend, who never did him more harm than perhaps to tweak his cherub's ear? Eh? Will he?

MOREL: (*Eagerly*) I say, Mémé, can you really do that? Get me the ribbon?

CHARLUS: Ah, but you'll have to practise hard, be a good little boy, make Paganini by comparison into a performer on the musical saw. No time for algebra, not a minute! You shall stay with me and practise your fingers to the bone. No more non-sense about $a^2 - b^2 = (a + b)$ times $(a - b)$. Vinteuil plus Morel equals Perfection, that's what it's to be. Well? What do you say? What do you say?

(*His voice dies away*)

MARCEL: His ruse (that of tempting Morel with a scarlet ribbon as one might tempt a donkey with a carrot on the end of a stick) proving successful, M. de Charlus was instantly irradiated with joy, the colour springing up like patches of rouge beneath the rice-powder on his cheeks. But his joy was to prove short-lived; since it was the insolence of the guests he had so carefully selected towards their hostess that brought about his down-fall.

(*Noise of party: greetings in response to Charlus*)

CHARLUS: Good evening, Mademoiselle de la Tour du Pin d'Auvergne. Good evening, Madame de Duras, is the Duke with you? I hope his arthritis isn't so troublesome — oh, good evening, Eliane, how magnificent you look, good evening Châtellerault, I'm glad to see you're cultivating a taste for finer things. . . . (*Sotto voce*) Splendid, ain't it, Marcel? I feel just like 'a few words in the vestry'— Ah, good evening, Madame de Quercy ... good evening, Madame de Reveillon — oh, good evening, my dear Oriane! — In violet velvet! One would say, Pope Joan!

DUCHESSE DE GUERMANTES: Mémé, how nice to see you, one finds you in the oddest places nowadays, they tell me. And my dear Marcel! How are you? Do tell me, which is Mother Verdurin? Do point her out to me ... *that* one? But she looks quite a respectable sort of person!

(Talk between Duchesse de Guermantes, Marcel and Charlus grows fainter)

DUCHESSE DE GUERMANTES: But I hear this is to be a stupendous event!

CHARLUS: You will hear Morel at his most amazing, I assure you, you've no idea — My dear cousin, you're holding up the queue. ...

MME VERDURIN: *(Simultaneously with above)* Gustave! Did you hear that? Oh, how revolting! How disgraceful! In my own house!

M. VERDURIN: Calm yourself, Sidonie, calm yourself, my dear.

MME VERDURIN: This is all Charlus's doing! Treating me like a cypher in my own drawing-room, I, who have given my life to art —

M. VERDURIN: Never mind. His turn is to come. ...

CHARLUS: It's refreshing to see you again, your Majesty. Oriane — the Queen wants a chat with you.

DUCHESSE DE GUERMANTES: Well, Ma'am, how delicious to see you after such ages! I didn't know Mémé had such a treat in store for us.

QUEEN OF NAPLES: My dear Oriane, you look charming and quite ridiculously young. Is Basin with you?

DUCHESSE DE GUERMANTES: Oh, he's somewhere about, Ma'am, looking as solemn as a sexton because he's going to hear some

new music. He's terrified of anything after *La Traviata,* he
thinks it's going to bite him.

QUEEN OF NAPLES: Charlus, would you be so kind as to make
my hostess known to me?

CHARLUS: Hostess . . . oh yes, certainly, my dear cousin: now
where the devil's she got to? Ah, she's just coming this way.
(*Raising his voice*) Madame! One moment, if you please.

MME VERDURIN: Did you speak to me Baron?

CHARLUS: Her Majesty the Queen of Naples desires me to present
you to her.

MME VERDURIN: (*Overwhelmed*) Oh! Your Majesty!

CHARLUS: May I have the honour to present, Ma'am, Madame
Verdurin, our hostess this evening. M. Verdurin.

M. VERDURIN: Your Majesty.

QUEEN OF NAPLES: I am so pleased that you should have invited
me, Madame. It was very kind. I am looking forward to hearing
delightful music in such a delightful house.

MME VERDURIN: You overwhelm me, Ma'am. I hope you may
enjoy your visit to my Temple of Music, as I dare to call it.

QUEEN OF NAPLES: But I'm sure I shall! Everything looks so
pretty that I am enjoying myself already.

(*Chatter rises*)

MME VERDURIN: Gustave, did you hear that? How simple and
unaffected she was? There's the difference between the true
Blood Royal and upstarts like the wretched Charlus and his
friends! I expect if the truth were known, half these precious
Duchesses are on the books of the police!

M. VERDURIN: My dear, she appreciated you *at once*; I saw it in
her face. She has the true instinct: one might almost say that
she would be 'one of us'. I wonder if *she* guesses what kind of a
creature Charlus is. . . .

CHARLUS: Good-evening, Sosthène, good-evening, Madame de
Silistrie, good-evening, my dear Gilbert, how's your cold? You

want to wrap up, these chilly nights. . . . Hostess? Oh — she was here a minute ago. Don't bother yourself, you can meet her later.

MME VERDURIN: Somebody else shall learn what kind of a creature he is, before this hateful evening is over. Mind you get hold of Charlie the *minute* the music's over, and tell Brichot to keep the Baron out of the way till we're ready. . . .

(Pause)

BRICHOT: You want me to talk to Charlus? *(Puzzled)* Well, of course a command from the Mistress is a ukase, but I hardly need a ukase to engage in converse with a man of such wide culture, not *stupor mundi*, perhaps, we must guard against exaggeration, but *stupor Lutetiae* indeed, who honours me by attending my humble lectures at the Sorbonne —

M. VERDURIN: That's all right, that's all right, we have our reasons, but don't you let him go until my wife tips you the wink.

(Noise of party rising)

MARCEL: Madame —

MME VERDURIN: What is it, Marcel? I can't talk to anybody now. I'm too strung-up. God knows how I shall get through this evening!

MARCEL: I only wanted to know — are the composer's daughter and her friend to be here to-night?

MME VERDURIN: No, they were detained in the country. I expected them to attend the rehearsal this afternoon — I'd just asked my family and all the miscellaneous bores, I couldn't have them crowding in here to-night — but they never came.

MARCEL: One would suppose, after their devotion to Vinteuil's memory, that they would wish to hear the first performance of his septet.

MME VERDURIN: If you ask me, their consciences overcame them.

They treated him like brutes, I'm told, when he was alive —
and whether he can appreciate their work of expiation *now* is
for theologians to decide.

BRICHOT: I say, strung-up or not, the Mistress is in good form, eh,
don't you think so, my young friend?

MARCEL: But Madame, it does seem so strange —

MME VERDURIN: Quiet, you! The musicians are coming in. I'll
talk to you later. If you remind me, I'll have something to tell
you about Mademoiselle Vinteuil and your little cousin. . . .

MARCEL: About Albertine!

MME VERDURIN: Sh-h-h!

*(Noise dwindles: silence. Applause as musicians appear on
the dais. The Vinteuil Septet begins)*

MARCEL: The Mistress sat stoically among her guests, not hiding
her face, but with head held high presenting a contemptuous
and stony countenance, as if to say, 'I, only I among you all,
know what music is', while she contemplated in her heart, perhaps, the 'execution' of M. de Charlus who, in his innocence,
stood with his longing gaze fastened upon Morel. Beside him,
still glowing, still golden, her piercing blue eyes taking a shade
of softness from the violet of her gown, Madame de Guermantes permitted herself a slight, secret, transient smile as if she
would let the world know that for her this new work of Vinteuil had delicious overtones, imperceptible by the commonalty
(Music fades) while the Duchesse de Duras contented herself
by staring at the impassive form of the Mistress as at some re-
constructed animal of prehistoric times exhibited in a glass case
at the World's Fair.

In a while I succumbed once again to the music. Vinteuil's
sonata, and, as I was to find later on, his other works as well,
had been no more than timid essays, exquisite but slight, towards the triumphant and complete masterpiece which was re-

vealed to me at this moment. At the conclusion of the *andante*, Madame de Guermantes crept to my side.

(*Subdued talk breaks out, excited, appreciative*)

DUCHESSE DE GUERMANTES: (*In a hoarse whisper*) It's fine, eh? What poor Swann would have given to have heard it? Do you suppose Mother Verdurin will put my name in the papers tomorrow? I shall never hold up my head again.

(*Talk fades. Rustling. Silence. The Septet continues: Variations on 'Petite Phrase', the 'Bell Theme,' and Conclusion*)

MARCEL: The septet had begun again and was moving towards its close: again and again one phrase or another from the sonata recurred, but always changed, its rhythm and harmony different, the same and yet something else, as things recur in life. Then this phrase broke up, was transformed, and became the mysterious appeal of the start. A phrase of a plaintive kind rose in opposition to it, but so profound, so vague, so internal, almost so organic and visceral that one could not tell at each of its repetitions whether they were those of a theme or of an attack of neuralgia. Presently these two motives were wrestling together — a wrestling match of energies only, to tell the truth. In the end the joyous motive was left triumphant, it was no longer an anxious appeal addressed to an empty sky, it was an ineffable joy which seemed to come from Paradise, a joy as different from that of the Sonata as from a grave and gentle angel by Bellini, playing the theorbo, would be some archangel by Mantegna sounding a trump.

(*Music comes to an end. Silence. Then prolonged applause. Through the applause*)

CHARLUS: Oh Charlie, Charlie, you were sublime — you deserve your ribbon, I shall see to it!

(*Chatter and applause rise higher*)

DUCHESSE DE GUERMANTES: Of course it's hard for most people to make up their minds about something new, ain't it? I adored it myself — what did you think, Ma'am?

(*Applause dies. Chatter high and loud*)

QUEEN OF NAPLES: Well, to tell you the truth, Oriane, I am afraid I am a little old-fashioned, I know what I like, as they say, but I never really know what I don't. . . .

DUCHESSE DE GUERMANTES: What about you, Madame de Duras?

DUCHESSE DE DURAS: (*A high, piercing voice, well dominating the chatter*) Oh well, it makes you think, doesn't it? I'm sure it's terribly clever. Do tell me, Oriane, do you think I can slip away without talking to the Verdigris, or whatever her name is? I promised I'd go on to the Tremoïlles.

MME VERDURIN: (*Whispering*) Oh, let them wait! Let them wait! Let Charlus wait!

QUEEN OF NAPLES: Madame.

MME VERDURIN: Your Majesty!

QUEEN OF NAPLES: I have come to say good-night, to thank you for your hospitality and for this feast of music that we have all been privileged to hear.

MME VERDURIN: Oh, Ma'am, my husband and I are more honoured than we can say by your kindness!

QUEEN OF NAPLES: I hope that I may have the pleasure of meeting you both again some day when I am in Paris. . . .

(*Her voice fades away*)

MME VERDURIN: (*Whispering*) You hear that, Gustave? The

Queen hopes to meet us again! Let Charlus put that in his pipe and smoke it!

M. VERDURIN: That gentleman will soon find out we don't need *his* social favours.

MME VERDURIN: And before this night's out he won't be in a position to bestow any, he'll be lucky if there's a single house willing to receive him. . . .

MARCEL: The Verdurins took their revenge upon M. de Charlus that night, taking Morel aside and informing him that his patron was making him a laughing-stock.

MME VERDURIN: (*Fading in*) I consider you cannot tolerate this sort of thing for another instant, you ought not to endure this degrading promiscuity with a tainted person whom nobody will have in her house —

MOREL: But why — why? I don't understand, I never dreamed —

MME VERDURIN: You are the talk of the Conservatoire. Another month of this life and your artistic future is shattered, whereas, without Charlus, you ought to be making at least a hundred thousand francs a year.

MOREL: But I have never heard anyone utter a word. I am astounded, very grateful to you —

MME VERDURIN: If you haven't heard anything, you're unique in that respect. He is a gentleman with a vile reputation, and the most shocking stories are told about him!

MOREL: (*Tearfully*) I don't know how to thank you. . . .

(*A silence*)

MARCEL: When M. de Charlus re-entered the drawing-room he came beaming down upon Morel, all in innocence of the snare that had been set for him.

CHARLUS: (*Fading in*) Well, are you satisfied, young glory, and presently young knight of the Legion of Honour? For very soon you will be able to sport your cross.

MOREL: (*Hysterically*) Leave me alone! I forbid you to come near me!

CHARLUS: Eh — eh — what?

MOREL: You know what I mean, all right! I'm not the first young man you've tried to corrupt!

CHARLUS: Charlie, Charlie, what are you saying?

MOREL: Men like you, they've only one idea, and that's to ruin artists. It's all over the Conservatoire, I tell you, they're sneering at me —

CHARLUS: But your cross, Charlie, your cross —

MOREL: Do you suppose I believe all that stuff? Didn't you tell the Verdurins you only wanted me to have it to please my uncle, and that my uncle was a *servant?*

CHARLUS: No, of course not, of course I didn't —

MOREL: You go and wallow in your own mire! I'm not going to be dragged down by you!

CHARLUS: Charlie —

MOREL: Keep away from me! Don't you come a step nearer, don't you dare. . . .

(His voice fades)

MARCEL: My sole consolation lay in the thought that I was about to see Morel and the Verdurins pulverised by M. de Charlus. Instead of which, an extraordinary thing happened. In a situation so cruelly unforeseen, this great talker could do no more than stammer —

CHARLUS: — What does it all mean? What has happened?

MARCEL: And the eternal pantomime of panic terror has so little altered, that this elderly gentleman, to whom a disagreeable incident had just occurred in a Paris drawing-room, unconsciously repeated the various formal attitudes in which the Greek sculptors of the earliest times symbolised the terror of nymphs pursued by the Great Pan.

But there was somebody who did overhear, and this was the Queen of Naples who, having left her fan behind, had thought it more polite to return for it in person. Seeing her opportunity to present Morel, Madame Verdurin came forward —

MME VERDURIN: I am Madame Verdurin. Your Majesty does not remember me —

QUEEN OF NAPLES: (*Icily*) Quite well. You were saying, Baron —

MME VERDURIN: Oh, Ma'am, I am so delighted to have this opportunity, will you permit me to present to you the hero of the evening, M. Charles Morel —

QUEEN OF NAPLES: Charlus, my dear cousin! You do not look at all well. Lean upon my arm. Be sure that it will still support you. It is firm enough for that.

MME VERDURIN: Your Majesty —

QUEEN OF NAPLES: (*Still to Charlus*) You know that, in the past, at Gaeta, it held the mob in defiance. It will be able to serve you as a rampart.

MARCEL: And it was thus, taking the Baron upon her arm and without having allowed Morel to be presented to her, that the splendid sister of the Empress Elizabeth left the house.

As I walked home through the streets, multifoliate with stars and with the million incandescent oranges of lamplight, I reflected that this evening, which had proved to be the life's justification and triumph of the humble music teacher, might prove to be the ruin of a great nobleman, monstrous in his vices but yet of generous and even of innocent heart; and, in fact, from the blow dealt him by the Verdurins, M. de Charlus was never able entirely to recover. Yet, for even the greatest tragedy of a friend can seldom detain the imagination as it can be de-tained by some trivial disquiet of our own, I found myself restless with envy of the dead, and even more depressed by the thought that I myself should leave no memorial.

I made up my mind to talk to Albertine, to forget my agita-tion in retailing to her the events of the past few hours; but I found her asleep in bed, her shoulders hunched in a manner both child-like and hostile, her knees drawn up to her waist and upon her face so sullen, so guarded an expression that I was about to withdraw without touching her. However, she awoke suddenly with a smile and held out her arms to me.

ALBERTINE: (*Drowsily*) My dear Marcel, I was dreaming. Did you have a nice time? . . . Why are you staring like that?

MARCEL: I thought you had gone away from me.

ALBERTINE: (*Almost asleep again*) As if I would ever leave my dear good boy, who has done so much for his ignorant little Albertine . . . what absurd things you do say!

MARCEL: Guess where I've been.

ALBERTINE: (*Dreamily*) I'm sure I don't know. Where?

MARCEL: At the Verdurins'.

ALBERTINE: (*Explosive*) I thought as much!

(*Pause*)

MARCEL: I didn't know that you'd be annoyed by my going to see the Verdurins.

ALBERTINE: Annoyed? What do you suppose I care, where you've been? It's all the same to me. Was Mademoiselle Vinteuil there?

MARCEL: So it was true! You wanted to go to the rehearsal this afternoon just to see her!

ALBERTINE: Oh, don't be so stupid! Anyway, I didn't go. I went to the Trocadéro, as you insisted.

MARCEL: And who did you see there?

ALBERTINE: Nobody, because after all that you made Françoise drag me out of my seat to go driving with you.

MARCEL: Léa was acting there! Now I know why you were so ready to do what I suggested.

ALBERTINE: And suppose she was? I've known her for ages, I told you that. So why should I have wanted particularly to see her again?

MARCEL: You're always hiding things from me. You remember that time when you went for three days to Balbec —

ALBERTINE: (*Blurting it out*) Which means you think I never went there at all! Of course I didn't, and I've always wondered why you pretended to believe I had. The driver had some business of his own and didn't like to ask you for a few days off —

MARCEL: (*Dazedly*) What are you talking about?

ALBERTINE: (*Racing on*) So out of sheer kindness of heart I invented a trip to Balbec and spent three days bored to tears with my friend at Auteuil! I thought you'd found out and taken it as a joke.

MARCEL: (*Regaining control of himself*) You are always deceiving me. For instance — you knew Mademoiselle Vinteuil was expected at Madame Verdurin's this afternoon.

ALBERTINE: Yes. I knew that.

MARCEL: Can you swear to me that it wasn't in order to renew relations with her that you wanted to go to the Verdurins'?

ALBERTINE: Of course I can swear it. I never had any relations with her!

MARCEL: Well, will you swear that it wasn't the pleasure of seeing Mademoiselle Vinteuil again that made you so anxious to go there?

ALBERTINE: (*Suddenly stubborn*) No. I can't swear. It would have been a great pleasure to see her again. And now leave me alone! I've had all I can stand.

MARCEL: Listen, there was something I found out from Madame Verdurin this evening. She told me. . . .

ALBERTINE: Don't bother to say it, *I* know! You found out that I lied to you when I pretended I'd been more or less brought up by Mademoiselle Vinteuil's friend! But I only did it because you were so keen on this man Vinteuil's music, I thought you'd think more of me if I pretended I'd known both the girls quite well, I thought it would draw us together, make me more important in your eyes! When I lie to you it's always out of affection for you, always, always, and you won't believe it. . . .

(Her voice fades away)

MARCEL: When I left Albertine's room that night, exhausted and terrified by her deceit and by her sudden anger, I remembered with sorrow that I had been unable to tell her what had been uppermost in my mind when I left the house of Madame Verdurin; that I had been present at the transformation of a life which had seemed full of waste and failure into a marvellous triumph, all the more resplendent because of the darkness and tears that, like a night of sodden winter veiling the brightness of a citadel, had hidden it until now. I found myself envying Monsieur Vinteuil with all my heart; for I knew that I had destroyed, through my love for Albertine, precious years which would never bear fruit, that, like Swann, I had wasted my life for a woman who did not really please me, who was not in my style.

Many years afterwards, when Albertine was lost to me, was dead, when even her ambiguous ghost had faded into oblivion, when a great war had been fought and had brought to birth a new world in which I felt myself a stranger, I accepted an invitation to a party given by the ex-Madame Verdurin, who, on her husband's death, had become Duchesse de Duras, and who after a second widowhood, was now the Princesse de Guermantes, the acknowledged leader of a society as inexplicable to me as the court of Genghis Khan or the fashionable hierarchy of New South Wales. . . .

(Behind closed doors, the Vinteuil Septet)

FOOTMAN: Madame la Princesse has ordered the doors to be closed until the music ends, Monsieur. If Monsieur does not mind waiting. . . .

MARCEL: Alone in the great antechamber, hung with Elstirs acquired by the Mistress long before he had become famous, I walked slowly up and down, listening to the voices of the past as I might have listened to the surging of all the five oceans in the iridescent matrix of a shell. . . .

(The Septet continues faintly)

ALBERTINE: *(An echo)* I won't have you driving me mad and upsetting yourself. What you ought to do is to try to write something. . . .

ODETTE: *(An echo)* You know you won't miss me, Charles, you've got your work to do, I should only be in the way. You can stay quietly here and finish your precious book on Vermeer —

SWANN: *(An echo)* Odette, my darling —

CHARLUS: *(An echo)* You are sure to have observed how affectionate Charlie has become these days, how grateful for any little favours I am able to bestow upon him, how truly like a son. . . .

M. VINTEUIL: *(An echo)* Germaine, you aren't going out like that? The glass is falling, it's going to rain. Do just take your shawl. . . .

LILIANE: *(An echo)* He's a silly, muddling, messy old fool. Say it! Let's hear his frail, delicate little girl with her ploughboy's wrists say it . . . say it . . . say it . . . say it. . . .

ALBERTINE: *(An echo)* I thought you'd think more of me if I pretended I'd known Mademoiselle Vinteuil quite well, I thought it would draw us together! When I lie to you, it's always out of affection for you, always, always. . . .

MARCEL: And all these voices reminded me that I had made

nothing of my life, that I should never become a writer, that the golden window high in the serpentine branches of the breathing night would be forever barred to me.

(There is the sharp tinkle of a spoon on china)

A servant, in his ineffectual efforts not to make a noise, had knocked a spoon against a plate. I was filled with a sudden, exquisite felicity, knowing in a single instant, pure, disincarnated and freed from the imperfection of exterior perceptions, an absolute joy.

All at once the magical window began to move down the sky, lengthening and widening as it glided towards me, the lamplight streaming out like the ribbons of the sun as the lattices themselves streamed open to admit me.

('Bell' motif of Septet begins, a little clearer)

MARCEL: And now, in the triumph of Vinteuil, which was the triumph of Time Regained, distilled for ever into the immortality of art in all its freshness and ineffable dew, so that not a single sorrow, not a single joy was lost or wasted but incorporated into its brightness as innumerable water drops, valueless as glass in themselves, are incorporated into the limitless emerald and saffron wonder of a summer sea, I perceived the way of my own work, of the task that lay before me, were Time allotted me in which to complete it. . . .

FOOTMAN: It's nearly over, Monsieur. I'll open the door just a bit, shall I, so you can hear it?

(The Septet, clear and full through the open door of the drawing-room, comes to an end)

Concluding Note

I DO not believe it is possible to recognise the greatness of Proust's stature if we treat him as a demi-god, as the idol of a cult.

Not to listen to him, not to give him our full attention, is indefensible, for no writer has ever spoken to his reader more personally. Balzac, perhaps, spoke as personally when he spoke to women — it seems to me that he knew more about women than any writer of any age — yet not he, not Tolstoi, not Dickens, not Dostoievski, insists on speaking so individually, so privately, to the reader as Proust does. He speaks to him of what he already knows but pretends not to know; he starts from a point buried somewhere in the reader's own emotional experience, so that he finds no impossible strangeness when he sets out with Proust upon the extraordinary journey.

André Maurois' *The Quest for Proust*, admirable though it is, is a *defence*. I do not believe there is any great fault to defend: *A la Recherche du Temps Perdu* is, in the minds of men and women able and willing to understand it, one of the great novels, if not the greatest novel, of the world. These programmes are simply critical studies in a new form, without defensive or offensive intention.

All the same, it seems to me dangerous to 'swallow Proust whole'. Often, when he seems to be writing for most of us, he is writing purely for himself; he has the trick of hypnotising us, when first we read him, into seeing in our own natures, our own desires, things that are not in us at all but only in him. He is, in fact, the greatest of subjective writers, and if we often feel that he speaks not only for himself but for us also, it is because many of those things that are true for him are universal truths; and because in each of us are many men and many lives, and as we grow older so, with experience, each of us adds more men and more lives to his own being.

I think it more than probable that *À la Recherche du Temps Perdu* may be a work demoralising to the younger reader. It is all too easy to feel that Proust has revealed to us, in the tablets of the law, that true love can never be reciprocated: that X cannot ever love Y at the same time as Y loves X: that 'Friendship' is an illusion, a mask for a forbidden sexual desire which, when that desire and the fact of its inevitable frustration is understood, will crumble away from the bitter and stony face beneath. This is because Proust writes with such great authority of what is true for *him* that we are tempted to take it as being true for ourselves. The reader old enough to know himself as well as a man may, will sense how often Proust has hit on the universal truth, how often upon a truth which is only for a minority of men, how often a truth which is one only for Proust alone. He will come to realise that, just as he cannot trust Proust upon mere physical facts (the coincidences of the keyhole, the imprisonment of Albertine in an epoch when such a thing would have been virtually impossible), so he must not repose an uncritical trust in him where the eternal verities are concerned. To accept the verdict upon love and friendship of *À la Recherche du Temps Perdu* would be as absurd as to accept respectively upon those subjects the verdicts of *Troilus and Cressida* and *Timon of Athens*.

These things have to be said. Yet the book as a whole is pervaded with truth: the truth of accomplishment and joy. The tragedies of loss in love, despair and degradation in age, are all too true for all too many: but it is remarkable that this novel, often in the past regarded as 'depressing', makes its most profound effect by touching the memory of ecstasy that is in us all. It is a 'young man's book'; it is full of rediscovery of the delights of the natural world and of the excitement of youth itself. In the end, it comes to a shout of pure triumph. With the shock of the madeleine, the uneven step in the Baptistry, the spoon against the plate, comes the tremendous and absolute victory over Time. It is caught at last, the golden net hauls it in, and there it lies, dense and glittering in its marvellous permanence, never to be lost again.

Appendix A

ORIGINAL CAST-LISTS

<small>All Programmes produced by Rayner Heppenstall</small>

1. The Duchess at Sunset

        First broadcast, Sunday, September 5th, 1948

Narrator	Esme Percy
Baron De Charlus	Austin Trevor
Marcel	Anthony Jacobs
Oriane, Duchesse de Guermantes	Lydia Sherwood
Basin, Duc de Guermantes	Ralph Truman
Mme. de Villeparisis	Ella Milne
Bréauté (Comte Hannibal de Bréauté-Consalvi)	Charles Lefeaux
Footman	Stanley Groome
M. Verdurin	Andrew Churchman
Mme. Verdurin	Betty Hardy
Dr. Cottard	Howieson Culff
Saniette	J. Hubert Leslie
Professor Brichot	Raf de la Torre
Mme. Cottard	Gladys Spencer
Albertine	Hilda Schroder
M. de Norpois	Carleton Hobbs

        Piano music composed and played by Arthur Oldham

2. Madame de Charlus

        First broadcast Monday, December 27th, 1954

Baron de Charlus	Max Adrian
Eugenie (Mme de Charlus)	Prunella Scales
Oriane (Mdlle. de Guermantes)	Lydia Sherwood
Marcel	Anthony Jacobs

WILLY HAYDON	David Markham
CHARLES SWANN	David King-Wood
EDMOND DE GONCOURT	Carleton Hobbs
HORACE PINAUD	David Peel
MME. DE VILLEPARISIS	Barbara Trevor
SAINTE-BEUVE	Felix Felton
BASIN (Prince des Laumes)	Godfrey Kenton
PRINCESSE DE GUERMANTES-BAVIERE	Maureen Robinson
MADAME DE MARSANTES	Sheila Byford
ALGERIAN BOY ⎱ OLD WOMAN ⎰	Denise Bryer
VICTOR HUGO	Felix Felton

Music by Michael Head

3. SWANN IN LOVE

First broadcast Monday, March 3rd, 1952

CHARLES SWANN	David King-Wood
MARCEL	Anthony Jacobs
BARON DE CHARLUS	Arthur Young
ODETTE DE CRECY	Diana Maddox
MME. VERDURIN	Betty Hardy
BASIN ⎱ BRICHOT ⎰	Roger Delgado
GENERAL FROBERVILLE	Raf de la Torre
MME. COTTARD	Gladys Spencer
'BICHE' (Elstir)	Keith Pyott
DR. COTTARD	Malcolm Hayes
M. VERDURIN	Richard Williams
SANIETTE	Bryan Powley
ANNETTE	Ann Totten
RÉMI	Ronald Sidney
COMTE DE FORCHEVILLE	Heron Carvic
ORIANE	Lydia Sherwood
PROSTITUTE	Penelope Metaxas

Music arranged by Michael Head

4. ALBERTINE REGAINED

First broadcast Monday, February 1st, 1954

ALBERTINE SIMONET	Olive Gregg
MDLLE. LE CHEMINANT	Ilona Ference
GILBERTE SWANN	Cecile Chevreau
MME. BONTEMPS	Betty Hardy
GISELE	Penelope Metaxas
ANDREE	Julia Lang
MARCEL	Anthony Jacobs
BLOCH	Richard Waring
AIME	Keith Pyott
OCTAVE	David Peel
LEA	Delphi Lawrence
FRANCOISE	Betty Hardy
MME. SWANN (Odette)	Mary O'Farrell
MOTHER OF MARCEL	Thea Wells

etc.

5. SAINT-LOUP

First broadcast Sunday, September 25th, 1955

SAINT-LOUP	Robert Eddison
RACHEL	Cecile Chevreau
BLOCH	Reginald Beckwith
MARCEL	Anthony Jacobs
BARON DE CHARLUS	Max Adrian
DUCHESSE DE GUERMANTES	Lydia Sherwood
DUC DE GUERMANTES	Oliver Burt
ALBERTINE	Olive Gregg

Other parts played by Ian Sadler, Raf de la Torre, Ilona Ference, and Denise Bryer.

Music by Michael Head

6. A WINDOW AT MONTJOUVAIN

First broadcast Monday, April 2nd, 1956

MARCEL	Anthony Jacobs
VINTEUIL	Edgar Norfolk

GERMAINE VINTEUIL	Elaine Macnamara
LILIANE	Mary Wimbush
ODETTE	Denise Bryer
SWANN	David King-Wood
MME. VERDURIN	Betty Hardy
M. VERDURIN	Richard Williams
ALBERTINE	Olive Gregg
BARON DE CHARLUS	Max Adrian
MOREL	Frank Duncan
DUCHESSE DE GUERMANTES	Lydia Sherwood
DR. COTTARD	Malcolm Hayes
PROFESSOR BRICHOT	Geoffrey Wincott
SANIETTE	Bryan Powley
THE QUEEN OF NAPLES	Mary O'Farrell
THE DUCHESSE DE DURAS	Ilona Ference
MOTHER OF MARCEL	Thea Wells
FATHER OF MARCEL	Oliver Burt
GILBERTE	Cecile Chevreau

Music by Michael Head

T

Appendix B

Remembrance of Things Past

Note: In the case of *Swann in Love*, the reader will find that I have frequently made reference to long passages in the novel which are adapted only very freely in my own text. I have sometimes given the whole of a Scott-Moncrieff passage where, in fact, I have used only a sentence or two and a few isolated phrases from it.

1. THE DUCHESS AT SUNSET

PAGE		REFERENCE
6	'It was still the light of day . . . enduring gold'	C. of P. I. 47
24	'You are perhaps afflicted by intermittent deafness'	C. of P. II. 142
25	'Duc de Brabant . . . et des Dunes'	C. of P. II. 122
28	'Cannot place to his credit . . . lofty in its conception'	W.B.G. I. 64

2. MADAME DE CHARLUS

PAGE		REFERENCE
37	'For a long time I used to go to bed early'	S.W. I. 1
40	'peculiar pink . . . into violet'	G.W. II. 179
40	'intelligence . . . a sort of burglar's jemmy . . . reputable drawing-rooms'	G.W. II. 184
40	'marry an artist . . . category of "detrimentals"'	G.W. II. 195
41	'Biscuits of Rheims . . . Tours'	G.W. II. 207
77	'Duc de Brabant . . . and des Dunes'	C. of P. II. 122

3. SWANN IN LOVE

PAGE		REFERENCE
82	'I am not interested in history . . . through me they met'	Captive II. 126

Key: Swann's Way: S.W. *Within a Budding Grove:* W.B.G. *The Guermantes Way:* G.W. *The Cities of the Plain:* C. of P. *The Captive:* Captive. *The Sweet Cheat Gone:* S.C.G. *Time Regained* T.R.

Appendix C

1. Proust's 'little phrase,' occurring in the Sonata for Violin and Piano in D Minor by Saint-Saëns, was used, freely arranged, by Michael Head in *The Vinteuil Sonata*. Our grateful thanks are due to Messrs. Durand & Cie, Paris, for the permission they gave us to do this.
2. *Valse de Charlus*. This was composed for *Madame de Charlus* by Michael Head.
3. *Pauvres Fous*, ballad, by D. Tagliafico. Favourite song of Odette de Crecy, *Swann's Way*, II, p. 25.
4. *Le Furet du Bois*. Guessing-game. Sung in *Albertine Regained* by the children of the Lycée Francais. Played by Albertine and her friends, *Within a Budding Grove*, II, p. 304.
5. *Le Biniou*, words by H. Guérin, music by Emile Durand, reproduced by kind permission of the copyright owners Editions Salabert—Copyright Reserved. Favourite song of Albertine, *The Captive*, I, 3.
6. Vinteuil's *Septuor*. Composed by Michael Head for *A Window at Montjouvain*.

Vinteuil Sonata

M. H.

Allegro risoluto

La Petite Phrase

M. H.

Tranquillo. Meno mosso

Valse de Charlus

M. H.

Tempo di Valse

Pauvres Fous!

D. Tagliafico

Moderato

I smile___ and I whis-per, Poor Fools,___ O whi-ther a-

-way For death___ comes all too swift - ly.___

286

Le Biniou

Les dou - leurs— sont des fol - les!— Et qui les e - coute

— est en - cor plus fou!— A nous deux— toi qui con - so - les,—

— Bi - niou, mon bi - niou,— mon cher bi - niou!—

Le furet du bois

Folk Song

Il court, il court, le fu - ret, Le fu - ret du bois, Mes-

-dam's il court, il court, le fu - ret, Le fu - ret du bois jo - li.

Vinteuil's "Septuor"

M. H.

A *Andante misterioso*

Violin

Viola

Cello

B

Violin

Horn

Harp

Flute

Appendix D

1. It would be outside the scope of this book if I attempted to go more deeply into Proust's chronology than is necessary for the placing of these programmes.

Those who would like to read something more thorough might study the most interesting chronology by M. Willy Hachez, in *Bulletin de la Société des Amis de Marcel Proust et des Amis de Combray* (No. 6, 1956). I am in general agreement with most of his findings and indeed, have worked backwards, as he has, from the final party, given by the Princesse de Guermantes (formerly Madame Verdurin) in *Time Regained*. The date of this must be 1920.

I do, however, differ from M. Hachez upon one important point. He feels that, if the internal chronology of the novel is to work at all, we must believe that 'Marcel', the narrator, was born ten years later than Proust himself: i.e., in 1881.

If M. Hachez's conclusion is followed, Marcel, at the 'final party', would have been only 39: far too young for the reflections he makes upon his own ageing, and too young for the remarks about 'old ———', made by other characters about him.

Now I can see no reason whatsoever why Proust should have made 'Marcel' so much younger than himself. A writer of a first-person novel with a marked biographical tinge tends quite naturally to give the narrator his own date of birth. To suppose that Proust was the exception seems to me a misunderstanding of the creative process.

We must, I think, start from acceptance of the fact that the chronology of *À La Recherche du Temps Perdu* is 'all over the place'. There are multiple contradictions, some of them, in the later volumes, the obvious slips of a tired man; others are less easily explicable. M. Hachez places, probably rightly, the party at which the Verdurins 'execute' M.

de Charlus (*The Captive*, II) in 1902: Proust dates it as 1900 by his reference to the niece of the Queen of Naples, Elisabeth of Bavaria, 'who shortly afterwards was to marry Prince Albert of Belgium.' (*The Captive*, II, p. 55). This marriage, in fact, took place in 1900, which would set the party, at the latest, in the early part of that year, if other and more oblique references did not contradict the date.

2. The 'Final Party'

The date of this must be, at the earliest, 1920: but is somewhat confused by a reference to Réjane 'touring triumphantly abroad'. Réjane, in fact, died in 1920 at the age of 63. Even if the Réjane reference (*Time Regained*, p. 371) is disregarded, the date of the party cannot be pushed much further ahead than 1920 since (even if it were possible to entertain the idea of Proust *setting it in the future*) this would make all the characters impossibly old.

For the purposes of my own work, I have assessed ages and birth dates of the various characters at the time of the 'final party' as follows:

	Age in 1920	Born
The Duc de Guermantes	83	1837*
M. de Charlus	80	1840
The Duchesse de Guermantes	72	1848
Marcel	49	1871†
Gilberte	46	1874†
Mdlle. de Saint-Loup	16	1904
Odette	70	1850
Mme. Verdurin (Pr. de Guermantes)	78	1842

* Age stated, *Time Regained*, p. 235.

† Where I am in substantial disagreement with M. Hachez.

I am prepared to agree that, if Marcel were born in 1871, his behaviour in the Champs Elysées and on the first visit to Balbec seems absurdly childish: but I can see no other means of accepting his commentary at the final party other than by the conclusion that at that time he was at least 49.

3. *Swann and Odette*

The question of the date of Swann's courtship is extremely difficult. Such historic references as there are are few and imprecise, although reference to the funeral of Gambetta (*Swann's Way*, I, p. 297) and Swann's reference to his dinners with M. Grévy at the Elysées (Presidency of Jules Grévy 1879–1887) would seem to place the courtship somewhere between 1882 and 1887.

Holding, as I do, the view that the Narrator was born in 1871, I have had to place the very beginning of the courtship much earlier than that, since my assessment must allow for the birth of Gilberte round about 1874: for my purposes, I have set the meeting of Swann and Odette round about 1873. I am aware that there is ample room for disagreement on such evidence as exists in Proust's text.

———

Some years ago, when I was beginning to make tentative notes, which I have not yet completed, towards a chronology of Proust's novel, I mentioned to Desmond Macarthy how bewildered I was by the innumerable confusions and discrepancies.

'I shouldn't worry too much about it if I were you,' he said: '*he never did.*'

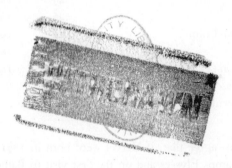

PRINTED IN GREAT BRITAIN BY ROBERT MACLEHOSE AND CO. LTD
THE UNIVERSITY PRESS, GLASGOW